MASTERING FUTURES TRADING

MASTERING FUTURES TRADING

AN ADVANCED COURSE FOR SOPHISTICATED STRATEGIES THAT WORK

BO YODER

McGraw-Hill

New York   Chicago   San Francisco   Lisbon
London   Madrid   Mexico City   Milan   New Delhi
San Juan   Seoul   Singapore   Sydney   Toronto

*The **McGraw·Hill** Companies*

1 2 3 4 5 6 7 8 9 10 DOC/DOC 0 9 8 7 6 5 4

ISBN 0-07-142034-7

This publication is designed to provide accurate and authoritative information in regard to the subject matter covered. It is sold with the understanding that neither the author nor the publisher is engaged in rendering legal, accounting, futures/securities trading, or other professional service. If legal advice or other expert assistance is required, the services of a competent professional person should be sought.

—*From a Declaration of Principles jointly adopted by a Committee of the American Bar Association and a Committee of Publishers.*

McGraw-Hill books are available at special quantity discounts to use as premiums and sales promotions, or for use in corporate training programs. For more information, please write to the Director of Special Sales, Professional Publishing, McGraw-Hill, Two Penn Plaza, New York, NY 10121-2298. Or contact your local bookstore.

This book is printed on recycled, acid-free paper containing a minimum of 50% recycled, de-inked fiber.

CONTENTS

Chapter 4

Chapter 5

Chapter 6

Chapter 7

ACKNOWLEDGMENTS

No one can learn to trade and survive in this tough business on his/her own. My life as a trader has been greatly enhanced by those who took the time to write about their trading. To those whose words have helped me find my style as a trader, I will be forever thankful. Barry Rudd and Jack Schwager for helping me begin to see trading as a valid career to pursue; Linda Raschke, Alan Farley, and Tony Oz for helping me escape the insane complexity I had in my chart reading; Mark Douglas and Dr. Richard McCall for helping define so many aspects of the mental game; Vadym Graifer and Christopher Schumacher for bringing an understanding of tape reading to my trades; "Buzzy" Schwartz for introducing me to the S&P's; Mark Cook for introducing me to the Bonds.

To the RealityTrader crew, Vad, Chris, Vic, Nesi, Allen, Russ, Jeff, thank you for making "work" such a joy. I feel so lucky to be in business with such talented and honorable people.

Finally, I dedicate this book to my family and Russell Van Der Biesen—without your unwavering support none of this would have ever happened.

PREFACE

Now I shall go far and far into the North, playing the Great Game. . . .
—Rudyard Kipling, *Kim*, 1901

In 1901, Rudyard Kipling wrote of the great game of espionage in *Kim*. Some have called spying the "second oldest profession," but I'm not buying this premise. I feel firmly convinced that somewhere deep in prehistory, before the first cloak was donned or the first dagger forged, Gronck traded a hunk of fresh meat to his neighbor Snarg for a handful of berries Snarg had picked in anticipation of Gronck's coming hunger. With this transaction the concept of trading was born, and the greatest of all games began. Trading has always been a fundamental cornerstone of commerce for any society, commerce being a basic necessity of any of civilization. Boiled down to its essentials, trading is the transference of risk and effort. Columbus was willing to risk it all for a chance to bring the spices of the Orient to a public willing to pay a "risk premium" for those goods. His spice buyers had no interest in assuming the risks it took to get the spices they craved, but were willing to pay a spice trader a high price to take these risks for them.

In the modern world this same process has been distilled to a pure form in the futures market. It started out as a way for the farmer to hedge the market risk for his goods. Due to the basics of supply and demand, a field of cotton was worth a lot less at the time of harvest because many farmers were trying to bring their crops to market at the same time. If a farmer could sell his crops *before they were harvested*, he could sell into the market at the higher prices that were seen in the off season. In return for this increased profit, he was willing to take the risk that the crops would fail and he would be unable to deliver on his obligations.

As the world progressed, these hedging instruments became more and more useful and popular. The financial instruments (bond futures, equity index futures) were developed to help financial instructions offset their risk, and the futures markets have blossomed into the vast ocean of risk takers, and hedgers that it is today.

This book is written for the risk takers.

—Bo Yoder

CHAPTER 1

The Nature of Speculation

A speculator is a man who observes the future, and acts before it occurs.

—Bernard Baruch

The word *speculator* comes from the Latin meaning "to spy out." Speculators are risk takers in the markets who are willing to try and predict the future. By doing so, they provide the liquidity needed for the market participants who wish to offset some of their risk (in much the same manner that an individual offsets the risk of losing his or her house to fire by buying fire insurance). I would define a speculator as any individual who assumes a position in stocks, futures, options, or any other financial instrument for the sole purpose of using that position for financial gain. They care not for fundamentals, news, or sentiment; these are but tools for them to form a directional bias. By becoming a speculator, you are participating in one of the purest forms of capitalism. Your infrastructure and overhead are very low; trading is a simple interaction between a buyer and a seller. Your business risks can be clearly defined and losses controlled in a way that many people in other businesses can only dream of. Your earning potential is limited only by your capital, liquidity, and willingness to assume risk. Contrast this with an opportunity you might see for a storefront retail establishment that sells bicycles. You must first find and lease and/or buy the space. Then you must build inventory, hire employees, advertise your business, gain exposure, and go through all the complicated processes needed to build a successful business. If your perceived business opportunity doesn't materialize, nobody will buy your bicycles. As the business fails, you will have to try to get out of your lease, let your employees go, and try to liquidate your inventory. To begin a business speculating in the futures market, all you need to do is select a broker to fill your orders, develop a trading plan, and capitalize your account. If your trading business is not profitable and you wish to shut down operations and move on, a phone call to your broker will liquidate your positions and the check for your remaining capital will arrive in the mail shortly thereafter. Because of the simplicity and ease of this process, many traders do not treat their trading as seriously as they would any other business venture, and they pay the price for their lack of preparation.

BEGIN AT THE BEGINNING

The futures markets are structured for consistency and simplicity to trade their underlying commodities in prespecified blocks called *contracts*. For example, one bond contract is the equivalent of a $100,000 block of 30-year Treasury bills (T-bills). This contract trades in the Chicago Board of Trade's pit from 7:20 A.M. to 2:00 P.M. Chicago time. If you buy one contract, you are entering into a legally binding agreement to take control of $100,000 in T-bills until the time of the contract's expiration. As a pure speculator, you are not interested in taking delivery of any actual goods, so you go into the market and offset your position before expiration by selling one offsetting contract. Your profit or loss is the difference between these two prices. Just as with any other product, if there are many buyers who are eager to buy, the price will rise to meet that demand. As soon as those traders who own the contracts discover that there are aggressive buyers, they will raise their prices and try to milk a little more profit from every sale. Vice versa, if there is a market awash with sellers, any traders who are interested in buying will be dropping their bids in an attempt to buy their contracts on the cheap. The speculator's job is to anticipate these supply-demand imbalances. Once it is determined that such an imbalance is likely to occur, speculators buy or sell contracts in order to position themselves for a profit, as the contracts are then marked up and sold to the hungry crowd.

The amount of capital you must have in your account to control these contracts is called *margin*. This down payment is a good-faith deposit required by the exchanges and your broker before you are allowed to enter a position. The level of margin required is set by your broker within a set of rules created by the exchanges themselves, and is based on the volatility and leverage inherent in the commodity you are trading. At the time of this writing, the margin needed to control one bond contract is less than $3000. The ability to buy $100,000 worth of T-bills for such a small initial capital outlay is both the promise and the bane of the futures markets. This powerful leverage can either be a tool for good or a very destructive force that can take you to bankruptcy in short order. Because of the leverage the futures market offers, it is possible to assume a level of risk that can result in a loss of much more than your original investment. Thus, like a firearm, leverage is a tool to respect and manage carefully, but it is nothing to be afraid of if handled responsibly. There are many horror stories about financial disasters in the futures world, but behind each you will find traders who either did not understand the risks they were assuming, or who became careless with leverage and paid the price. The scary aspect of trading a leveraged instrument keeps many away due to an almost superstitious fear. By doing so, they miss out on some of the most liquid and tradable markets available to the professional speculator. The beauty of trading is that you and you alone, control your level of risk exposure to the markets. It is an endeavor of unparalleled freedom. You choose what style to trade, you choose how many contracts to buy, and you choose how many positions to have open at any one time. The more risk you assume, the larger your potential for gains or losses. Because of this fundamental truth, there is a constant balancing act that each trader engages in as he or she balances acceptable risk against the possibility for reward. Many beginners get stars in their eyes and see only the upside in every trading opportunity. They forget to analyze what will happen if they are wrong, and when the market turns on them, are unprepared to control their losses, sometimes resulting in catastrophe. The beginner often expends all his or her effort trying to predict the market's action and will ignore the money management side of the business. The professional trader takes the opposite path. Beginning with risk control and plans for profit management, the act of market forecasting is often the last step taken before initiating a position.

Once you have developed a risk management plan and adopted an analysis style that produces a directional bias, you are ready to initiate a trade. Your task is then to back your directional bias with money as you interact with the market to buy or sell your contracts. Some futures contracts are traded in a physical pit, where floor traders (or locals) fill your order by finding another trader willing to take the other side of your trade. With brightly colored jackets and frantically gesticulating hands signaling an interest to buy or sell, these pits are a swirling vortex of human energy and emotion. You call your broker with an order, and this information is transmitted to the floor. This order is then routed to a local who physically interacts with another trader in the pit to buy or sell your contracts. The floor traders flash hand signals and yell out their bids and offering prices along with the size they are willing to trade. In order to close out the transaction, each party must make eye contact and then make a record of the exchange. This process can take several minutes, but when it is complete, your broker will notify you that your orders were filled. Since there is an element of time involved, often the price you see on a quote screen will have changed by the time your order hits the market. Any difference between the price you expected to pay and the actual fill you receive is called *slippage*. This slippage is one of the hidden costs of doing business as a trader and is a factor that must be considered as you decide which trading strategy to employ. There are a number of contracts now that are being traded entirely in a virtual electronic pit. When you send an order to your broker for these contracts, it is usually done via an electronic order entry platform. Your orders, along with those from every trader who is active in the market, are sent to a central electronic exchange. These orders are sorted by price and then by time. If you are long the S&P E-Mini and wish to sell your contracts at 900, your order goes into a queue. If the size at 900 was 15 contracts, and you add your order to sell 10, the size posted will change to 25 as soon as your order is accepted. The traders who are selling the 15 contracts are ahead of you in line, but as soon as those 15 contracts are taken at 900, you will be at the top of the queue and your contracts will begin to fill as other traders take the offer. With near instant fills, sharply reduced levels of slippage, and great liquidity, electronically traded offerings are one of the fastest growing segments of the futures game.

OPTIONS FOR ORDER ENTRY

You have a number of choices when you wish to buy or sell in the futures markets. If you want to buy, and are willing to take whatever the current offering price is, a market order will find the contracts available on the offer and fill you from that liquidity. A market order will continue to chase the offer indefinitely until your order is filled in full. If you want to be filled for sure, and are willing to risk taking some slippage, a market order will get the job done as quickly as possible.

If you are willing to run the risk of missing the trade in order to better control your fill price, a *limit* order is the way to go. This sets a specific price beyond which you are unwilling to buy or sell as you initiate your position. If there are any market participants who are willing to sell you their contracts at your limit price (or better), then your order will be filled. If there are none, the order will sit out there unfilled, waiting for a time when somebody is willing to meet the limit price you posted. For example, a buy limit order for two NASDAQ E-Mini contracts at 976 indicates that you are willing to buy two contracts at any price up to, but not to exceed, 976.

A *stop* order is a conditional order that can either be tied to a market or limit order. Once the market trades at your stop price, it triggers the stop, and a market or limit order is transmitted to the exchange. A stop market order to buy three corn contracts at 260 would enter the market as a live market order to buy three contracts as soon as 260 begins to trade. A stop limit order to buy three contracts with a trigger at 260 and a limit of 261 would enter the market as a limit order to buy contracts at a price not to exceed 261 as soon as 260 begins to trade. Stop-based orders are very useful for entering positions and protecting capital when used as stop loss orders.

The final form is a linked order pairing, or OCO, order. (This acronym stands for "one cancels other," and can be used to tie several orders together. The title or description may vary from broker to broker.) Using this form of order pairing, you can set a stop loss order *and* a limit order to exit the trade as your profit objective is reached. If one of these orders is filled, it triggers an action to cancel all the other orders linked to it. This

FIGURE 1.1

order style is one of my favorites, as it allows me to enter a trade, set my stop loss and target levels, and go to the beach! My broker will manage the trade for me while I enjoy my afternoon.

Let's go through a few examples.

The S&P E-Mini futures are setting up for a breakout. I know there is a likelihood that as the market breaks through the resistance at the top of the range there will be many buyers. I'm afraid I will miss the trade if I use a limit order and am willing to take the added risk of slippage that a market order incurs. I feel the reward in this trade, if it succeeds, will be worth risking any slippage I may see. The breakout level is 863, so my order is set as a buy stop market with a trigger set at 863.25. If the market breaks above 863 and prints 863.25, my order to buy will go live. The market does indeed break, and I am filled at 863.75 (1) as the market gets heated, and I take two ticks of slippage. (See Figure 1.1.) As soon as I am filled, I move to protect my trading capital by setting my stop loss order. My stop loss level will be under 861.50. This order will be structured as a stop market to sell. With a stop loss trigger for this order set at 861.25 (2), my capital is now protected in case the market proves my bullish opinion wrong. The

FIGURE 1.2

price goes as high as 866.50 (3) and begins to show signs of topping. It's time to take my profit. I can see that the market is mixed and trading in a range. I feel strongly that if I put in a limit order at 866 I will be filled, so I enter a sell limit order for my contracts at 866, and within a few minutes that price is met and the trade is closed at 866 for a profit.

In the next example the bonds are selling off into an area of support. I wish to enter this trade as the price tests support at 109 30/32. I send in a buy limit order for 109 30/32, which is filled a few minutes later. (See Figure 1.2.) (1) I set my stop market order for my protective stop loss at 109 15/32. (2) The trade is moving higher within 15 minutes of my entry, and I feel comfortable leaving my screens, so I set up an OCO pairing. I link my protective stop loss market order at 109 15/32 with a limit order to sell my contracts at 111 15/32 if my profit objective is reached. Now my trade is boxed. It will either hit my stop loss level or my profit objective, in which case my limit order will be filled as my profits are taken. As this order is filled, the OCO link will automatically cancel my stop loss order as my account goes flat. I leave my computers as the market is trading at 110 12/32, and head out to the golf course. Later that afternoon when I return, I find that the market did indeed trade up in the afternoon, but failed to reach my profit objective by the close. My protective stop loss order, as well as my limit order, will remain active for the following day's session. The morning of the following day, my profit objective was reached, and my limit order was filled. (3) The instant after the confirmation came through, the OCO sent an order canceling the stop loss order, leaving my account flat with no open orders.

This "Fire and Forget" style is one of my favorite ways to trade. You set up the trade, analyze your risk and reward parameters, get yourself filled, then box yourself in with a stop loss order to take your loss and a limit order to take your profit, and then get on with your life! This is also a very low-stress way to trade as you are not glued to a quote screen. . .living or dying with each uptick or downtick. It makes your plan easier to follow, and will help to keep you from falling into many of the common mental traps that the market sets with such ease. It weeds out the impulsive elements from your trading, and by eliminating these errors, you will see a very distinct change for the better in your performance.

CHAPTER 2

Who Are You?

> If you don't know who you are, Wall Street is one of the most expensive places to find out.
>
> —*Warren Buffett*

Now that we understand some of the basics of market interaction, we can begin to get to the bread and butter of speculation. When markets are bullishly controlled, they rise. When markets are bearishly controlled, they fall. They trend during this time within a certain envelope of chaotic noise, and always retain a very random character within the context of their trend. How do we harness this pseudorandom movement to consistently pull money from these markets?

First you must understand, accept, and embrace the randomness of the markets action. All the skill and experience that a market master brings to bear still cannot deliver absolute certainty about direction due to the random nature of price movement. What the master has that the novice lacks is a powerful edge: an analysis structure to bring order to the chaos and ensure that there is a positive expectancy for every trade that is taken.

This has to be the hardest lesson I learned as I taught myself to trade. In almost every other endeavor, we will see a positive or negative outcome based on our effort, skill, commitment, and so forth. But as a trader, you are engaged in a business with an element of randomness that can wreak havoc on your emotions and confidence. You can scan diligently, focus intently on the tape, take the trade with a totally objective state of mind, *and still lose*. This is not your fault; you do everything you can as a skilled trader to produce a winner, yet you will still take losses. You must learn not to take these losses as any type of personal failure. You will experience a great many of these *good trade/bad outcome* scenarios in your career. At first it is only human to believe that the losses were caused by something you did, perhaps a signal from an indicator you missed. The sooner you totally accept the premise that every trade is a random event within a certain set of probabilities, the sooner you can begin to press your edge in the markets to maximum efficiency.

ROLL THE DICE

As I work with traders who are just beginning to realize this truth about their trading, I have them go through an exercise that I find to be extremely helpful. Take a single six-sided dice, and roll it 100 times. Write down on a piece of paper the result of each roll, scoring 1 through 4 as winners, and 5 and 6 as losers. This exercise ensures a mechanically perfect probability of 66.7 percent that any given roll will end up as a winner. Here is a set of 100 as an example. Now, remembering that this is a statistically perfect test, look over these results.

2W	4W	6L	3W	5L	2W	2W	4W	4W	6L
4W	6L	3W	4W	4W	2W	3W	3W	2W	5L
3W	5L	1W	3W	6L	6L	6L	2W	3W	2W
3W	4W	3W	6L	3W	2W	3W	2W	5L	3W
5L	5L	4W	4W	5L	6L	2W	3W	1W	6L
4W	3W	3W	5L	1W	2W	6L	3W	2W	6L
1W	2W	5L	1W	3W	1W	1W	6L	6L	5L
4W	1W	1W	6L	6L	2W	1W	3W	2W	4W
3W	4W	2W	4W	1W	2W	1W	4W	6L	3W
1W	4W	6L	2W	6L	2W	4W	2W	1W	6L

Let's assume that this is the result from 3 months of trading. Every profitable trade yields one unit of profit. Every loss decreases the account by one unit. The first observation is that the win rate in this sample is running rich. With 71 winners and 29 losers, this block of 100 trades actually had a 71 percent win/loss ratio. The next thing to note inside this sample is how winners and losers tend to cluster together. About two-thirds of the way through the sample, you will find a win cluster of 13 trades in a row without a single loser! Think how great you would feel trading this strategy through a 13-trade win streak. You might begin to form all sorts of opinions about *why* you were winning, and why you should expect this winning streak to continue. Your ego inflates along with your account balance; you

10

start pricing exotic sports cars and begin to plan how you are going to spend your fortune. Yet a reality check reminds us that this was a controlled experiment, so we know there is no particular reason for this win cluster to have formed where it did. It was just a short-term statistical anomaly. In this experiment we know that we have a positive expectancy and will see a positive outcome over time. But the most important lesson is that within this overall positive expectancy, there will still be periods of euphoric gains and depressing losses. Thus is the manic depressive nature of this business. The sooner you understand this truth and begin to accept and manage these cycles, the better your chances for consistent success.

To further explore this concept, let's look at another sample of 100 dice rolls.

6L	5L	2W	6L	5L	5L	4W	5L	4W	6L
5L	2W	2W	3W	5L	5L	6W	4W	6L	4W
2W	4W	2W	2W	1W	2W	4W	3W	3W	6L
2W	2W	6L	6L	4W	5L	5L	1W	3W	6L
2W	5L	4W	2W	6L	4W	4W	1W	6L	5L
5L	4W	4W	1W	1W	4W	3W	6L	1W	3W
3W	2W	2W	2W	1W	6L	5L	6L	4W	6L
4W	4W	2W	6L	1W	5L	3W	1W	6L	2W
5L	5L	6L	3W	6L	3W	2W	6L	4W	4W
2W	3W	5L	5L	5L	1W	6L	1W	1W	3L

This sample ran pretty lean, yielding only a 60 percent win/loss ratio. There was still a 10-trade win cluster, but think how you would have felt as you suffered through the first 20 trades, losing again and again. If you are trading 30 times a month, then this sample took you through your first month without showing you any success whatsoever; in fact, you had to endure a six-trade losing streak! Does this lack of performance in the short term mean the edge in this example has been lost? No! It's still the exact same trade with the same statistical edge as the first sample.

With a 66.7 percent chance for a one-unit gain on any trade, it can be said that each trade has a statistical yield of 0.334 units. For every $100 you risk on each trade, this system should produce $33.40 over time. This example strategy has a clear positive expectancy, and over time *if you stick to the plan*, it will show you a profit.

When I'm studying a market tendency that I think could be used as a setup, I always wait before drawing any conclusions until I build a sample size that is large enough to buffer the win and loss clusters. Then I get a much more realistic expectation about how the pattern trades during good times and bad. I have found that 20 to 50 examples are needed in a sample before any accurate analysis or projections can be made. Since the markets are always changing, time is also an important element to consider as you test out a new strategy or setup. If your new trading idea can remain profitable with acceptable drawdowns for 3 months in a row, the chances are very high that this new edge you have discovered is robust enough to back with your money. In a period spanning 3 months you will see many different market environments, and any strategy that can perform well in all these different market phases is likely to continue producing for many months into the future. After several months of testing and observing you will have a much more realistic idea of the accuracy and average risk-to-reward ratio that this new strategy offers. Once you have those two numbers, you can calculate your edge and begin to project your expected profitability.

WHAT TIME FRAME SHOULD YOU FOCUS ON?

Once you understand the concept of probable randomness, it is time to choose an analysis style that you will use to find profitable trading setups. It will take time and experimentation to discover the style that best fits your personality. Don't try to cut corners here. The better your trading style suits you as a person, the lower your levels of emotional stress, and the better your results will be. Trading is the business of backing strong opinions with money, and as a result just about every trader has a strong opinion that his or her way is the *only* way to trade. You must begin to search out your style with the clear understanding of this fact, and the fundamental truth that there is no right way to trade. Some styles seem ludicrous on the surface yet provide a steady income to their inventors. If a style fits you and produces consistent profit…trade it.

The first choice you must make as a trader is to choose which time frame to operate in. Do you wish to become a position trader with an average holding period measured in days to weeks? Or perhaps a daily based trader with holding times measured in hours to days? Or lastly, a small time frame day trader with holding periods measured in minutes to hours? Each style has its pros and cons, and each has its own risks and rewards.

The position trader has the advantage of time. The weekly setups she trades take time to form, time to set up, and time to follow through. The size of the stops and the expected reward make slippage a nonissue, as each tick is such a tiny piece of the move she is trying to capture. News blips, head fakes, and whipsaws will not affect her positions as these spikes in price will just be seen as noise in the deep time frames. Her directional bias will eventually be proved right or wrong by the market, and the chance of some other market event causing her to stop out is small. She can take just about any position size she chooses, as there is liquidity that is unparalleled on the weekly charts. Her risk-to-reward ratios are among the best available, but it takes patience and guts to hold on for the big trend moves. On the downside, there will be a variety of tradable patterns in the smaller time frames that she will miss as she holds the wiggles. These wiggles present a profit opportunity for those trading the daily charts, and the setups in these time frames will be missed by the position trader. A position trader may only find two to three quality setups in a year for each market traded. So, if a pattern is missed, it can be quite a while before the next setup shows itself.

The daily based trader has an agility and speed that the position trader lacks. There are many more profit opportunities each day, week, and month on the daily and hourly charts that a daily based trader can exploit. This constant turnover allows the overnight trader to constantly keep his money working in the market. He is trying to position himself in only the markets that are likely to be moving today, and in an ideal world would see a gain in the positions he has entered every day. If he misses a setup, there will be many others to choose from. When the market is hot he can string together a multiday winning streak of 10 or more profitable trades without a loser. When the market is tough, he will have to survive periods of time where none of his patterns are following through, and a depressing drawdown begins to form. The emotional highs and lows of the daily based trader are more pronounced than those experienced by the position trader. The time commitment of a daily based trader is much higher. Hours of market research each night and real-time analysis of setups are the norm for this style of speculation.

Take another jump up in intensity and you will find the day trader. This trader is an emotional athlete, an individual who is able to take a beating one minute, then turn on a dime and make it all back and more. This is the most intense, fast-paced, and potentially profitable style available to the professional trader. It is highly leveraged, and this trader's edge is often a function of speed and willingness to accept risk without confirmation. Spikes and intraday whipsaws that are ignored by the daily and weekly based traders are life and death for a day trader. Market savvy and timing must be honed to a precise science, and it is for this reason that you will find many of the most successful day traders to be those with the most experience.

These styles all have their pros and cons, and some traders may choose to specialize in one particular time frame, while others will build a strategy that draws from several of these styles. There is no wrong way to trade if you can do so with acceptable stress levels and show a profit. By experimentation and research you will find the time frame that fits you best as a trader.

TREND FOLLOWER VS. FADER

Once you know what time frames you wish to focus on, it's time to decide what strategy to use as you look for setups. The best traders in the world are still just dealing with a set of probabilities within the context of a random environment. They use price patterns as a way to filter out price action to identify when the odds are stacked the highest in their favor. Each time two market participants come together and do business, that transaction is recorded. This *print* can be seen on the time and sales window your charting provider offers. This so-called tape is the foundation for every price and volume chart. The chart simply displays graphically what extremes in price were printed during a specific period of time. By learning to interpret this information, you can glean a great deal of information about who is operating in that market, and in which direction the underlying supply-demand balance leans.

There are two basic ways to trade a market. The first is to identify and follow the trend. Markets tend to trend strongly, then move into a period of choppy congestion before the trend resumes. A trend follower tries to capture these price thrusts. She hopes that by capturing the sharp trend moves, she can make enough money to sustain her during the periods where the market stops trending and just chops. A trend follower makes her money when the markets are moving, and loses or treads water when the markets are basing. Trend followers try to get positioned in the line of least resistance, and grind out profits as they wait to score a home run once in a while as a strong trend moves in their favor.

The second way to trade is to fade the market. These traders are banking on the fact that markets spend much of their time basing, as they build strength for the next trading phase. This is a grinding style and there are few home runs; they trade instead for many small gains. A trending market is a losing environment for a fader; instead they thrive in the basing chop that a trend leaves behind. A fader tries to get positioned against an exhausted trend in order to capture the moves caused by the trend followers as they take profits and execute stops.

Every time frame, style, setup, and strategy that you are familiar with acts as an arrow in your quiver. The successful traders that I know have built a trading style that incorporates facets of many different strategies.

They are familiar with many different strategies even if they never trade them. As a result, they gain great insight into how the different players in any given market are likely to trade, and use that knowledge to trade profitably against the majority.

CHAPTER 3

Understanding the True Nature of Risk

In the last analysis, our only freedom is the freedom to discipline our-selves.

—*Bernard Baruch*

Of the many variables that traders deal with, there is only one that they have complete control over. And that is risk. When you put on a position, only you decide where to open the position, set your stop loss, and how many contracts to take. In order to properly control and manage your market risk, it's vitally important to truly understand the exact nature of the risk you are assuming.

The first step is to analyze the character of the market. How smoothly does it trade in the time frame in which you are interested? Does it have a tendency to gap? From these two observations you can make a determination about the likelihood of an uncontrolled loss due to excessive slippage or an overnight gap. If this risk is unacceptable, either pass on the trade or look in a deeper time frame for a possible setup with a larger stop.

The next hidden risk to look for is correlation risk. Do you have positions already open that will move off the same market stimulations? If you already have a position open in wheat, adding a corn position increases your exposure to the grain markets. If something bad happens and your wheat position stops out, it is likely the corn will follow suit. This effect is even more pronounced with equity futures, so be careful to keep your correlation exposure limited to a level of risk that is comfortable for you.

The last and most important risk to watch for is news risk. News can shock a market and send it reeling. If you employ a trend-following style, news reactions will almost always move against your position as the other trend followers jump ship to avoid the news. Make sure to keep a calendar with the scheduled news events that will affect your market [such as Fed reports, crop reports, and economic numbers such as producer price index (PPI)].

Once you have satisfied yourself that you're not stepping into a trap and assuming a level of hidden risk that is inappropriate for you, it's time to open a position in a manner that optimizes your edge. What is *edge*? Your edge is the positive expectancy inherent in your trading style. As you research and develop a trading strategy, you look for recurring market behaviors that help put the odds for a profitable outcome strongly in your favor. Once you have chosen your style and understand where your edge in that strategy lies, you can begin to employ the active risk management that will most efficiently turn your edge into hard currency! Controlling your risk exposure is key to maximizing the profit potential in any trading style. Every dollar you can avoid losing is a dollar less you have to make up on your next profitable trade.

One month I kept track of all the setups I saw that were valid and fit my style of trading. Then, I made a note of what happened to the patterns on which I chose to pass. Out of the seven trades that I passed on, six would have resulted in a stop. So that month, by choosing to stay away from all but the choicest setups, I saved myself from six losses! If you risk 1 percent of your account on your trades, and can miss one bad trade a week that you otherwise would have taken (and stopped out of), you will have avoided an accumulated 52 percent loss by the end of the year! The more experience I gain as a trader, the more convinced I am that loss avoidance is what separates the haves from the have-nots. There is a paradox here. Many of those who try to learn to trade are risk-taking self-starters with a strong work ethic. They are used to working hard and being busy. They feel a strong urge to be in the markets all the time to keep their money where the action is. But by doing so, they are also participating in the markets during some rotten periods when the setups are all failing. They take losses they should be avoiding because they would feel like they were shirking their duties to let days or weeks go by without taking a trade. So the first step in the chore of risk management is to decide if you should take the trade at all.

HOW MUCH MONEY SHOULD I PUT AT RISK?

Once you are ready to trade, you need to pick a level of dollar risk that you are comfortable with, and that is appropriate to your account size. For trades based off a daily or intraday chart, risking 1 to 3 percent of your account's cash value is a level I have found to work very well. This is a conservative risk level, and one that lets you absorb a horrendous losing streak without damaging your ability to trade. Keeping losses under control is paramount to success as a speculator. You can't interact with the markets without taking losses, yet if you let those losses spiral out of control you put yourself in a position where you can't get your account back to the breakeven point. Assuming a trader can make 50 percent a year with consistency, his 1-year maximum drawdown level is 30 percent. If his account started the year with $100,000 and then saw losses of 30 percent or $30,000, he would have to trade the remaining $70,000 for an entire year in order to make back this loss. This is one of the reasons why trading has such a high failure rate. Newer traders don't have a proper respect for risk, and end up taking 30 to 50 percent drawdowns. Then in a desperate attempt to beat the clock and get back to even, they increase their size even more and blow out their accounts. In my experience working with traders of all backgrounds, those who are solely focused on the money have the lowest success rate, and the shortest life spans. The folks I have worked with who have broken through and have become consistent are those who love the game. They have a passion for what they are doing, and they see the money as a by-product of their success. As a result the money flows into their account with an ease that the money-grubbers will never know.

Personally I am comfortable taking a 10 percent drawdown, and so I take risks that will keep me within that envelope of comfort. If I sustain a 10 percent drawdown, I am only a couple months' maximum from the breakeven point, which leaves the rest of the year to build up a profit. Keeping my drawdowns within this zone limits my performance, as it dictates what levels of risk are appropriate for me to assume. I could perhaps see a larger return if I was willing to take larger risks, but if I experienced a slump while trading with increased size, I could take losses that would affect my ability to continue trading and supporting myself. This is a business where slow and steady wins the race, so I have structured my trading to provide me with enough cushion to sustain just about every kind of trading adversity.

POSITION SIZING FOR CONSISTENT RESULTS

How does one control losses in such a consistent, reliable manner? Position sizing. It is extremely important to maintain a consistent dollar risk per trade in order to most efficiently work your edge in the markets. As a technically driven trader, your stop sizes will vary widely based on the volatility of the market and the time frame in which you are operating. Let's go through a case study to more easily understand this concept.

Two accounts are funded with $100,000. One trader will trade five contracts on every setup. The other trader will scale the position size in order to risk 1 percent of the account or $1000 on every setup. During the S&P E-Mini trading session, there are three flag patterns that these traders take. The first one has a 4-point risk, and yields 6 points of profit. (One ES point is worth $50 per contract.) The next has a 2-point risk, and yields 2.25 points of profit. The final trade has a 10-point risk, and ends up stopping out. Let's contrast the two traders' results on these same three setups.

Trader 1

First trade	6 points of profit on five contracts yields $1500 in profit.
Second trade	2.25 points in profit on five contracts yields $562.5 in profit.
Third trade	A 10-point loss on five contracts equals a loss of $2500.

Trader 2

First trade	In order to risk $1000 on a 4-point stop, five contracts are taken.
	6 points of profit on five contracts yields $1500 in profit.
Second trade	In order to risk $1000 on a 2-point stop, 10 contracts are taken.
	2.25 points in profit on 10 contracts yields $1125 in profit.
Third trade	In order to risk $1000 on a 10-point stop, two contracts are taken.
	A 10-point loss on two contracts equals a loss of $1000.

These two traders took the same setups, yet saw two very different results. Trader 1's account shows a loss of $437.5, while Trader 2 has a profit of $1625. You can see from this example how radically position sizing can affect your profitability. Over the last few years I have worked with hundreds of traders, and I have seen many otherwise talented chart readers fail to make money with any consistency because they were sizing their positions improperly. If you are trading a style that yields different stop sizes and you trade a fixed number of contracts for each opportunity, you are doomed to follow lady luck around. Each trade *should* have an equal chance to succeed within their set of probabilities. However, in my painful personal experience, Murphy's Law will cause the largest stops to be taken first. And these losses will inevitably suck back all the profits from the trades with smaller stops that provided a profit.

In order to understand your edge and exploit it to its fullest, it is critical to keep your dollar risk consistent across all your trades. I feel that this scaled-size method of position sizing is fundamental to success. As an added benefit, since every trade risks the same amount, no one trade can hurt you more than any other. This can be a great help as you try to maintain your emotional objectivity. To further simplify this process and distance myself from the money at stake, I like to analyze my trading in terms of risk units. A *unit* is defined as the size of the initial risk taken. If you enter a trade in the bonds with a risk of 12 ticks, and the trade is closed for a 24-tick gain, then this trade yielded a 2 to 1 gain or +2 units. If you are trading a $100,000 account, and choose to risk 1 percent on each trade, then your unit size is $1000. A trader employing a scaled strategy for position sizing would see a $2000 profit on every 2 to 1 trade (2 units of profit).

DISCOVERING BREAKEVEN

Once you begin to analyze your trading in terms of risk units, defining your market edge is very easy. Look back at your trades for the last month. Count your winners; then divide this by the total number of trades to get your win/loss ratio. Next, calculate your average gain for the month in terms of risk units. Now do the same for all your losses. Divide your average gain by your average loss to get your risk-to-reward ratio. With these two important ratios you can determine your mathematical edge and project your profit expectancy for the next month. As you play with these numbers you will begin to see the power of the risk-to-reward ratio. If your risk-to-reward ratio is 1 to 1, then your profitability is determined solely by your accuracy. If you trade 100 times and win on 51 of those trades, you will show a profit. Maintaining the 65 to 75 percent accuracy that you need to make a good profit with a 1 to 1 strategy can be difficult, which is why I particularly like to target the 2 to 1 level for my profit targets.

If you target an area of greater than 1 to 1 as your profit target, you place an extremely powerful edge behind your trading. For instance, if you scale your position size for consistent dollar risk, then your statistical breakeven point for a 2 to 1 strategy is only 34 percent.

BREAKEVEN FOR A 2 TO 1 STRATEGY

Risk on 100 trades is $1 and profit is never more or less than $2 for gainers (2 to 1):

66 trades produce a $1 loss = $66

34 trades produce a $2 gain = $68

Bottom Line: 34 percent accuracy produces a gain of $2 (less trading costs)

BREAKEVEN FOR A 1.5 TO 1 STRATEGY

Risk on 100 trades is $1 and profit is never more or less than $1.5 for gainers (1.5 to 1):

60 trades produce a $1 loss = $60

40 trades produce a $1.5 gain = $60

Bottom Line: 40 percent accuracy produces breakeven result (less trading costs)

BREAKEVEN FOR A 3 TO 1 STRATEGY

Risk on 100 trades is $1 and profit is never more or less than $3 for gainers (3 to 1):

75 trades produce a $1 loss = $75

25 trades produce a $3 gain = $75

Bottom Line: 25 percent accuracy produces breakeven result (less trading costs)

So you can clearly see how a strong risk-to-reward ratio can deliver you a very profitable outcome even if your trade accuracy is very low. As you research and develop your trading strategy, look for and analyze the accuracy and average risk-to-reward ratio that this strategy offers. These two variables will quickly help you determine if the strategy has a positive expectancy. Most of the traders I have worked with could find setups with consistency that would follow through to the 2 to 1 level. Of all the trader errors I have seen committed, taking gains that do not justify a trader's risk is by far the most common. It's an insidious cancer that kills a trader's account in a death of a thousand cuts. Its classic symptom is that of the chronic breakeven trader. This trader works hard and has a respectable win-to-loss ratio. But somehow, the gains that are taken never do anything but bring the account back to the breakeven level. The gains are missing a key element in the positive expectancy equation. They have reasonable accuracy, but just not enough risk-to-reward ratio to justify their trading. This is a pathetically simple concept, but one that can be stated as a trading rule:

Never take a gain unless it is large enough to justify the risk you assumed at the outset of the trade!!!

Your accuracy and average risk-to-reward ratio will help you determine what level of gain justifies banking a profit. The sweet spot for every strategy will be different, and your setup research will help you determine where that sweet spot lies. Look back over your past performance and discover how your profit or loss would have been affected if you had targeted the 1.5 or 2 to 1 level. Most of the traders I have worked with came back in shock after this exercise. If they had held on in a do-or-die manner for their target zone, they would have seen profits two to three times larger than the actual gains they banked. But the kicker is, in order to have achieved these results, they would have to have held through some dreadful wiggles and whipsaws. The market delights in shaking loose as many traders as possible before making its money move. By holding your position, for every heartbreaker that runs only to fall back to your stop level, you will find many that do make it eventually to your target zone. And if you employ a 2 to 1 profit objective, then every gain you take will erase your last two losers.

DEALING WITH A DRAWDOWN

These lessons were hammered home to me one month early on in my career. I began to struggle with my first real losing streak. I lost consistently for a solid month. I kept good discipline and controlled my losses well, but every day I would end up as some kind of loser. I'd trade well in the morning, then see all my profits slip away in the afternoon. I'd lose all morning, then make some of it back in the afternoon. It was the most discouraging, demoralizing, and heartbreaking experience I had ever been through. I began to question everything. Was trading nothing but a big scam? Was I the world's biggest idiot? Everybody around me seemed to be cleaning house, and there I sat taking loss after loss. I kept reducing my position size, risking less and less to protect my capital. At the end of this month of hellish misery, I finally threw up my hands and took a week off. After a week with no computers, no charts, and no thoughts about market direction my mind was refreshed. I could see in my logs a few errors I was making. I needed to be more patient and not chase my setups, stick to my stops, and stop trying to save money by aggressively trailing my stops. With these simple changes in place I began trading again. That first week back was one of my best ever! In that 1 week, I made back every cent that it took me a month of pain to lose. That lesson was the one that made me as a trader. From that point on I never was afraid of the markets. I understood the power of my risk-to-reward ratio and how easily I could undo the damage caused by a drawdown. If you talk with successful traders, they will all have a story about one galvanic experience that changed the way they thought about their trading and took them to a whole new level of profitability. Mine was living through that terrible month, and then being able to erase it so quickly and easily. That was a life-changing experience for me.

So these are the two ways to produce consistent profits as a trader: have a very high win-to-loss ratio with a small risk-to-reward ratio, or have a very high risk-to-reward ratio with a small win-to-loss ratio. Every profitable trader I know falls somewhere between these two extremes. A lot of folks need to keep ringing the cash register, and are more comfortable with a higher win rate/lower risk-to-reward style. Others are unfazed by stops, and are willing to sit through a string of small losses in order to capture the huge risk-to-reward ratio of a trend move. Again, consistent performance will be a function of who you are as a trader. Once you look within yourself and are able to find out where your comfort zones lie, you can begin to build a trading style that fits your personality. Once you build a style that you can implement properly without mental errors, trading becomes very simple. Once you discover the edge that works best for you, go out to the markets and press it!

CHAPTER 4

The Tools of a Market Timer

It's not the strongest of the species that survive, nor the most intelligent, but the one most responsive to change.

—*Charles Darwin*

A trader once said, "The markets are exactly the same as they were when I first started trading…constantly changing!" This sums it up very well. In my experience the markets are different enough that every 6 months or so I have had to adapt my trading strategy to maintain my profitability. As a devout worshiper at the church of what's working now, I have always been disappointed by the outdated patterns and strategies I found in other books about trading. As I began to build my analysis style, I realized that it was much more important to understand *why* the patterns formed than try to predict market direction through simple pattern recognition. This gives you a level of market understanding that will transcend any particular pattern. You will then be able to utilize the pattern with or *against* the crowd, as you choose! In order to employ this "Twisted TA(technical analysis)," you must first understand the basic chart patterns, and why they form.

The foundation of any chart-reading method is a simple price and time chart with a volume histogram.

For this type of chart, a price and volume reading is taken at regular intervals, and these values are strung together from left to right to create a line chart. (See Figure 4.1.)

A line chart can be a useful tool when you wish to simplify your view of a market. However, since it only has one data point for price per unit of time, it is harder to see into the market psychology. The next step taken in charting notes the opening price, highest price, lowest price,

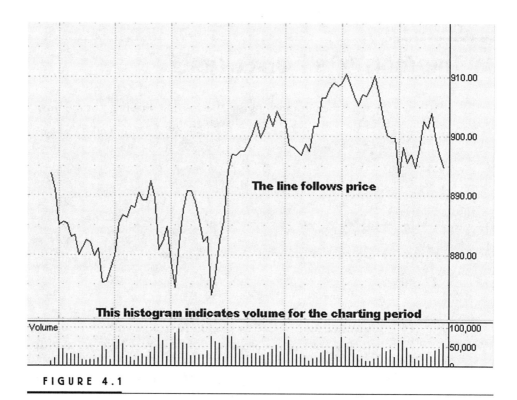

FIGURE 4.1

and the closing price for each charting period. This bar chart has a vertical line drawn for each charting period. The extreme high and low of this line denotes the highest and/or lowest price traded during the charting period. A small horizontal tick on the left-hand side of the line is recorded at the opening price, and a tick on the right-hand side denotes the closing price. Figure 4.2 illustrates the same price action as depicted by a bar chart.

Candlestick charting (which is what I use) takes the bar chart one step further. It draws the same vertical line to illustrate where the extreme highs and/or lows occurred, but draws a box around the opening and closing levels that creates the candles' "body." This body is filled in with white for a price increase and black for a day that opens high and closes low. These colorful candlesticks with their bodies and tails make price patterns much easier to identify. They tend to create an almost icon-driven environment for your eye as you scan. With practice you will be able to pick out the reversals in a chart almost instantly, adding to your edge as a trader. Figure 4.3 shows the same price action but drawn as a candlestick chart.

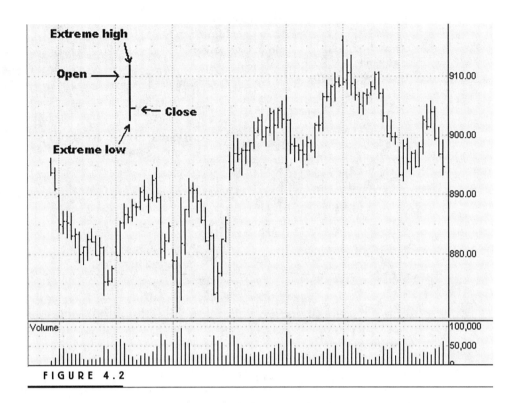

FIGURE 4.2

Other than highlighting powerful trend moves with color, the most important aspect of candlestick charting for me are the tails. (See Figure 4.4.)

Tails allow you to see at a glance if the market is rejecting price. If the market sells into an area of support where there are more buyers than sellers, then the market will move higher, leaving a bottoming tail on the chart. If the market rises into an area of resistance and there are more sellers than buyers, then the market will fall, leaving a topping tail to show you where the price has been.

When a topping or bottoming tail is seen after an extended move, it often signals that a reversal is occurring. These price pivots often cause reversal candlesticks to form, which can add needed confirmation that a trade should be considered.

The Doji, or iron cross reversal, is formed when a market opens, moves into and is rejected by an area of support or resistance to close right back where it opened. The more asymmetrical the Doji is in the direction of the trend change, the better the confirmation of a reversal. (See Figure 4.5.)

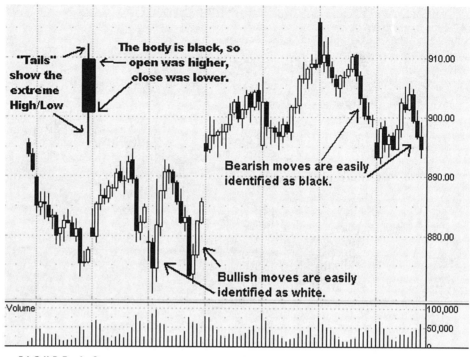

"Tails" show the extreme High/Low

The body is black, so open was higher, close was lower.

Bearish moves are easily identified as black.

Bullish moves are easily identified as white.

Volume

910.00
900.00
890.00
880.00
100,000
50,000

FIGURE 4.3

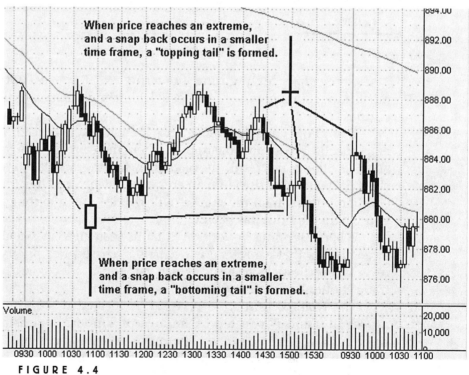

When price reaches an extreme, and a snap back occurs in a smaller time frame, a "topping tail" is formed.

When price reaches an extreme, and a snap back occurs in a smaller time frame, a "bottoming tail" is formed.

Volume

894.00
892.00
890.00
888.00
886.00
884.00
882.00
880.00
878.00
876.00
20,000
10,000

0930 1000 1030 1100 1130 1200 1230 1300 1330 1400 1430 1500 1530   0930 1000 1030 1100

FIGURE 4.4

28

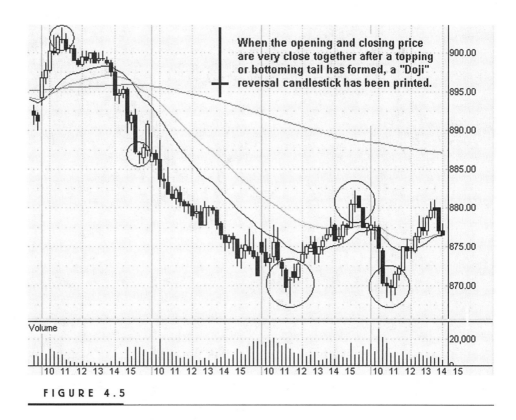

When the opening and closing price are very close together after a topping or bottoming tail has formed, a "Doji" reversal candlestick has been printed.

FIGURE 4.5

The second most common reversal candlesticks are the hammer. This candle is formed when the price moves into and is rejected by an area of support or resistance to close well beyond the opening level. This leaves a candlestick with a large bottoming tail and a white body for a bullish reversal, and a candlestick with a large topping tail and a black body for a bearish reversal. (See Figure 4.6.) These reversal candlesticks are most accurate when they form after a sustained multibar price thrust. When the market is under bearish control, the majority of the candlesticks will be colored black. As the bearish power wanes, these reversal candlesticks will help you identify when the bears begin to lose control and the trend change begins.

Both the Doji and the hammer candlestick show special reversal power when they form within the range of the previous day's trading. These Inside Range Bars (IRBs) add a second level of confirmation to a possible trend change. The IRB proves that a market is trading in an area of support or resistance. Since the entire bar's range is contained within the previous day's candlestick, it shows that the trend was unable to push the price beyond the previous day's extreme for a new high or low. This

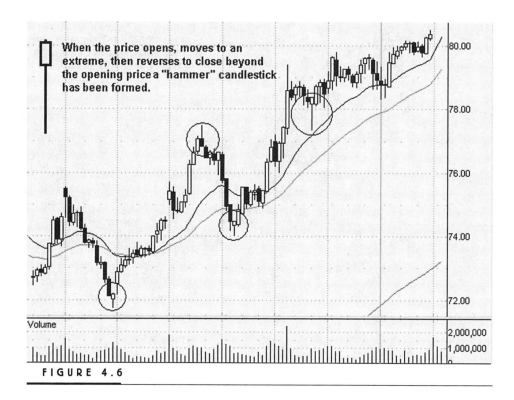

When the price opens, moves to an extreme, then reverses to close beyond the opening price a "hammer" candlestick has been formed.

FIGURE 4.6

lack of follow-through shows that the trend is losing power and therefore should be stalked for a reversal. (See Figure 4.7.)

TREND ANALYSIS

Once you have chosen the charting style that suits you best, you begin to scan your charts for price action that will tend to indicate future direction. There are many, many books written about patterns and pattern recognition. Many traders use these patterns quite blindly, almost taking them on faith alone. They think they are discretionary traders, when in reality they are taking a much more systemized path. For me, a price pattern is a trend instigator, a market event that draws attention and helps to focus the reaction. The market is very much like an amoeba; it just lays there and undulates until something pokes it and then it reacts to that external stimulus. Your job as a chart reader is to find the point at which the charts prod the amoeba sufficiently to provoke a consistent, tradable reaction.

At my core I am a trend trader, so it is very important that you understand trends and how to identify them as you progress through this book. An *uptrend* is classically defined as a market that continually forms higher highs

Inside Range Bars (IRB) are another way the trend demonstrates its lack of power.

FIGURE 4.7

and higher lows. Simplistically, a chart that starts off low on the left-hand side and ends up higher on the right-hand side is trending up. (See Figure 4.8.)

A *downtrend* is defined as a market that continually forms lower highs and lower lows. Simplistically, a chart that starts off high on the left-hand side and ends up lower on the right-hand side is trending down. (See Figure 4.9.)

Markets are always cycling between overbought and oversold within the context of their trend. It is this cycle between too high, and too low that allows a trader to take money consistently out of a market. When a market moves up rapidly, traders begin to chase the offer as the momentum builds. Sooner or later, all the short-term players will have been filled for as many contracts as they choose. As each order is satisfied, another bull removes itself from the mix. The price spike will have created paper profits for many of the longs. As the momentum wanes, these bulls will begin to sell out their positions in order to convert paper profits into cash. It is through this process that price exhaustion occurs. At some point, there will be a moment in time when the market has nobody willing to buy. At this moment the equilibrium shifts, and the price will pivot down as the market swings to the downside. It is at this moment, and its mirror opposite as a market capitulates short term that we seek to identify. These

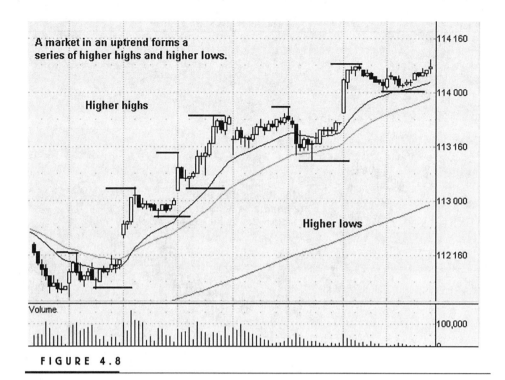

A market in an uptrend forms a
series of higher highs and higher lows.

Higher highs

Higher lows

Volume

FIGURE 4.8

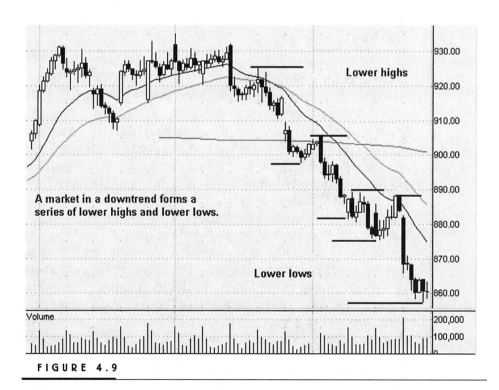

Lower highs

A market in a downtrend forms a
series of lower highs and lower lows.

Lower lows

Volume

FIGURE 4.9

are some of the lowest risk entries the market makes available, as the snapback effect of a market coming off overbought or oversold will deliver you a trending move.

In order to find these swing points, you need to begin to look at your charts as a series of moves to significant highs and lows. With practice, these swings will jump out at you, and their extremes will point out important price zones to focus on.

The amateur looks at the chart shown in Figure 4.10 and sees little.

The professional looks at the same chart and sees many tradable swings. Note carefully in Figure 4.11 every pivot point where price rolled over from bullish move to bearish, bearish to bullish. These extremes in price will give you your levels of chart support and resistance to watch.

The simplest and most basic price pattern to exploit the market's tendency to snap back from support and /or resistance is to sell into a rally to chart resistance or buy into a selloff to chart support. The psychology behind these trades is simple: Many amateurs buy or sell without a trading plan or stop loss order. When a trade goes against them, they tend to wait for it to come back before exiting.

When they miss a trade, they will tend to buy any time the price returns to the setup level. These actions, combined with the forces of a short-term overbought or oversold situation as described above, give that amoeba a major poke to deal with. (See Figure 4.12) for an example of a rally to chart resistance.

Then, a market in an uptrend breaks out with a large gap. This causes many to miss out on the trade. After a time, the price comes back to test the setup level, and many pile into this second-chance entry. This buy-side imbalance is what creates chart support in this example. (See Figure 4.13.)

To identify areas of chart support and resistance, remember this saying: "Resistance once broken becomes support, support once broken becomes resistance." For instance, look for areas in the past that acted as support or resistance; then if a prior resistance level has been broken and is being tested from above, be on the lookout for support to manifest itself.

Train your eye to break down your charts visually into price swings. As price moves to an extreme and reverses, the short-term trend will change and the market will pivot back in the opposite direction. This area of price rejection will identify the support and resistance levels that were significant in the past. (See Figure 4.14.) Watch carefully each time one of these levels is tested. A great deal of information about the hidden supply and demand in a market can be gleaned from these simple price points.

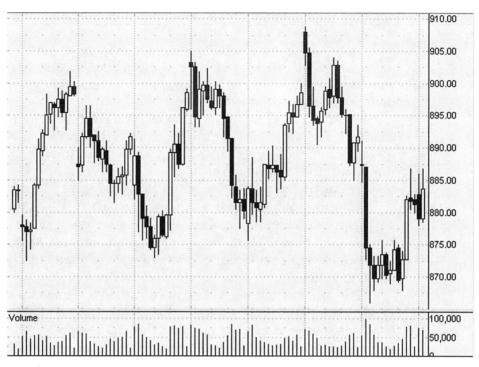

FIGURE 4.10

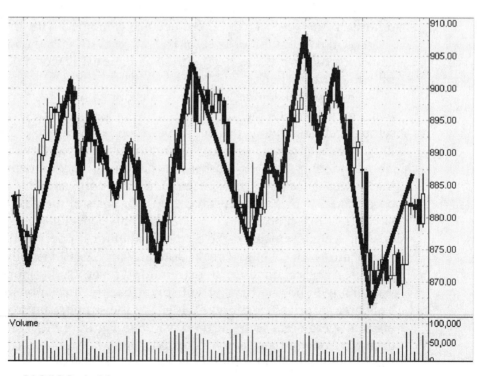

FIGURE 4.11

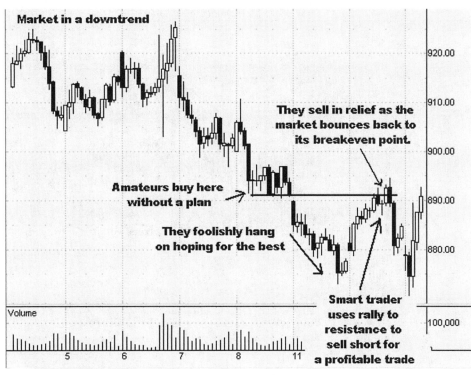

Market in a downtrend

They sell in relief as the market bounces back to its breakeven point.

Amateurs buy here without a plan

They foolishly hang on hoping for the best

Smart trader uses rally to resistance to sell short for a profitable trade

Volume

FIGURE 4.12

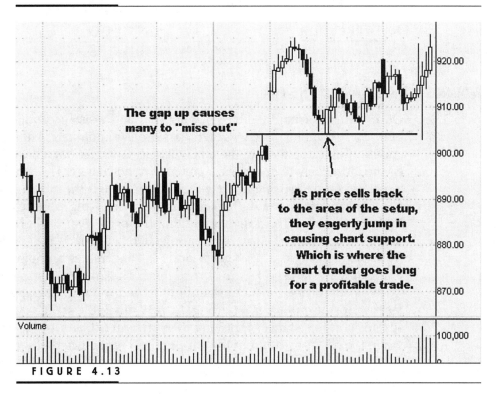

The gap up causes many to "miss out"

As price sells back to the area of the setup, they eagerly jump in causing chart support. Which is where the smart trader goes long for a profitable trade.

Volume

FIGURE 4.13

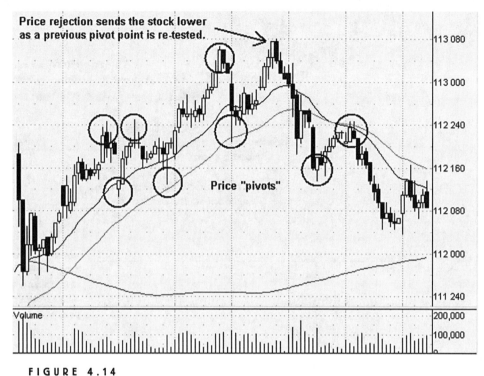

Price rejection sends the stock lower as a previous pivot point is re-tested.

Price "pivots"

113 080
113 000
112 240
112 160
112 080
112 000
111 240

Volume
200,000
100,000

FIGURE 4.14

ADDING INDICATORS TO THE MIX

Once you understand the basics of support and resistance, you can begin to build more complex strategies on these simple foundations. Adding indicators and candlestick patterns to the mix will help you filter out which support levels are most likely to provoke a significant trend change. The simplest of these indicators (and the one that I rely most heavily on) is the moving average.

The moving average is calculated by selecting a data point (open, high, low, or close) and then averaging the price over a selected period of time. As time passes and a new candlestick is formed, one bar is dropped from the series and a new bar is added. This creates a line on your chart that can act as a center point for a trend. The 20-period moving average (MA) is one of the most commonly followed moving averages, and is by far the most useful for my trading. In very much the same manner as chart support and resistance, a moving average will act as support or resistance when tested. In addition to the support and resistance that it provides, the 20 MA gives me a consistent way to gauge the power and health of a trend.

FIGURE 4.15

The daily chart in Figure 4.15 illustrates how the daily 20 MA gave four clear trend change indications over a period of 4 months.

1. A rally to 20 MA resistance turns the market lower for a multiweek decline.
2. A powerful gap up above the 20 MA gave a strong indication that the bulls had regained control of the market.
3. After a strong move to the upside, the market corrected and tested the 20 MA, which twice acted as support. After each test, the 20 MA triggered a surge of buying and a resumption of the trend.
4. After a buying wave which took price to new highs, another correction formed. This time, however, the support offered by the 20 MA was broken. This break of support was a clear indication that the buying surge had ended and the market was ready for a wave of selling.

As this example illustrates, the 20 MA acted not only as a roving area of support and resistance but also as a pass-fail area for the trend. It is this double usefulness that makes the moving average the most fundamental indicator.

Many of today's charting packages offer exponential as well as simple moving averages. The simple moving average is just the price (normally of the close) summed and divided in order to derive the average price. An exponential moving average (EMA) weights the recent data to provide a faster and more responsive indicator. I find these exponential moving averages to be slightly more accurate than the simple moving averages (SMAs) for the smaller periods. On any chart, in any time frame on my trading system you will find a green 20 EMA, a red 40 EMA, and a blue 200 SMA. Having traded with many other indicators, I still find myself coming back to these three moving averages when I trade. They give me an enormous amount of information upon which to base my directional bias, and offer a roving level of support and resistance against which to enter and exit.

If I overlay a 20 EMA on top of the 20 SMA that we analyzed previously (see Figure 4.16), you can see how the EMA more accurately pro-

FIGURE 4.16

vided support in mid-November and acted as resistance during the base in December. The differences can be subtle, and it is a matter of taste, but I find the exponential moving averages give me a slight edge over traders using the simple moving averages.

As the chart in Figure 4.16 shows, the 20 EMA acts as a centerline when a market is trending. It is a moving mean that the market will move toward and then away from as it cycles from overbought to oversold within the context of its trend. Before we continue onward, we need to explore the concepts of market expansion and contraction, capitulation and euphoria, overbought and oversold. What is overbought or oversold, and how is it useful to a trader?

EUPHORIA AND CAPITULATION

Markets are continually cycling in every time frame within the context of a trend. There are waves of buying which take the market higher; then as the bulls' power wanes, there are waves of selling that take the market lower. It is at these extremes that a market offers its most attractive trading opportunities. The reason for this lies in the psychological ramifications of euphoria and capitulation. For example, a market is basing quietly when a catalyst event sparks a surge of buying interest. The most informed and agile traders will be buying during this first wave. As the news of this new bullish sentiment trickles down to other market participants, they will also begin trading this market to the long side as they try to participate in the beginning of a new trend. As the trend continues, more and more bulls will use the pullbacks to enter. All of this action builds strong buying momentum to the upside, and as the trend heats up the momentum players will begin to enter as they try to capture a piece of the now rocketing move. At this point, all the swing trade setups have been triggered and their orders filled, the position traders have seen entry signals as well, and the momentum players are hammering the offer as they chase the market higher. All of these forces combine to create a market with many buyers and very few sellers. Because there is no liquidity on the offer, bulls late to the party are forced to pay extraordinary prices in order to establish a position.

The market at this point has become faddish. In the same way parents will line up for hours or pay an extraordinary premium for *the* hot toy at Christmas, greedy and foolish traders will pay through the nose in order to get long when they are afraid they are missing the move of the century. As this euphoric situation develops, there will come a time when all the bulls' orders have been filled and nobody is willing to chase the market further. In an instant, the market that had been dominated by the bulls becomes a market with few buyers. The lack of depth on the bid creates a vacuum into which the price is quickly sucked. Thus, the top is formed and the scramble to take profits begins. Again, the most informed and agile traders will be the first to take profits. The profit-taking will trickle down the food chain as the selling pressure builds in a mirror image to the move up. As the market entered euphoria, it was driven by those panicked that they were missing out on the move. After the market flips and the selling pressure builds, the market is driven by those panicked by rapidly diminishing paper profits (or outright losses). At some point this panic will come to a head, and the market will become saturated by selling with very few buyers to be seen. As the market capitulates, the last wave of sellers screams, "Get me out at any cost!" After these orders are filled, for an instant the market will have no selling pressure. In the same manner that price was sucked down after euphoria, this capitulating market gets sucked up as buyers try to get filled on a virtually nonexistent offer. This turns the market to the upside, and the cycle begins all over again. The smaller the time frame the more frequent the market will cycle from

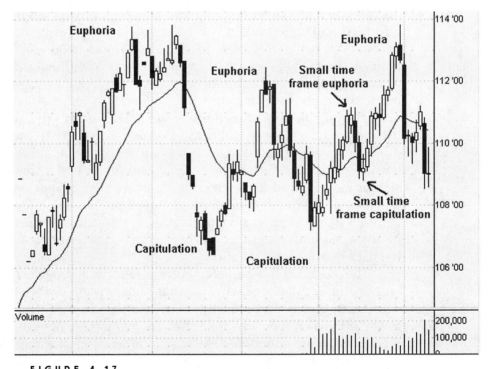

FIGURE 4.17

15 - minute chart becomes oversold
as the daily 40ema is tested.
The small time frame capitulation
into larger time frame support
increases the odds for a trend change.

15-min chart

FIGURE 4.18

euphoria to capitulation (overbought to oversold). You may observe four complete cycles within 1 trading day on a 15-minute chart, while it may take many months or years for a market to cycle from euphoria to capitulation at a weekly level.

In the daily chart of the 10-year Treasury note shown in Figure 4.17, you can see how the market moved from euphoria to capitulation again and again over several months. Each of these turning points offered an excellent trading opportunity as the market completed a super swing from daily euphoria to capitulation.

TURNING SIMPLE TREND ANALYSIS INTO A PROFITABLE TRADING STRATEGY

With the basic building blocks of capitulation and euphoria, support and resistance, you can build many profitable trading strategies. When a market exhibits signs of capitulation in the smaller time frames while testing an area of support from its bigger time frames, you have one of the lowest risk entries possible. Both these forces will bring buyers to the market, and so your trade starts off on a good foot. All you can ask yourself as a trader is to correctly identify the direction and health of the trend, and then nab the best entry possible as you try to position yourself in the line of least resistance.

In the multi time frame example shown in Figure 4.18, the 15-minute chart becomes extremely oversold after a sustained wave of selling takes it lower without any wiggles to take the pressure off. This selling wave begins to show signs of capitulation just as the daily 40-period exponential moving average is tested. The combination of an oversold market's tendency to bounce and the buying likely to be attracted by the larger time frame moving average support greatly increases the odds for a significant trend change in this area.

The simple correction trade (buying the dips or selling the rallies) is the basis for many a trading system. At its heart it is a trend-following strategy; the correction trade's premise is based on the fact that a trending market is likely to continue trending until major support or resistance is tested.

In the 1-minute chart of the S&P E-Mini shown in Figure 4.19, we begin with euphoria and a double top (1). As the market rallies sharply, volume

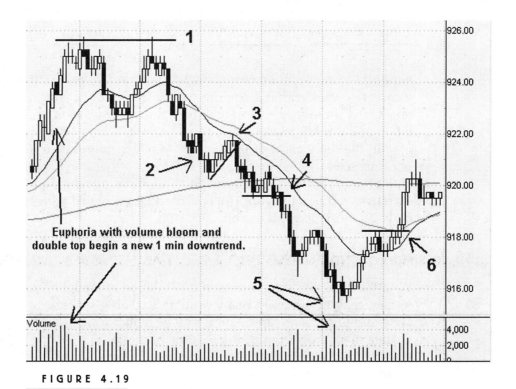

Euphoria with volume bloom and double top begin a new 1 min downtrend.

FIGURE 4.19

42

rises dramatically and smart traders begin to exit their longs. This selling pressure eventually overcomes the bullish power, and the market tops out. Next, a wave of profit taking hits the market as those less informed begin to react to the topping pattern. Some traders just freeze. Without a clear trading plan, they have no clear objectives for their exit. Having missed the top, they are unwilling to close out their longs, having given back so much of their paper profits. After the wave of selling has finished, the market bounces. As price retests the previous high, all the traders who were winging it sigh in relief and exit as the highs are tested. This selling pressure creates the most classic chart pattern of them all—the double top. This retest of resistance can be seen at many major trend changes. It acts as final confirmation of a change in trend.

Since a trend is comprised of a series of higher highs and higher lows, the double-top pattern signals that the market has failed to reach a higher high and is likely to turn. Short sellers attracted to the double top begin to sell into a market already weak and saturated with the sell orders of the second-chancers. It begins to sell off in earnest and falls in a straight line until it becomes oversold in the area of the 200 SMA (2).

Traders begin to take profits as the market reaches moving average support, and a corrective wave begins to form. This is the pullback, the wiggle, which offers a low-risk entry into a trending market. Traders are watching this rally as it tests the overhead resistance at the 20 EMA (3).

They begin to sell as that resistance is tested, and the trend resumes. Those with scalp expectations begin to cover as the lows are tested, using the prior level of chart support as a profit objective. Again the market becomes a bit extended to the downside and starts to correct. When a market becomes oversold, it needs to resolve itself through correction. It can do so in one of two ways. The first and most common is a price correction (3). Price moves in a countertrend manner as the market reverts to the mean. The second way price can correct is through time (4). If the profit takers who bring buying pressure to the market are counterbalanced by bearish order flow, the market will find a range of equilibrium and begin to base sideways. This, like the rally to resistance or pullback to support, is a trend continuation pattern. After the market has based long enough to relieve the overbought and/or oversold pressure, price will tend to break out of the range and the trend should continue as it seeks major support or resistance levels. You can see how in both these examples, once the lower trend line was broken the overall trend quickly resumed. A bullish time correction and breakout can be seen after the market bottomed (6). Notice also that the market formed that bottom after giving out clear signs of capitulation (5) as the volume bloomed, and bottoming tails began to form.

More often than not, you will not notice the euphoria or capitulation action until it is too late to take the trade. Instead, these blowout reversal patterns will become your signposts for reversal as you begin to stalk the market for continuation patterns that will allow you to profit from the new trend.

While all of these continuation patterns can be lumped together as pullback or correction trades, for clarity they can be separated into three subgroups: pennants, flags, and triangles.

THE PENNANT

A pennant is a time correction in which the market bases in a more or less horizontal range. (See Figure 4.20.) This base near highs or bullish breakout pattern is one of the oldest in the technical analysts' arsenal. After a sharp upthrust or pole is seen, the market is overbought and ready for a rest. It begins to trade in a sloppy channel as profit takers begin to sell their shares to the accumulators who are using the base to build positions of size in anticipation of a breakout. The classic way to trade a breakout or pennant price pattern is to buy a break of the upper trend line, with a protective stop

FIGURE 4.20

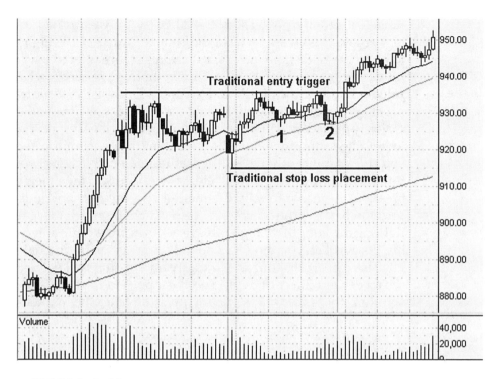

FIGURE 4.21

loss order placed beneath the lower trend line. (This pattern can be easily inverted to generate a short trade when a market produces a base or pennant near lows.) In a momentum-driven market, buying breakouts and selling breakdowns can be a simple and effective way to trade. However, the pennant is probably the most commonly followed price pattern in any intraday market, and since so many traders are watching, it is advantageous for you to play these pennants in a slightly hybridized manner.

Consider the textbook breakout pattern shown in Figure 4.21, which formed and set up over the course of several sessions. Using a traditional breakout strategy, a long would have been triggered around 936 as the highs of the range were broken. The breakout move offered approximately 12 points of profit potential by the close on Monday. However, using a traditional stop loss placement strategy, your stop would have been in the 915 neighborhood. So even though as a traditionally managed breakout this setup made you money, it offered a poor risk-to-reward ratio due to its large stop.

If you had identified this pennant pattern early, and were willing to stalk it intraday, two much more elegant entries presented themselves on Friday. After a lows-to-highs move that terminated into the highs of the range, an orderly pullback to the 20 EMA (1) was formed. At this point a higher low was created within the pennants range. This higher low helped to focus the bullish power against the resistance offered by the high of the range. If you missed the first pullback, there was a second chance (2) as the price fell to test the 40 EMA. By entering against these intra-range pull-backs, you put two significant edges behind your trade. First, since the majority of traders will be focused on the traditional entry trigger, it is easy to get filled intra-range and as a result slippage is minimized. Second, by entering significantly below the traditional entry trigger, you will be sit-ting on a small open profit as the crowd begins to take their entries. If the breakout is unable to rally the market and the pennant ends up as a fail-ure, you have a profit cushion within which to scratch the trade. Instead of fighting for your fill along with every other breakout trader who is watch-ing this market, you can focus on the action as the traditional setup occurs. In a successful breakout, the liquidity on the offer will get very thin, you'll see an excited flurry of buying on the tape, and the price should shoot out significantly as the setups' buying pressure takes the market higher. If you

FIGURE 4.22

never see any excitement on the tape, or if the buying surge occurs with little positive price movement within, the chances for pattern failure are high and a scratch should be considered.

THE FLAG

A flag is simply a pennant that fails to maintain its horizontal channel. I define a bull flag as a channel-bound correction that pushes back in a countertrend manner at an angle of 30 degrees or less. A bull flag retraces bearishly within the context of an uptrend; a bear flag retraces bullishly within the context of a downtrend. In Figure 4.22, you can see a textbook bull flag (1), which corrects in a channel-bound manner, tests the 20 EMA, and then sees an almost immediate trend resumption. Again, just like a pennant you can either take the traditional entry trigger as the market breaks above the upper trend line or try to nab the trade as it tests support. In this instance, a buy at the 20 EMA would have put you in excellent position going into the area of the traditional entry trigger. After a solid rally, the market became overbought again and a new correction formed (2). This time it was a pennant-type correction, and you can see once again how the optimal entry was available as the 20 EMA was tested.

THE TRIANGLE

The final continuation pattern that I feel is most important to understand is the triangle. (See Figure 4.23.) As you begin to gain experience, you will notice again and again how market trends tend to breathe as they work themselves out. There are sharp increases in volatility as price thrusts are printed, then some form of correction as the market catches its breath after a move into an overbought or oversold position. The most obvious way a market can burn off some overbought energy is through a price correction. But sometimes a market is so strong that all it does is pause for a few days before moving higher. During these powerful impulse moves, triangle patterns are often the only tradable setups. As you can see in the chart in Figure 4.23, an extremely powerful bull move was under way in this market. After the initial price thrust (1), there was a 3-day pause in the trend. During this time, volatility sharply decreased, forming a symmetrical triangle. Just as markets tend to cycle from overbought to oversold, their volatility cycles as well. When a market gets very quiet, it is usually building energy for a sharp volatility breakout as some technical trigger brings action and focus back to the market. Each of the triangles highlighted on the chart below had different durations, but each shows a period of

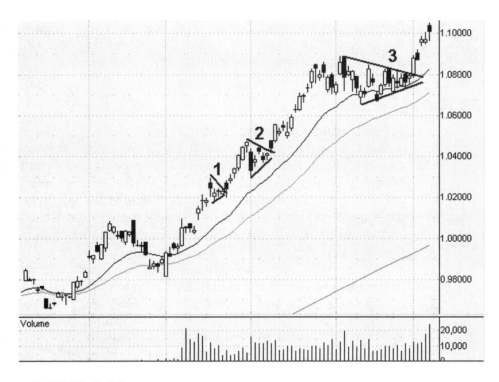

FIGURE 4.23

sharply declining volatility. Sooner or later, the two trend lines converge and there is a sharp price thrust in the direction of the initial trend line break.

The triangles shown in Figure 4.23 are all symmetrical triangles. After the initial price thrust, the volatility decreases symmetrically without any particular bias from the bulls or bears. However, if the bears have control of the market when a triangle forms, the volatility constriction will take on the appearance of a descending triangle.

In the example shown in Figure 4.24, the market is in the process of filling a dramatic gap to the upside. The market falls and finds a zone of support near the moving average around 895. This congestion near support exhibits the hallmarks of a descending triangle. First, it is a consolidation after a sharp move to the downside. The consolidation is formed with a series of lower highs (1), yet refuses to make a lower low. It is this declining upper trend line and horizontal lower trend line (2) that gives the descending triangle the diving platform it needs to set up and trend. The classic trigger for a descending triangle is a break of the lower trend line (3). Stops are traditionally set a few ticks above the upper trend line.

FIGURE 4.24

Whenever possible, I like to take a more aggressive entry against the upper trend line resistance on a rally within the triangle. For these more aggressive entries, I will usually set my protective stop loss above some previous test of the upper trend line.

When the bulls have control of a market as volatility begins to constrict, an ascending triangle will often form.

The pattern illustrated in Figure 4.25 is the mirror image of a descending triangle and has the same power to produce an accurate directional bias. After a move up, a series of higher lows begins to form (1). This establishes the lower trend line of the ascending triangle. The overhanging resistance creates a horizontal line beyond which the price is unable to trade. This creates the upper trend line of the triangle (2), and defines the classic trigger point. As with the descending triangle, the classic trigger for this pattern is a break of the horizontal upper trend line, (3) with protective stop loss orders set a few ticks below the lower trend line (1). Whenever possible I like to try and nab an elegant entry off the support offered by the lower trend line. As with the descending triangle, I then place my protective stop loss order below a previous test of trend line support.

FIGURE 4.25

AGGRESSIVE ENTRIES

Whenever I have a strong sense for the market and its trend, I like to become more aggressive as I stalk entries into these continuation patterns. Let's look at an example from a strongly trending move that offered two such continuation scenarios.

The first opportunity comes in the form of a bull flag. (See Figure 4.26.) This channel bound correction back to moving average support is classically triggered by a break of the upper trend line around 882 (2). Stop loss orders would have been set a few ticks under the lower trend line around 880. An aggressive trader would have been focused and ready to buy as soon as signs of support were seen in the area of the moving average. By the time support could have been identified and reacted to, the aggressive trader could have filled the position around 880.75 (1). The stop level and profit expectations for this pattern remain the same, so by taking a more aggressive entry, the focused trader has more than halved the risk by taking the stop from 2 full points to only .75. The trade sets up and works out nicely. Profits are taken as the market breaks above a previous swing high

FIGURE 4.26

(3) around 884. The more conservative classic flag entry would have yielded 2 points of profit for a 2-point risk (a 1-to-1 trade). The aggressive trader risked .75, and banked a gain of 3.25 points (a more than 4-to-1 gain). Nine times out of ten, this dramatic increase in risk-to-reward ratios more than offsets the increased risk you assume when entering a trade before it sets up. A more aggressive entry strategy will result in a decreased accuracy rate, but can have a much larger profit potential over time if the risk-to-reward ratios can remain high. Let's say that a classic trader and an aggressive trader had both taken this bull flag with positions scaled to assume $1000 in risk. The classic trader would have taken in $1000 in profit whereas the aggressive trader would have banked more than $4000 in the same pattern with the same amount of dollar risk assumed at the outset! There is also a positive mental edge I have seen develop in the clients that I coach as they begin to take more aggressive entries. Not only does it reduce your risk, thus allowing you to take larger positions to increase your potential for gain, but there is something very positive about reaching into the market and snatching the trade before the classic trading crowd picks up on the pattern.

The second continuation pattern in the example above is an ascending triangle. Again, the classic entry strategy is to wait for the upper trend line to break. The aggressive trader, however, would have taken the trade long as the market based into the uptrending 20-period exponential moving average around 883 to 883.50 (4). Although not offering the dramatic increase in performance that the bull flag offered to an aggressive trader, this pattern still offered an aggressive entry that is .50 to .75 below the classic trend line set up around 884 (5). As the market set up the ascending triangle, there was a violent spike to the upside. A very wide range bar was printed on higher than average volume. This euphoric action offered a good exit signal for the swing trader hoping to capture the move out of the setup (6). Again, the classic trader was able to take profits in the 1 to 1 area while the aggressive trader took in better than 2-to-1 gains.

This example also shows how sticking to the plan can cause mental anguish! Having taking the proper action and exiting as the market exhibited signs of euphoria (6), traders then had to sit and watch the market rise another 2.5 points. This frustration in missing what is perceived as potential profit needs to be put into perspective. If you traded these two continuation patterns aggressively, you would have just banked 5 units of profit. This is a more than respectable yield for just two trades. The professional trader sees his or her trading as a *process* with each trade acting only as the tiniest piece in an overall puzzle. In the same vein, each trade's sole reason for existence is to deliver a unit or two of profit. Unless you're willing to hold for an extended period of time and sit through many corrections, gains of better than 3 to 1 will be rare. Your job as a swing trader is to capture the swing. Buy near the lows of the flag, then sell as the flag reaches the resistance offered by the previous swing high. If the market goes up steadily for a week after that, it really should not bother you. You planned to capture the swing from support to resistance. You sized the position properly to a predetermined level of dollar risk, and banked a proportional gain as the trade met your definition of success. Since you had not planned on targeting a larger move, it is a waste of time to mourn any missed gains. They were not targeted by your plan, so as far as you are concerned they do not exist.

ELLIOTT WAVE ANALYSIS

So once you are adept at identifying generic pullbacks to support or resistance—bull flags, bear flags, triangles, and bullish and bearish pennants—which of these patterns should you actually pay attention to? Enter Mr.

Elliott! In the early 1930s and 1940s, a gentleman by the name of Ralph Nelson Elliott developed a theory of market structure that has remained popular to this day. It is a deep and fascinating subject about which many books have been written. For practical purposes, I only use one facet of Elliott's discovery—namely the tendency for trending markets to form five price waves to the upside before a more complex correction is likely to form. By harnessing this tendency, we can choose which pullbacks to target for a continuation-type trade. In the above example, the market is stuck in a sliding range until a breakout occurs mid-Friday. In my view, this breakout triggers the next period of bullish trend. If you subscribe to Elliott's theories, then the third and fifth waves will likely offer the best profit potential. For this reason the first two continuation patterns shown in Figure 4.27 (1 and 2) after a new leg begins will offer the highest odds for success. If you think this through logically, it makes sense. If the market is indeed trending with a series of higher highs and higher lows, or lower lows and lower highs, then after two successful pullback trades the trend will have matured quite significantly. The more astute traders will have been trading aggressively off the first and second pullbacks, and will

FIGURE 4.27

FIGURE 4.28

now be exiting into the fifth wave as the market becomes overbought. Only the less informed and therefore weaker players will continue to look for pullbacks after the first and second opportunities have come and gone. At this point the trend has matured and profit-taking forces will be lurking just below the surface. Any lower high or indication of weakness will get sold aggressively as those who positioned themselves against the first two pullbacks take their profit. Remember this simple rhyme: "Pullback's three? Let them be" and you will avoid many of the sucker patterns that print, set up, and then flush (3).

PEEK REVERSALS

After the base near highs or lows, the double top is probably the most widely known and followed price pattern, but the best double top or bottom variation is what I call a peek top. For this pattern to form, the price must break above the previous high or low and then quickly reverse. This price pattern is the best example of one of my philosophies for reading any chart. It is easily summed up in one sentence: "That which should go up, *should go up!*" When a market breaks out above a previous swing high, that is a buy signal for many trading styles. This should bring buyers to the market, and price should respond quickly to that buying surge. But what if it doesn't? Then lick your lips and get ready to trade because the market has just given you a peek at its cards! Without constant buying pressure, The trend will crumble. So if the market broke to new highs and did not have the strength to continue higher, it proves there is a serious lack of bullish sponsorship. Since a lack of sponsorship will allow the trend to crumble, a peek top or bottom offers a very low-risk entry into a possible change in trend.

On this 5-minute chart of the S&P 500 (see Figure 4.28), there were four peek reversals in the space of 2 days. The first was formed (1) after the market broke to new highs, then reversed for a quick pullback to 20 EMA support. It then rallied, took out the high of the day by just a few ticks, and closed out the candlestick with a topping tail. You can see how quickly the selling took the market right back to chart support. Then the market put in a false breakdown below that chart support forming a peek bottom (2). This peek reversed the market hard into the close.

The next day the market opened off a gap down. It spent the first hour printing nothing but trendless chop, then a powerful surge of buying hit the market. This buy spike took the market into small time frame euphoria, which was finally halted by... (a gold star to anyone who noticed the chart resistance left over from the previous day). In a giant highs-to-lows move, it retraced the buy spike 100 percent. The price then broke below the low for the day and quickly reversed (3), forming the third peek bottom. Price took its time getting back to the highs, but it finally did so (4) and formed the fourth peek top of this chart. Again, the power of the peek took over as the market slammed back down off the highs around 920.

If you've noticed a theme here, congratulations! Almost every price pattern I trade is based around the concept of buying a market when it is short-term oversold into an area of support, or selling a market when it is short-term overbought into an area of resistance. The concepts of overbought and oversold are quite subjective and can be debated at length. An *oscillator* is a technical indicator that attempts to identify objectively when markets are trading at overbought or oversold levels. There are many, many oscillators available in every charting package. Personally, I found that once I trained my eye, I was able to identify overbought or oversold with much more precision and accuracy than by simply relying on an oscillator for overbought or oversold identification. However, I found the Stochastic Oscillator to be very useful for me as I built experience and trained my eye.

UTILIZING A STOCHASTIC OSCILLATOR

The Stochastic Oscillator is perhaps the most popular momentum indicator in the technical analysts' arsenal. If you look at price charts during a strongly trending move as a market moves into euphoria, you'll see that the majority of the candlesticks will close near their high. The Stochastic Oscillator's formula tracks where a market has closed relative to its price range over a specific period of time. When a market is continually closing near its highs, the Stochastic Oscillator will have a very high reading, alerting you to the fact that a euphoric condition may be nearing. When a market is continually closing near its lows, the Stochastic Oscillator will have a very low reading, alerting you to the fact that a capitulation may be coming. The classic settings for the Stochastic Oscillator are 14 periods with a three-period smoothing value for the secondary line. Oversold is usually defined as a reading of 20 or lower, while overbought is defined as a reading of 80 or higher. Figure 4.29 shows what those settings look like when drawn on a 15-minute chart of the S&P 500.

The darker of the two lines is the %K, and the lighter is the smoothed %D. The most basic use of the Stochastic Oscillator is to wait for an over-

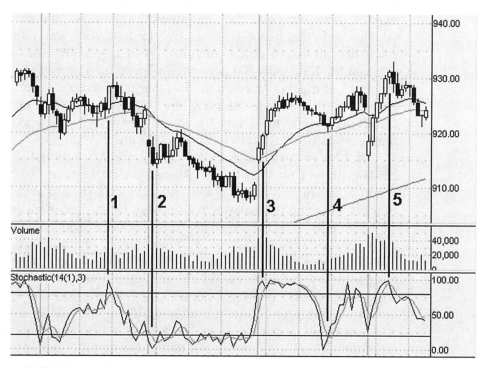

FIGURE 4.29

bought or oversold signal, then take entry as the %K crosses the %D in the direction of the anticipated reversal. This strategy never proved very useful for me, as the signals can come one after the other, or be very premature in a runaway market. A good example of this is seen in the third example (3). There is a gap up in price, and the Stochastic Oscillator reaches the overbought level within the first 30 minutes of trading. The %K breaks below the %D, giving a short signal in the face of a sharply trending market.

I quickly found that if I ignored the stochastic signals themselves, and instead used the Stochastic Oscillator as a filter, it became a much more useful tool. You can see how the strong rally candlestick took the Stochastic Oscillator into overbought territory (1) just before the topping tail was printed and the market turned lower. Had you entered that trade as a short, the next oversold reading (2) gave you an accurate indication that the market was ready to wiggle. Exiting based on that oversold reading would have helped you avoid the following bear flag. The oversold reading after the strong move off the gap (4) would have alerted you to begin focusing on a pullback entry. On the last day (5), there was another

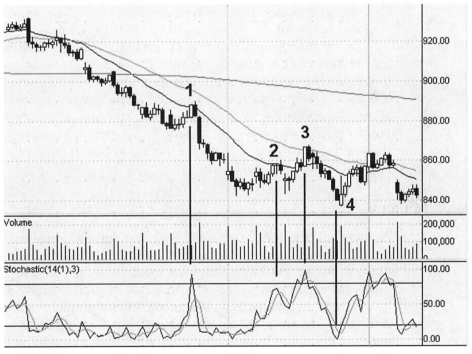

FIGURE 4.30

gap down and violent rally. The overbought reading there started you thinking about a short as the euphoria waned.

For a real-world example, let's look at the 60-minute chart of the S&P 500 E-Minis in Figure 4.30. It is obvious that this stock is in a downtrend, so we want to be looking for bearish continuation patterns. The first rally back toward the 20 EMA (1) is accompanied by a sharp spike in the stochastic indicator that takes it above the overbought threshold around 80. This overbought reading helped to confirm the bear flag as it tested the area of resistance offered by the 20-period exponential moving average. This bear flag followed through nicely, and after the selling finally exhausted itself it formed another perfect bear flag back to the 20-period exponential moving average (2). However, as you can see, the stochastics never passed the overbought threshold, and this nonconfirmation kept you out of a poorly performing setup. After the false setup off the 20-period exponential moving average, price rallied up to test the 40-period exponential moving average just above. This time the stochastics *did* spike above the overbought line to help confirm the rally to resistance setup, which quickly followed through to retest the lows for the day. The lows for the day were then broken, but this breakdown was short-lived. The breakdown or reverse scenario offered a nice peek bottom to go long against (4). Once again, a glance down at your stochastic indicator helped confirm the oversold nature of the market as the peek bottom formed.

So the stochastics can act as a useful indicator for confirmation as you try to filter out all but the trades with the highest chances for clean follow-through. They act like a set of training wheels as you begin to train your eye and develop your feel as a trader. Some systems will also let you set alarms based on the stochastics output. You can set your system to alert you when the market begins to trade into overbought or oversold territory, thus saving time as you focus on the markets only when the chances are optimal for a successful trade.

FIRST FAILURES

Another set of reversal patterns I find particularly useful are not based on support or resistance at all, but rather the inability of the trend to break through for a new higher high or lower low. The first lower high that forms at the end of a sustained uptrend is a signal to many market participants that a trend change is imminent. After a period of sustained buying during an uptrend, just about every trend-following style will have triggered an entry and be sitting on open profit. When the trend finally begins to lose steam, there will be a final pullback trade that sets up and follows through, but is unable to break out and form one last higher high. As the uptrend forms its first lower high, anticipatory traders will begin to take profits off the table. As a topping tail or Doji reversal candlestick forms, a second group of traders will be aggressively trailing their stops beneath that candle's low. The last chance for the trend usually occurs as the 20 EMA is tested. At this point, the last group of traders remaining from the uptrend are clinging to the hope that the support the moving average offers will be strong enough to turn the stock higher for an eventual break new high. Let's analyze an example of this first lower high pattern from the daily chart of the S&P 500. (See Figure 4.31.)

After a sustained uptrend, the S&P 500 prints a much deeper than normal correction during the month of December. (Usually, an uncharacteristically correction act is an accurate indication that a first lower high will be formed.) The correction eventually found support and bounced rather sharply at first. It ran out of steam just below the swing high from early December. It ended the day with a Doji (1), which brought in enough selling to take the price back to test the 20 EMA. You can see how this moving average offered some support, as a small bottom tail formed the day

FIGURE 4.31

59

the moving average was tested. However, 20 EMA was easily broken during the next day's trading, and this final failure of support triggered an intensive wave of selling. An aggressive strategy would have been to trigger a short entry under the lows of the daily Doji, with a protective stop loss order set above that Doji's high. A more conservative trader could have used the break of the 20 EMA as confirmation for entry. Once again, a protective stop loss order set above the Doji candlestick's high would offer good protection against pattern failure.

You can easily stand the first lower high pattern on its head as a long pattern. The psychology behind a first higher low is precisely the same. After a sustained downtrend, there is profit to be taken and the first higher low sends a strong signal to the bears that the party is over.

The 15-minute chart of the S&P 500 shown in Figure 4.32 shows a classic first higher low trade from entry to exit. It begins with a sustained downtrend that takes the stock down to an eventual low around 817. Note the volume bloom as the stock gaps and sells off violently in the morning. There is a quick bounce off the capitulation lows and then off a final wave

FIGURE 4.32

of selling, which takes the price back down toward the lows. The capitulation and its subsequent bounce have broken this market away from bearish control, so it is unable to break down below 817 and forms its first higher low (1). Again, the aggressive traders would take entry above the reversal candlestick's highs, with protective stop loss orders set below that candlestick's low. More conservative traders might wish to wait for a break of the 20 EMA. Each entry trigger is valid, and as you can see will offer profit potential for a successful first higher low. After a sustained rally off the first higher low, the market confirms its change in trend with a small correction back toward the 20 EMA (2). Utilizing Elliott's wave theory, we would wish to exit into the buying surge off the second pullback. The rally up to test the 200 SMA (3) offers a perfect target for this trade's exit. You can see how the market kept within the Elliott wave mold as it formed a final sucker pullback (4), then a first lower high (5) as it traded in the resistance offered by the 200 SMA. Note how the first lower high (5) pattern offered some nice profit potential to the short side as it sold off, formed a bear flag, and continued to fall into the close. The first higher low began a new uptrend in this example, and a first lower high ended it.

All the patterns described above are derived from the basic building blocks of market action. They are universal tools that a trader can use to trade in any time frame, in any market. Some markets may favor one pattern more than another, but the basics of support and resistance, overbought and oversold, exhaustion and capitulation remain the same as long as there are human beings interacting within the context of a market. So having discussed the concepts of trade generation it's time to take the next step—converting your market opinion into hard cash!

CHAPTER 5

Entry Tactics and Trade Examples

> The point of investing is not to guess the future, but to act on new information before the whole world pounces on the idea.
>
> — *Todd G. Buchholz*

My rules for entry are simple as my patterns and tactics are derived from the basics of market action. I want my trading style to be easy to execute, and to be sustainable through any number of market environments. All the exotic setups and tweaky trade strategies I have experimented with over the years have eventually broken down, and I ended up going back to my basics. I began to understand the value of building expertise with the simplest trading setups, as these were the most available in every time frame and provided a strong edge in just about every market environment. My standard trigger for entry is a simple bar break. When I identify an area of support or resistance that I feel is important, I watch for a reversal candlestick to form. Once the candlestick is finished, I have the confirmation needed to take an entry. (See Figure 5.1.)

I will enter the trade when the price breaks above the reversal candlestick's high (1). My protective stop loss order will then be set below that candlestick's low (2). This bar entry strategy is based on the premise that the stock has reversed, and the candlestick is the proof. Therefore, if the market is able to break below that reversal candlestick's low, my opinion will have been proven false and I would need to take my loss. Sometimes the market doesn't pivot cleanly, as the second inset shows. As an inside range bar forms, the trader has two options. Leave your trigger for entry above the original reversal bar's high (3), or tighten your trigger above the inside range bar (4). The tighter entry trigger will offer a smaller stop, but has a higher chance of false setup. This, as everything in trading is a judg-

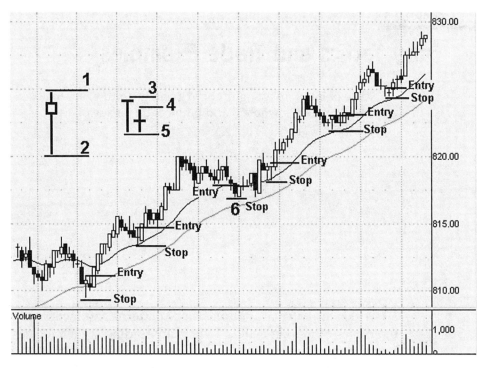

ment call, is a tradeoff between richer risk-to-reward ratios and lower accuracy. For either entry trigger, the stop remains the same, set a few ticks below the first reversal bar's lows (5). You can see how the pullback trade (6) tested the 20-period exponential moving average, then continued to sell off *without triggering* as it formed one more bar of selling. As the reversal formed, placing a buy stop above the reversal bar's high gave you an excellent entry point as the trend continuation occurred. You can also see how many profitable pullback entries were available during this clean uptrend.

In the chart shown in Figure 5.2, we have a real-world example of an inside range bar setup. After a bear flag that rallies to test the 20-period exponential moving average, an inside range bar is formed. Trailing your sell stop under that bar's low (2) with a protective stop loss set above the original candlestick's high (1) allowed for a better entry with a tighter stop than the original reversal bar.

Since my trades are almost always based around tests of support or resistance, setting my targets for profit taking is usually quite simple. As a swing trader, I am trying to capture a move from support or resistance or

FIGURE 5.2

resistance to support. Since the trade example above was a rally to resistance in the context of a downtrend, my logical profit objective would be the support area offered by the price gap from a few days back (3). As you can see, this area of support not only signaled exit but it also formed a reversal candlestick and offered a buy-off support. In an orderly swinging market, you can often flip your positions from long to short as the market ping-pongs from support to resistance within the context of its trend.

So with the basics in place, let's move through some examples of trade entry and exit within the context of a changing trend.

CASE STUDIES

In the example from the S&P 500 shown in Figure 5.3, we start off with a market that rapidly becomes quite oversold. After a rather large gap, the selling continues until the bounce begins. I would definitely be stalking the rally for a short opportunity against the 20-period EMA. The bounce was short-lived, however, and the 20-period EMA was never tested.

FIGURE 5.3

The price fell as the bounce began to fail, but was unable to break or even retest the previous swing low. This higher low (1) was the first indication that the trend was about to change. The changing trend was confirmed as price broke above the previous swing high to form a higher high. This resistance, once broken became support, and this support was tested as the price began to correct (2). Using the bar break entry strategy, a buy stop set above the reversal candlestick with a protective stop loss order set below its lows put you in the trade very near to the lows of the correction. Where was the logical target to use as a price objective? The first and most likely to be tested is the resistance offered by the previous swing high (3). The second and more optimistic target would be for a move up to test the gap resistance around 868 (4). Either target was a valid choice. In a stereotypical move, the market quickly and easily retested the previous swing high. Then it wiggled back down to test the break-even point, before turning higher to eventually reach the gap fill profit objective. Here is a perfect example of the balance between smaller gains and the ease with which they reach their target, and the games the market will play if you hold out for larger gains. In this example, both price objectives were met, but you were forced to endure a lot more price discomfort before a larger gain was seen.

After the gap was filled, another correction formed as price moved back to test the 20-period EMA (5). For this trade the most logical profit objective would be a test of the 200-period SMA lurking overhead. This profit objective was easily reached as the pullback bounced off moving average support (6). By exiting into the 200-period SMA, you left quite a bit of profit on the table. *Never* let this bother you! You shouldn't mourn that which you never targeted! Your initial trade plan was to initiate a long on a pullback to moving average support, then exit for profit into moving average resistance. That trade was a bang-up success; what happened after that has no relevance since it was not a part of your original trade plan. I cannot emphasize this point strongly enough: Clearly define your opinion and develop your trade plan before any entry is taken. Then, manage the trade according to your original plan, and congratulate yourself if your profit objectives are met. I have worked with many traders who allowed these false "I couldas" to spill over into their next couple of trades. The errors they committed as they responded to the mental pain they felt from missing out would inevitably cost them more in real dollars than any fantasy gains they felt they missed. When a trade goes according to your plan and is closed at the profit objective, pat yourself on the back and begin to look for your next play.

The next play in the S&P 500 was a pullback to the support offered by the 200-period simple moving average...*or was it?*

Let's step back and look at the day's action with our Elliott wave glasses. If we believe the trend changed as a higher high was formed, then our first pullback (2) was wave 2 in an Elliott cycle! The next pullback (5) would have been wave 4, and the last high odds pullback in the trend. Because of our knowledge of Elliott wave theory, we would have avoided the pullback to the 200-period SMA. This proved to be the best choice in hindsight as the market was unable to retest the previous swing high. By keeping track of our probable wave count, we not only avoided a mediocre setup but we are also expecting a more serious A-B-C correction to form. Thus, the lower high (7) offers a high odds setup for a short trade. A sell stop placed under the reversal bar's lows, with a protective stop loss set above that bar's high was a great way to initiate the trade. If the opinion based on the Elliott wave theory is correct, then this should be a meaningful correction. If that is the case, then it is likely that the support offered by the 200-period SMA, the 20- and 40-period EMAs will be broken. If this is the case, where is the most logical support level to use as a profit objective? In my opinion, the pullback lows (5) around 866 will offer support to a falling market and will act as a good profit objective for this trade. A limit order to cover just above 866 would have been filled easily (8) for another profitable trade.

It is this objective analysis of trend—Elliott wave count, support and resistance—that allows the skilled trader to capture a great deal of market movement within one bull-to-bear cycle, all the while controlling risk and maximizing gains. Each trade in this example offered a good risk-to-reward ratio, and the pullback entries had reversal candlesticks to use for entry trigger or stop loss placement.

A MORE CHAOTIC EXAMPLE

Having an example of perfect order and trend change is nice for illustrative purposes, but as anyone who has ever executed a live trade knows...the market delights in throwing you curve balls! Let's look at an example of a market moving from order to chaos, alignment to misalignment, payout to payback.

As shown in Figure 5.4, we began our analysis with the first pullback after a bottom has occurred (1). The market pulled back to test support

FIGURE 5.4

offered by the 20-period EMA, and formed a reversal candlestick to confirm the support. A bar entry strategy would have triggered a long above that bar's high, with a protective stop loss set below that bar's low. As a profit objective, a retest of the previous swing high seems probable. That profit objective was met without too much of a struggle, and the market broke out to form a higher high, then pulled back again to the 20-period EMA (2). Another reversal candlestick formed, and another profitable pullback trade resolved itself. In the next session, the price gapped up, then sold off rapidly to test the 20-period EMA (3). Again we saw a reversal candlestick form, and a bar break entry strategy would have triggered a long as a high of the reversal candlestick was broken. The price immediately reversed, and the trade would have stopped out soon thereafter. Having trended so perfectly before, now the market is exhibiting strong signs of chaos. Wider than average price bars and a disrespect for support and resistance offer clear signals that a payback cycle is looming. The price then spiked radically off the lows to run back up toward the high for the day. The next pullback tested the 40-period EMA, and formed a picture-perfect reversal candlestick (4). This long would have set up as the highs of the reversal bar were broken. It offered little more of a rally than the previous trade, but would never have reached the profit objective, and would have been closed either as a scratch or as the stop loss order was triggered. After such a nice period of order, two quick stops in a row were a strong signal to stop trading in reaction to the payback cycle. The first of the pullback trades offered a 3 to 1 profit, while the second delivered little more than 1 to 1. So even though you just had two winners and two losers, your net gain for the four trades would have been 2 units. Your risk-to-reward ratio buffers the losses incurred before you are able to identify the presence of a payback cycle.

Let's move forward in time and see how this period of chaos resolves itself.

In Figure 5.5 you can see how the range-bound action of this payback period formed a perfect symmetrical triangle. The breakout from the triangle (1) offered a quick profit as it retested the highs of the range; however, after identifying the beginning of a payback cycle I would have been demanding pullback entries and never would have taken this breakout-type long. After the highs of the ranges were tested, the price collapsed and began a period of amazingly trendless chop (2). Just as a bearish or bullish trend comes to a head as capitulation or euphoria occur, a period of chaos will often come to a head in a mishmash of laughable chop. This chaos crisis was confirmed as a bullish price thrust took price up for a breakout of above-the-range highs (3). Having had a full cycle of chaos culminating in

FIGURE 5.5

a chaos crisis, it was time to begin looking for pullbacks. After the breakout, the price pulled back to test the 20-period EMA (4). Order began to return, as the price easily retested the highs without much of a fight.

Let's look at another scenario. (See Figure 5.6.) In this instance we have several overnight gaps to deal with. Price gaps show the market discounting after-hours sentiments with the first print of the day. Generally, they will trade in the opposite direction of the gap to fill the gap soon after the open. When they are unable to fill, a breakaway gap situation will unfold, often delivering a strongly trending move in the direction of the gap.

DEALING WITH OVERNIGHT PRICE GAPS

In this example, the market gapped down and continued to sell off. After finding some support midmorning, it reversed and rallied to fill the gap (1). It then pulled back to test the 20-period EMA before breaking through the gap resistance to begin a new uptrend. When trading pullbacks, I generally use the resistance offered by the last swing high as my target. When trading for a gap fill, my target is set near the closing prices from the pre-

FIGURE 5.6

vious session. If the gap fills back to these levels, gap support and/or resistance will begin to manifest itself and possibly cause a trend change, so I need to take my profits.

The first clear setup the new bullish trend offered was an extra nice pullback as the market took five bars to correct back to the 20-period EMA. This pullback (2) had not reached the target by the close of trading, but gapped up to exceed that target level the next day. What followed was a classic gap fill. After the gap up in the morning (3), the price rapidly fell to fill the gap and test the 20-period EMA (4). Any time you're in a trade overnight and the stock gaps up beyond your profit target, *take the gift*! Chances are quite high that the gap open will be the best price available to you. Use the gap to take a windfall profit and then begin looking for your next trade. The gap fill back to the 20-period EMA (4) offered another good chance to get long and participate in the trend. The market was able to break above the previous swing high, then pulled back to offer another pullback entry (5). Since this would be the third pullback in a new uptrend, our Elliott wave theory tells us the chances for follow-through on this test of the 20-period EMA are lower. So any entry taken off this final pullback should be managed with a more scalpy mind-set. I rarely trade the third pullback, so would have more than likely missed this opportunity. The following day this market experienced another gap. This time, however, there was no fill. The market moved aggressively lower as a breakaway gap brought in waves of selling. Breakaway gaps are strong enough shock events to be able to change the trend from bull to bear in many instances. So once it became obvious that this was a serious breakaway gap, it became time to look for rallies to resistance. For a time, the selling was strong and sustained without any wiggles. Later in the day, however, the market began to bounce from its oversold position. This rally continued up until the 20-period EMA was tested (6). This test of moving average resistance reversed the trend long enough for a test of the 200-period SMA (7).

So we see here how gaps affect our pullback trades. What about trading the breakaway gap outright? (See Figure 5.7.) These breakaway patterns are fairly rare, but offer a great potential for risk or reward if entered properly. Since gaps that fill tend to do so within the first 30 minutes of trading, triggering an entry based on the 30-minute range offers an accurate filter for breakaway gaps. The quieter and more narrow the 30-minute range is, the better your chances for breakaway gap follow-through. The example in Figure 5.7 was from a 15-minute chart of the S&P 500 E-Minis. As you can see from the chart, after the gap went down, the market was stuck within a tight range for the first 30 minutes of trading. Not only did it stay within a tight range but also the topping tail in the second bar tells us it actually made an attempt to fill the gap! Since the move up was rejected, it further bolsters the argument that a breakaway gap situation is unfolding. A sell stop set underneath the 30-minute lows (1) with a protective stop loss order set a few ticks above the 30-minute highs (2) is all that is required to prepare for a potential setup.

After the setup, the market followed through beautifully. Having fallen sharply all morning, it began to drift lower through the noonday doldrums. Then as the afternoon session began, it began forming another leg to the downside. The selling became quite frenzied an hour or so after the breakdown, and a sharp volume spike confirmed the market's capitulation (3). This capitulation event offered a perfect trigger for an exit. As a rule of thumb, breakaway gap patterns tend to offer gains between 1.5 and 3 to 1. Once you are up better than 1.5 to 1, you can begin to focus more carefully on the market as you look for signs of capitulation or euphoria.

POSITION TRADES

Having dealt with a number of examples from intraday as well as daily time frames, let's switch modes and look at some position trade examples.

FIGURE 5.7

While a swing trade seeks to capture a single price move from support to resistance or resistance to support, a position trade seeks to follow a deep trend within the market. When you're in a position trade, you're willing to hold wiggles and sit through periods of chop that a swing trade would not survive. Let's look at a major trend change in wheat futures, and how a position could have been entered in order to capture that trend. (See Figure 5.8.) We begin with the market in a distinct downtrend. The price is declining as the market prints a series of lower highs and lower lows. An unusually large rally occurs—a rally that is able to break the 20- and 40-period EMAs for the first time in months. This is the first sign that the trend may be changing, so position traders will begin to focus on the market as they wait for confirmations of a trend change. This confirmation is printed several days later as a higher low forms (1). Position traders begin to buy contracts in anticipation of a major trend change. If the market was able to break to a new low, it would then invalidate a higher low as well as the support which caused the initial price thrust that was able to break the moving averages. Therefore, the most logical spot for protective stop loss orders would be under the last major low (2). The price quickly rallies to break above the last daily swing high. This action forms a higher high to

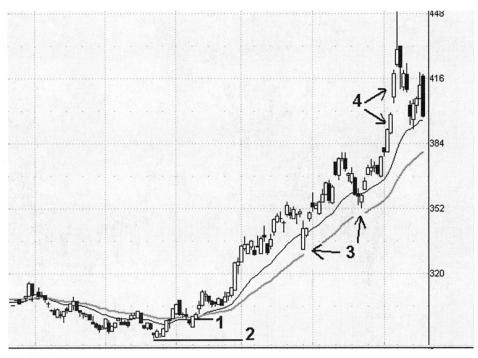

FIGURE 5.8

go with the previous week's higher low. This action confirms the change in trend as the stock starts a daily uptrend. While a swing trader entering off the higher low (1) would be taking profits as the market forms this higher high, a position trader sees this as confirmation of a beginning trend and stands pat. The uptrend begins to build, and offers two potential swing trade entries (3) as the trend continues to print higher highs and higher lows. After a little more than 3 months in its current daily uptrend, wheat begins to move into euphoria. The rally, which has been smooth and consistent to this point, becomes quite frenzied. Daily bar width increases dramatically, further confirming euphoria. As euphoria becomes obvious (4), the position traders exit their positions banking a tremendous risk-to-reward profit (10 to 1 or better!).

Once a market moves into euphoria, position traders begin to look for signs of reversal as euphoria often signals the end of an uptrend. Our next example comes from the soybean meal market. (See Figure 5.9.) After a period of clear euphoria (1), the market pulls back near its 20-period EMA, then rallies to form a lower high (2). Using the same logic as the previous trade, position traders begin to take short positions with protective stop loss orders set above the euphoria's highs. The trend has indeed changed, and the market begins to form a series of lower highs and lower lows. Eventually the market moves down to test its 200-period SMA (3), which offers an excellent position to take profits on this successful position trade. You can begin to see some of the benefits of a position trading style: large risk-to-reward profits when your market opinion is proved correct, but on the downside each market may only offer one to three position trades in any given year.

In the previous two examples, we saw a trend change occur as the market formed its first higher low/lower high. In this instance, we see how a false break out/peek top can also reverse a trend. Through the month of January, silver formed an ascending triangle. (See Figure 5.10.) This pattern should have been the precursor to a bullish breakout; however, when the market finally set up to the upside, it was quickly faded and a peek top was formed (1). A dramatic panic move followed as the bulls digested this extremely bearish signal. When the market finally found support and bounced, a lower high (2) was formed. In an interesting pattern, the market formed a higher low followed by a lower high (3).

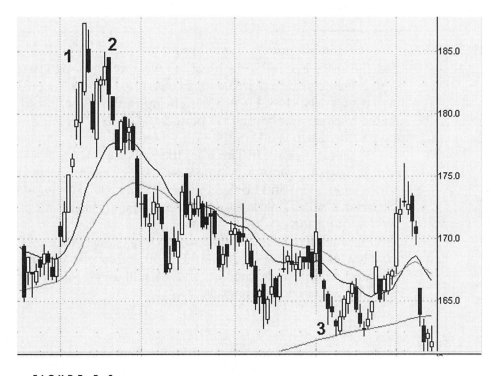

FIGURE 5.9

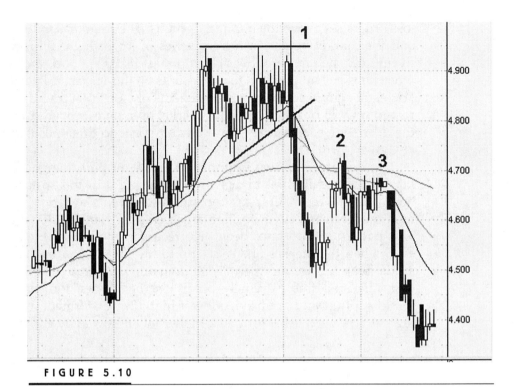

FIGURE 5.10

Had the price been able to break above the previous lower high (2), it would have confirmed a change in trend and any short positions should have been covered. But it was caught up in the 40-period EMA, and was unable to break above the 200-period SMA, so short positions remained open as the downtrend continued to mature.

So there you have it! These are the tools and tactics I use for trade generation. They are simple and universal as they are built upon the basics of market movement and human emotion. They have served me well in both bearish and bullish market environments and are easily adaptable to fit the sweet spot for the market at any time.

But, the dirty little secret about trading is this: Stock-picking skills are probably less than 20 percent of the profitability pie! The money management and mental skills that you possess will determine whether you are a loser or a winner in the markets.

CHAPTER 6

Can It Really Be This Simple?

Take the obvious, add a cupful of brains, a generous pinch of imagination, a bucketful of courage and daring, stir well and bring to a boil.

—*Bernard Baruch*

For several years now I have worked as a consultant for a number of traders, trying to help them find ways to achieve their trading goals. Many of them come to me frustrated, angry, and extremely cynical about their trading and the market in general. They may have seen me give a presentation describing my trading tools and the patterns and indicators I use. They are usually aghast at how simple my style is and always suspect I'm holding out some super secret indicator or price pattern. They are convinced that there is some secret squiggly green line on my personal charts that will foretell the future. If only they could pry this secret from me, all their problems would vanish!

I have discovered that there is a very consistent learning cycle that just about every trader goes through as he or she goes from consistent loss to consistent gain. Perhaps by identifying the stages, I can help some of you shave a few months or years off your learning curve. It has been amazing for me to see so many traders going through the exact same struggles as they move from one stage to the next. Even though the learning curve can be lonely and many traders feel they are the only people having problems with their trading, *we all* start out in the mystification stage. In the beginning we understand little about market structure and our price charts are a meaningless mishmash of colored lines and squiggles. The ability for anybody to look into that mess and divine the future seems a manifestation of the blackest magic. Yet as you begin to read trading books, watch the markets, attend some seminars, and accumulate some knowledge about the markets, your chart-reading ability will grow and the patterns you have learned about will begin to pop out at you.

You now enter the hot-pot phase. You scan the markets and start noticing one particular setup that seems to be working well. You start to focus on finding this one pattern, and bing, bang, boom, the next few instances all set up and run! You are thinking, "OK, this is it. The last five trades I saw with this pattern all made big money; I'm taking the next one!" You step up to the plate and before you can blink, your stop is hit. This cycle repeats itself again and again. What's happening is that you are committing a classic payout error by waiting to see perfection in the pattern before taking a trade. The problem is that perfection only shows in a win cycle. And so just as the win cycle finishes its run, you're jumping into the market just in time to eat the next losing streak! This cycle of observed pleasure and experienced pain puts your emotions and mental objectivity into a blender. It's the same process as a child who touches a hot pot on the stove top and gets burned. After getting hurt once or twice the child becomes afraid of the pot, not understanding that it is the heat from the stove that makes the pot painful.

After studying so hard and putting so much effort into your trading only to have this universal failure in the patterns *only when you take them* will take you into the cynical skepticism stage. This is where the majority of beginning traders get stuck and wash out. They feel betrayed by the market, the books and materials they tried to learn from, and the folks whose opinions they followed. All these inputs claim their ideas lead to profitability, yet every time a cynical skeptic takes a trade it's a loser! What makes these losses all the more maddening is that all the trade setups the cynical trader observed before taking a trade worked perfectly! Since one of the most painful human experiences is to fail when success looks easy, this embarrassment is diverted by the cynic into anger: anger at the evil market manipulators who gunned for the stops, anger at the teachers who taught the tactics that are causing them so much pain. All these people *must* be charlatans, fakirs who are exploiting their clients in a way that would make P. T. Barnum proud! This blame game may be satisfying to the ego, but to engage in this whining removes any chances for your success! If you become convinced that there are omniscient external forces working against you, then why would you bother to analyze your *own* trading to look for ways to improve? This excuse-driven mind-set is a dead-end viewpoint, and one that takes many promising traders out of the game.

Those that persevere move into the squiggle trader phase. Since they experience what feels like universal failure in the price patterns they choose to trade, they figure that there is some secret weapon, some holy grail, that would help them filter out these bad trades. Once they find the magic potion, their accounts will explode and they will achieve every goal and dream they have for their trading. They believe the reason they have been losing is simply ignorance. They begin an obsessive study of trading methods. They buy every book, attend every course that mentions a pattern or indicator that is new to them. They try desperately to buy success. This is the same process as a golfer who spends $600 on a new driver so he or she can hit the ball 10 yards farther into the woods! These patterns and indicators are all useful tools, but by themselves cannot make a trader profitable. As you begin to stack indicator after indicator on your charts, you begin to suffer paralysis by overanalysis. There are so many inputs to consider that you just can't make a decision. Or even more likely, once in a position your mind will seek out those indicators that agree with the direction of the trade. This behavior is a hallmark of scared money. Without a clear acceptance of the risk assumed, these traders dart around in search of anything or anybody who can tell them their trade is a good one. This serves two destructive purposes: (1) It transfers to others the responsibility for the trade, and (2) it will shake you out of trades as your indicators begin to conflict. The MACD says buy, the stochastic says sell, ADX says the market is trending, yet the OBV is indicating an overbought situation. The result of this mess is a gibbering trader whose brains have been reduced to a quivering puddle by the end of the trading day.

As you can see in Figure 6.1, this chart is buried by its indicators! Too much information! With all these potentially valid inputs, which indicators do you trust? What if they are in conflict as a pattern appears? (By the way, this happens *constantly*.)

This squiggle trader phase (although unprofitable) is an important step in a trader's development. It teaches traders about all the styles of trading that are popular, and gives them great insight into what other traders are doing and what techniques and tactics are most popular. This information and experience will prove invaluable later on as the trader begins to mature and starts to trade traps and other panic-inducing patterns. This exploratory phase is also important because it is at this point when traders begin to find out who they are, what trading styles suit their psyche the best, and which tactics they should focus on as they go forward.

The squiggle trader phase is another morass from which many traders never break free. They spend the rest of their lives as traders searching for *the answer*, and even though some may be profitable while they search, they only realize a fraction of their potential as traders. At this point those who have what it takes move to a new level of personal

FIGURE 6.1

responsibility. They take all the knowledge they have accumulated up to this point and begin to experiment on their own. They try to adapt well-known, popular patterns to their own style. They are comfortable with their analysis skills and really begin to specialize and focus on the strategies that fit them the best. Much of the growth during this phase is focused inwardly, as the trader explores the mental and emotional side of his or her trading skill set. I call this last step the inward bound phase. It is in this stage that the trader will discover the true holy grails of trading: risk management, the payout-payback cycle, and the power of a trading plan! As an inwardly bound trader, you begin to take total responsibility for your trades. You understand that you can control your risk in the markets, so when you put on a trade you have accepted fully the possibility for loss. You are the one who respects your stops, you are the one who sticks to your trading plan, and you are the only one able to manage your trades with objective consistency. Once you move to this level, the impulsive emotional trades that once caused so much damage are now gone and true trading errors have been limited to one or two a month. You begin to have realization experiences as you move to new levels of market understanding that take your profitability up a few notches. All these advances are not fundamental changes in technique, but rather tweaks that help you enhance your edge as a trader.

The final stage in a trader's learning curve is mastery. Trading becomes second nature for you. Your trading style becomes such an ingrained part of you that it doesn't take a conscious effort anymore to follow your rules. You can trade effectively when there are distractions that would have been deadly even just a year or two before. You can make money in the morning when you're not quite awake; when people are in your office watching; with music in the background; when you have a cold, a hangover, or while talking on the phone. When you pass into this final phase of your career, trading itself becomes a thoughtless endeavor. Your trade planning and research are what take your time and focus; they become your scrimmages with the market. The trading itself is just the natural action or reaction to market behavior that your scrimmaging taught you would optimize your edge. Athletes use this same process, as they expend great effort planning their strategies and practicing their skills so that the instincts are there to make the big play instantly without thinking. This level of trading skill takes time to develop, and it is during this time that your intuitive side begins to show itself. You will not always be able to explain the feelings, but from time to time you will get a very strong sense that the market is about to move. These gut trades are infrequent but can be extremely profitable. As you begin to get to this level, start experimenting with these opinions, taking them with small size, and begin to build trust in your newfound instincts.

PAINFUL LESSONS

How do I know so much about all these phases of trader advancement? I have lived through all of them. All my opinions and theories about trader development have come from personal experience. During this journey I experienced intense pain, frustration, dejection, depression, and misery. It seems that every giant step forward was preceded by an intense emotional crisis. This manic-depressive cycle from absolute hero to complete zero is a little discussed fact of trading life. Learning to manage these cycles was critical for me if I wanted to make this my career. You must learn to accept the cyclicality of trading and not personalize or internalize the pain associated with the loss clusters that are a normal aspect of any trading method. To do so will lead to many mental and physical difficulties, because the stress you have to live with will consume you. I stumbled through the learning curve by myself, over the course of a year learning many of my lessons the hard way. After that first year of hellish frustration

I began to interact with other traders. As we compared notes I became aware that I was not alone. They were going through the same difficulties, and we shared many of the same frustrations. We had all underestimated the difficulty and complexity of the business of speculation! The reason the potential for great profits exists in trading is because it is such a difficult thing to master. If it were easy, everybody would trade profitably and the potential payout would fall dramatically. So be thankful a small elite group takes home the bulk of the gains available from the markets! Become a member of this exclusive club, and the market will reward you very richly.

After I reached a level of success and competence on my own, I began to help other traders as they struggled with these same issues. I saw so many of these traders repeating the same mistakes that I had been guilty of in the past. This mirrored experience helped me clarify the symptoms of each phase in the learning curve, and I began to find ways to help others move up one level at a time. Interestingly enough, among the traders I was helping, technical analysis and the skills of trade selection were rarely the reasons for failure. In almost every case the barriers to profitability were due to mental errors or poor money management.

FROM SEC FORMS TO CHART READING

I began my trading career as a Graham/Dodd fundamentally driven equities investor. Working solely with stocks, I totally bought into the theory that fundamental value was the key component behind stock movement. I became very adept at reading and analyzing all the company books and SEC forms that I believed held the keys to the castle. I even interned in the research department of a local money management firm. I learned two major lessons during this time. One was how slowly and deliberately the decision processes on the street worked. If a stock was discovered and fit the value concepts of the firm, then it would be presented and discussed at a weekly meeting. Then the partners would do some research and due diligence of their own, and all would come to a decision at the next weekly meeting. These folks were dealing with true asset management, so this careful approach was totally appropriate, but I immediately saw a niche for a trader who was independent and had the agility to enter the stock before these larger players had the time to come to a consensus. This was my first step on the road that led me to becoming a pure independent speculator. The second important lesson I learned at the office came as a shock at the time. I discovered to my consternation that even if a stock was ridiculously undervalued, it could still move a lot lower with the greatest of ease! There were lousy companies that saw huge increases in their share prices and great companies whose stocks got slaughtered. I had spent so much time learning about how to fundamentally value companies, that these illogical moves were very mystifying to me. I tried to find logical explanations for these movements, but then I realized that stocks move up simply because there are more buyers than sellers, and the reasons for buying often seem illogical and stupid. But just because they seem crazy to you doesn't mean you will lose any less on your position if you are on the wrong side! I was going through a painful period when I began to question every bit of information I had been working so hard to learn. During this stressful time I went to the bookstore and bought *The Market Wizards* by Jack Schwager. In this book was a quote from George Soros that hit me right between the eyes. "Economic history is a never-ending series of episodes based on falsehoods and lies, not truths. It represents the path to big money. The object is to recognize that trend whose premise is false, ride that trend, and step off before it is discredited."

Yes!!! This was it, my reason for the phony moves in my stocks. This book with its stories of trading was to me like water for a man just rescued from the desert. I began to understand that this is what I wanted to do. Trading was how I would make the markets work for me. If solely accumulation and distribution drove price moves, then I would learn to read the charts and ride those trends into the sunset!

As my mystification period came to an end, I started to move into the hot-pot phase. I'd read about flag patterns and go into hyper mode. Scanning for flags, watching how the market dealt with a setup, I'd watch and try to learn. Every once in a while (usually after an observed win cluster), I'd gird my loins and take a flag for real. Inevitably the market would respond with a quick loss! I'd back away, nursing my burned fingers. This went on and on as I tried all kinds of different trading strategies. This painful drudgery taught me a great deal about technical analysis, but also instilled in me a fear and paranoia about the markets. I really felt singled out and persecuted by the market. Invariably after I was stopped, I would notice that the next trade would work wonderfully. Every blasted trade I'd take would stop it seemed, and this after I saw nothing but winners! How did *they* know I was taking a trade so they could stop it out? I was becoming afraid of the hot pot, becoming gun-shy as I entered a trade. I was wincing every time I pulled the trigger, expecting to lose instead of trading to win!

I spent a great deal of time in the hot-pot phase as I looked for a holy grail—that one magic pattern or indicator that would take me from loser to winner in one easy step. This phase of my development, although painful, was a critical time of learning for me. I experimented with just about every possible style for trading a market. I became familiar with all the strategies that traders bring to the markets, and began to notice a cyclicality that was inherent in every single one of these approaches. I began to develop my understanding of the payout-payback cycle and the most exciting period of my development began.

TRUST, THEN VERIFY!

The scientific method is a systematic approach to quantify observed data. At first you observe a perceived phenomenon and come up with a hypothesis about it. Then you begin to experiment as you research and look for data that can prove your hypothesis correct. After you have enough data to basically corroborate your opinion, your hypothesis becomes a theory. Finally, if you can ever find enough data to prove irrefutably that your original observation is absolutely true, then your theory becomes a law. What follows is for me personally a law, and I strongly believe it is the same for all traders, but with an absence of proof I feel I must still call it a theory. If I speak in absolutes, it is because these have become laws for me and my trading. Please, please, *please*, take everything I say (indeed, this entire book!) as one trader's way to take money from the markets. Believe nothing I say or anybody else says blindly; instead take these ideas and test them on your own. Beware of anybody who tries to convince you that one style is the only way to trade. It is imperative for you to take the lessons and ideas presented in this book and make them your own. If you don't prove these ideas to yourself, then you will never trust them deeply enough to trade them well.

For every style of trading there is a perfect market environment. When the market is aligned to your style, everything you touch will turn to gold. Your patterns will set up and run without stress to your target zones. Your excitement and confidence will soar as your win cluster grows. But these glorious periods seldom last long. Stops will begin to appear again and then perhaps a loss cluster. This constant cycle from zero to hero and back again is why trading is the manic-depressive business it is. This constant shift from in alignment to out of alignment is what I call the payout-payback cycle.

I spent countless hours and lost a lot of money trying to find ways to beat the payback cycle. I tried to find ways to adapt with the market and change my trading style so I would stay aligned to the market as closely as possible. What I found was at first distressing. I was just chasing my tail, because as soon as I figured out that breakouts were working, they would stop following through and would be pullbacks that would start rocking the Casbah. By the time I figured this out, the shift would be on again to a new pattern. It took me a while to realize it was hopeless to try to become all things to all markets. I stepped back and began to observe this cycle from the easy money of the payout, to the total frustration of the payback. I began to look at all my trading strategies with different eyes. I started to look at which strategies stayed in the payout phase most often, and for the longest time. This research really opened my eyes. Every strategy or setup I looked at had this built-in cycle of a winning streak followed by a losing streak, then back to another period of easy gains. If you think about this for a moment it makes sense. A continuation pattern setup like a flag will perform well when the larger time frame market is trending strongly. If the daily chart has set up a buy signal, and is trending you might get three or four successful flags in a row before the upthrust wears itself out. Once the momentum from the daily chart is worn out, these smaller time frame flags will begin to fail. The transition from win cluster (payout) to the loss cluster (payback) has begun. As the market tops off and chops, the flags will fail miserably. Then as a trend reemerges, the flags will begin to pay out again as a new win cluster begins to form.

Once I became aware of the smooth cyclicality of the payout-payback cycle, my outlook began to change. I began to see the money flow in these patterns as the tide in an ocean of money. I began to see this payout-payback cycle as simply the manifestation of a natural ebb and flow inherent to market action. One would certainly never try to fight the tide of an ocean, so why was I trying to fight this tide of money? I started to question my previous tactic of shifting strategies. I began by picking a few trading strategies that I knew were consistent performers in a variety of market environments. Then I really tried to get in tune with the payout-payback cycle that each strategy exhibited. I found with relative ease that I could identify when the market was not aligned to that style and was beginning a payback cycle. By reducing my trade frequency during this time I could avoid taking several losses as these otherwise valid patterns set up, then stopped. I became aware of the power of avoiding loss. Every time I eluded a stop on an otherwise valid setup, it acted as a 1-unit gain to my account. Since I avoided taking the drawdown, my next winning trade would be banked as 100 percent profit! Avoid one stop a week, and you would show a 52-unit gain over the performance of another trader who had stepped up to take these losers.

I also came to believe the payout-payback cycle is responsible for many of the fundamental errors of emotion and discipline that hurt so many traders. They get caught up in the euphoria of the payout and begin to get aggressive just as the odds begin to shift against them. They get discouraged in the payback cycle and abandon valid, profitable strategies as they try to avoid the pain of losing. Having worked with so many traders as they struggled during their learning curve, I've seen this behavior repeated over and over. Here is a example.

JACK AND JILL COMPARE NOTES

Jack is a trader with a $50,000 trading account. He has just discovered a new strategy and he plans to begin trading in the S&P 500 index futures. He sizes his positions to risk 1 percent of his account on each trade. He has been trading for a while, but is still relatively inexperienced.

Jill is a trader with a $50,000 trading account. By coincidence, she trades the same strategy that Jack has just discovered. She sizes her positions to risk 1 percent of her account on each trade. She has been trading for a number of years and fully understands the concept of the payout-payback cycle.

Their month begins well; the first few days are easily profitable. Jill correctly identifies this as a payout market, is more aggressive in her entries, and is also more willing to hold the wiggles and let the positions work in her favor. Jack is on top of the world! After working out this new strategy, the first couple of trades are winners! He was right (he always knew he was right), and now he is going to make some serious money! By the end of the first week, the win cluster is in full force. Out of the five trades the strategy gave that week, only one resulted in a loss. Jack's account shows a 4-unit gain for the week, while Jill's aggressive management of these same trades has produced a 4.6-unit gain.

As they begin the next week, Jill is slightly wary. After such a nice payout, the transition to payback must be coming soon. Jack, on the other hand, has increased his size since his new strategy has been performing so well. The first trade of the new week stops right away, and the following day produces a small gain, but the action is choppy and unstable. Jill sees the setup begin to struggle and decides to trade tomorrow's signal at half size. Jack knows every setup will lose once in a while, so the action of the last 2 days does not bother him.

The next day, the setup fails badly. Jill takes this as confirmation of the shift from payout to payback, and plans to take the rest of the week off. Jack feels hurt by this recent failure. With his increased position size, these losses hurt a lot more than normal. But he remembers the euphoric success of the first week, and this keeps him going. He is unwilling to reduce his position size, because he wants so badly to make up his recent losses. He toys with the idea of adding even more contracts to tomorrow's trade, rationalizing that if it is a winner these gains would take him back to breakeven. His better sense prevails, and he decides to take the same size as yesterday. Over the next 2 days, while Jill is off having a good time away from her computers, Jack is home taking two more losses as the payback cycle heats up. His head is spinning. What happened? Did he make some mistake in his trade management? Has the pattern stopped working? His account shows a 5.5-unit loss for the week. Not only has he lost all of the profit from the last week, but now his account is in the red! He decides to stop trading and reassess the situation. Maybe a little more research will help him identify why he lost last week. He strongly suspects there will be some combination of indicators that could have filtered out the losing trades. He spends all weekend poring over charts as he tries to find a way to beat the payback cycle. During this time of emotional upheaval for Jack, Jill has been out enjoying her life. She spent a day at the beach, had dinner with friends, and plans to volunteer at her favorite charity on the weekend. Her mind is clear, and her soul is refreshed. On Sunday she looks at her charts and sees that she missed two losing trades. She still shows a 1.5-unit loss for the week, but feels happy that her identification of the payback cycle was correct. She suspects that after such a string of losers, the shift back to the payout cycle is coming, and plans to take Monday's trade with her normal position size.

Monday arrives, and Jill takes the trade. The payback cycle is not quite finished yet, and she is quickly stopped out for a loss. Jack is dead tired from a weekend of intense study in front of a computer screen, and decides to watch the setup for a while before jumping back in. He feels smugly pleased that he was smart enough to avoid this loss. He decides to spend the rest of the week watching the setup. He wants to see some confirmation of success before he takes any more trades. Jill is unfazed by the loss on Monday. She still feels the payback cycle is on the wane, and the payout cycle is just about ready to kick in. She plans to take her normal-sized trade for tomorrow's setup. The next day the setup struggles, but ends up producing a profit. The following 2 days some economic news hits the market, and the setups all set up and run to perfection! Jill begins to see the happy signs of the payout cycle returning. Jack is relieved to see this strategy producing profits again. He is quite frustrated that he missed the last two setups, as the follow-through was so powerful. He decides to take the trade on Friday with half size, just to get his feet wet. This decision is influenced in large part by the pain he experienced in missing the last two trades. He wants to make up for the good trades he missed, and so impulsively jumps back into the Friday trade. After two solid days of trend, the market is tired, and the Friday setup stops. Now Jack feels foolish. In retrospect he can see that his decision to trade on Friday was an impulsive, emotionally based one. Even though his loss for this week is only .5 unit, the mental damage has been great. By missing the good trades and getting slapped on the wrist by the one trade he took, his confidence has taken a big hit. He also is faced with another losing week on the books as he moves into the weekend. Jill has had a week of ups and downs, but has felt in control of her trading. This week was nothing stellar, but it produced a gain of 2 units for her, which nicely covered the loss from the week before. She feels the payout cycle is back in effect, and looks forward to Monday's session. Jack spends the weekend trying to run away from his feelings. He feels lousy about how his trading is going, and this colors his ability to enjoy the weekend.

The following Monday, Jill is back in action. Her trade is easily closed for a profit, and she happily looks forward to the rest of the week. Jack's funk just grows as he misses another winning trade. "I *could* have had that," he whines, and his feelings of embarrassment begin to turn to anger. Tuesday's trade is also a winner, and now Jack cannot take the emotional pain. "Forget it," he says. "I'm going to trade tomorrow no matter what…This market is *not* going to get the best of me!" He takes the next trade, and sees it quickly closed out for a nice profit. "Ha-Ha!" he says, "that's more like it!" He is now deep into an incredible emotional roller-coaster ride. He has lived through the cycle from hero to zero, and bears the scars of the anger, frustration, embarrassment, and wish for revenge that this cycle creates in so many traders. While all these storm clouds have been swirling around Jack's trading, Jill has been nonchalantly plugging along, trading her plan. Her proper identification of the payout cycle has allowed her again to become more aggressive. She takes just a little more profit than normal out of each winner, and this yields a 3.5-unit profit over the first 3 days of the week. Again, after seeing such a strong win cluster, she begins to trade a bit more cautiously going into the Thursday and Friday sessions. It is likely that after a period of gains such as this, the transition back to the payback cycle will begin again soon. And indeed Thursday and Friday are mixed: one produces a gain, while the other results in a loss. She is happy with the 3.5-unit profit she has for the week, and plans to trade lightly next week, as the move to the payback cycle seems to be inevitable. Jack is back in the game and shows a 1.5-unit gain for the month. This puts him right near the breakeven point for his account. He has a resigned, dogged air now. He is going to trade every pattern next week do or die, and damn the consequences. This mind-set is at its heart a way to avoid responsibility, by trusting to fate, and taking no control over the management of your trading. A resigned "whatever will be will be" mind-set should be a real danger signal to any trader.

The final week is just a disaster. Only one out of the five trades produces a profit. Jill is ready for this payback cycle, and manages it well. She ends the week with a 2-unit loss. By passing on trades once she identified the payback cycle, she avoids at least 2 more units of drawdown. During this week, Jack has his head down. It has been too painful for him when he tries to think, so he turns his mind off and just takes loss after loss. The week costs him 4 units, and he quits in disgust. "This is all just a scam; nobody can actually make money doing this!" He storms off in disgust. Another trader washes out. Jack washes out not because his trading plan was invalid, but because he was unaware of the payout-payback cycle. He fell into every mental trap the market sets for a trader; he sat out during the payout cycles as he waited for confirmation. After seeing a win streak, he jumped into the market just as the payback cycle was beginning. During this time he lost almost 5 units in his account, while Jill with her ability to identify the payout-payback cycle banked a 6.6-unit gain on the same trade signals.

As you can see, managing the payback cycle is crucial to maintaining a consistent level of profitability. During a normal month with very standard payout-payback cycles, proper payback management will result in a much larger return than will a trader who is blindly pressing on. But once or twice a year you will encounter a payout-payback supercycle. The market is gripped by chaos. The smooth transition from payout to payback and back again is replaced by random gains and losses. Your strategy experiences a total breakdown, and your trades are stopping out right and left. This chaos supercycle is often what causes traders to take a year killing drawdown. It is in this chaos period that you begin to hear about disaster gaps, devastating limit moves, huge drawdowns, and other trading disasters. I traded through one of these chaos periods recently, and have seen these ill winds blow through the markets in the past. Here is how I dealt with this cycle when it happened to me for real. (And in front of all my coaching clients as well, which ramps up the stress level by quite a few notches!)

A SUSTAINED DRAWDOWN

It started out with a five-trade losing streak. It is very uncommon for me to get stopped five times in a row, so I began a very thorough trade review to make sure I was not committing some destructive trading error. Finding nothing to pin my losses on, I took the losing streak as a statistical anomaly. I did not find any errors in my trade selection and would have taken every trade again, so this period of losing must have been just a period of bad luck. My next five trades were all winners, so I felt reinforced in my view that the previous losses were nothing more than a streak of bad luck. However, even though the trades following the losing streak were all profitable, none of them reached my profit objective. Each trade was closed by a trailing stop as poor follow-through kept me from taking the profits I had hoped for. The next week was also mixed, with both gainers and losers. The week ended again with a net loss as I was not getting enough follow-through from my gainers to offset the losses taken from my stops. After another careful trade review I felt I had picked great trades, but just did not see enough movement away from the entry point. I began to notice that the setups I had passed on also had not followed through. So my losses were again not due to poor trade selection. I took this as another signal that things were out of whack and the market was in a period of chaos that was affecting my trading. The next week started out with a win streak that took me almost all the way back to the breakeven point for the month. Then another large losing streak quickly followed. This time my drawdown was more than 6 units. Again, *very* unusual! To add to the unusual aspects of this adversity, this was the second major losing streak in a single month! I knew then that something was seriously wrong; this was a very aberrant result for me. It was time to take aggressive action to protect my capital from any further losses. I began to trade half sized lots as I tried to feel my way out of the drawdown. This was a timely move as I quickly began another five-trade losing streak. After this losing streak hit I knew the market was out of whack. This was my third major losing streak in 1 month! It was time for me to walk away from a market that had proved to be too edgeless for my style of trading. There were three possible explanations for this drawdown. Either the market was totally out of alignment with my style, the market had changed and my strategy had no edge anymore, or I was making some trading error that I was unable to identify. A few days off would help me regain my perspective and perhaps with a clear mind I could restore objectivity and figure out what I was doing wrong. At this point my stress levels were very high. Not only had I taken a larger than normal drawdown in my own account but I had been falling flat on my face in front of all my clients who were paying me to help them become better traders! They had a very hard time understanding why I was withdrawing from the market. Why didn't I want to knuckle down and work extra hard to get back to breakeven for the month? How could I give up when I was down? After seeing these anomalous results for my trading style, I knew the market was working its way through a chaos supercycle. Having identified this chaos, I knew I had little to no edge for my style at the moment. My job was to stop the bleeding, control this drawdown, and repair my mental state so I could trade well when order returned.

Markets always swing from depression to euphoria and back again. Thank goodness they do, because this cycle is what gives us the ability to take money from the market on a regular basis. After every losing cycle comes a period of winning. The nastier the losing cycle the nicer the winning cycle will be. I knew this was a brutal chaos period, so I expected to see a huge payout cycle after the chaos had worked itself out. Drawdown periods are always a trying time for the newer traders that I work with. No matter how many lessons I give that explain the payout-payback process, many will interpret these explanations as excuses. They are still unwilling to accept the law of the payout-payback cycle, and labor under the mistaken belief that master traders should be able to make money every day. I know some of the more hyper newbies will lose interest and will abandon the strategy. They will bound off in search of a new secret weapon and will continue to chase their tail as they look for a way to become profitable. On the other hand, those who stick it out during the drawdown periods will see firsthand how losses were managed under adverse conditions. When order returns, they will have learned a very powerful lesson about controlling a drawdown during a period of market chaos. They may not apply this knowledge for some time, but one day they will experience their own slump, and this memory will return and save them from a huge drawdown!

LOSING TO WIN

Trading is at its core a losers' game. Those who are best at losing will walk away at the end of the day with everybody else's money! These slump periods are something every trader will have to deal with, and are most often the times when traders wash out. They give up trading just before a massive payoff cycle kicks in. It's another one of the sick trading paradoxes that keeps the success rates for trading so very low.

Identifying that chaos period and walking away from the markets for a few days saved me from taking an additional four to six stops by my estimate. Again, my trade review did not come up with any obvious errors in trade selection or management. If the market had changed and was now eating my normal style for lunch, I was left with two choices: change my trading strategy to fit the market's action, or hunker down and wait for conditions to change. My trading style was very carefully crafted; it suits me and has served me well over time. Why would I choose to abandon it now because of 3 tough weeks of trading? Why discard what has been consistently profitable until it has really proved it's a failure? I decided to continue to stay on the sidelines in cash until I saw signs of order returning to my markets. After a few more days of waiting, the action began to look more orderly, and I decided to start trading again. I began trading with half lots as I eased back into the markets. My first few trades were successful, and I saw follow-through returning to the market. After seeing these positive results, I decided to increase my risk and began to take full lots again. I ended the month with a string of winners, covered my drawdown, and ended the month with a slight gain. Going into the new month, my mental state was very good. I had traded through a chaos cycle before, and knew I had managed this one well by controlling my losses before they got out of hand. I was focused and ready to be at the top of my game for the payout that I knew was coming. As the new month began, I extended the winning streak that had closed out the month so strongly. By the end of the first week I was up more than half my average gain for a month! The payout cycle was in full force as the chaos disappeared.

A nice mix of winners and losers followed as the payout-payback cycle returned to normal. My gains for the month continued to build. By mid-month, I was up more than twice my average monthly profit! This was a textbook chaos supercycle, a month of misery and edgeless trading followed by wonderful trends and large win clusters. By managing my drawdowns, and more importantly my mental state during the period of chaos, I was able to maximize the profits available to me during the payout cycle. This payout cycle was quite large, and more than made up for the time and effort wasted in the prior month's chaos period. Your job as a trader is to tread water during the times when the market is not in alignment with your style, then be ready to trade aggressively when the gains of the payout cycle present themselves. Graph the equity curve of a consistent trader and you will see a pattern of base, jump, base, jump, base, jump. Most of the gains will be seen in a cluster as win streaks manifest themselves. Hopefully, this real-world example can hit home for some of you. Learning how to manage a severe slump period, either self-induced or as the result of a chaos period, is the key to consistent success as a trader. If you allow yourself to get down and out during a period of adversity, you will miss the huge profits that lurk on the other side, as the markets come back into alignment to your style.

CHAPTER 7

Plan Your Trade, and Trade Your Plan

> It never was my thinking that made the big money for me. It always was my sitting. My sitting tight! Men who can both be right and sit tight are uncommon.
>
> —*Jesse Livermore*

To avoid the pitfalls that entrap so many traders, a clear trading plan is a must. The majority of the trading world doesn't have the discipline to plan a trade and then stick to that strategy, so instead they stagger around the markets falling into every emotional trap that is set.

What is discipline? The big "D" is a subject that has been beaten to death in books, courses, and seminars. But nine times out of ten, the dire warnings about discipline deal with blowing stops, doubling down on losers, and taking position sizes that are far too large for your account. Since I have spent time working with aspiring traders, I have found that the discipline needed to succeed is an entirely different thing. Those afflicted with the inability to take a stop, or the gambling urge to put on big size without a real plan will blow out their accounts so quickly that they never even have time to learn the basics of trading.

If you blow stops in the hopes that the market will come back, you are dead. If you double down to lower your average price as you wait for a bounce, you are dead. If you take giant positions that expose you to an inappropriate amount of risk, *you are dead!* Don't waste your time. Take the entire contents of your trading account and donate the money to a worthy charity. They will at least do something useful with your funds. It never ceases to shock me how people who are quite careful and frugal in the rest of their financial lives will casually put thousands at risk in the market with no rational thought or plan to back up their positions. Maybe it is the funny money electronic nature of the markets. If they had to plunk down

$100 bills as they took their positions I bet their mind-set would be entirely different.

The discipline that helped me succeed is based not on avoiding suicidal trading behavior, but rather is based on acceptance. First of all you must accept that losses are a constant part of this business, and that they will occur at random within a set of probabilities. Once you accept this fact, you can move to a point of objectivity that will keep you from personalizing your losses. In the beginning it is natural to assume you lose because of a mistake you made or some indication you missed. You take each loss as a personal failure and will often let this embarrassment spiral out of control until you become a confirmed skeptical cynic. It takes time and experience to begin to see the payout-payback cycle and really understand that losses are often unavoidable. There will be many great trades that you take that close out with a bad outcome. Good Trade/Bad Outcome (GTBO) trades cause more heartache than any other trading setback.

The next thing you have to accept is your level of dollar risk. Choose a unit size that will not cause you to sweat at every downtick or uptick. Next, you have to remember the definition of a stop loss order. "A stop loss order is set at a price level where the market will prove your original opinion wrong." If you truly believe this definition, then the market will not be able to wiggle you out of your positions by simply looking scary. Holding to your stops is critical to your success. I cannot begin to count how many trades have been a few ticks from my stop, yet turned back to close out with a nice profit. There is a strong urge to just get out when you see a trade failing. But you must have the discipline to stay the course and not jump your stop. This is one of the trading disciplines that I rarely see discussed. Failure to hold your stops is an insidious evil, one that dooms you to die the death of a thousand cuts. You never take big losses, but by giving up on your trades prematurely, you never get the profits you need to offset the constant stream of small controlled losses.

The last hidden discipline that I see causing so much trouble is profit snatching. Folks get so beat up mentally by the market that they are desperate for a profit—any profit. They grab whatever gains the market shows out of the setup, and in doing so take profits that do *not* justify the risk they assumed at the outset of the trade. This again is an aspect of trading discipline that gets overlooked, but will doom you to a slow slide in your equity. Your losses are set by your stop loss, yet your profits are never given a chance to run. Thus, the risk-to-reward ratio is ruined, and an otherwise profitable strategy can show a loss week after week. Different strategies have different profit expectations, and part of the strategy planning process is to define what level of profit is needed to justify your initial risk.

DEVELOPING A TRADING PLAN

This then begs the question: How does one begin to develop and optimize a trading plan?

First, you need to do some research and come up with a trading strategy that puts the odds in your favor. There are two ways a strategy can produce a positive expectancy: a high win-to-loss ratio or a high risk-to-reward ratio. After you back test a setup or strategy that seems to have a positive expectancy on paper, it's time to begin the forward-testing process. Start by trading the setup on paper or with very small positions, logging very carefully where your entry and exit points would have been. Make sure to subtract reasonable slippage and commissions costs from the equation as you try to determine profitability. After you have 20 to 30 setups in your trading log, you can begin to analyze the potential in the setup. First, you need to look at the win-to-loss ratio, and compare it with the results from your back testing. Count out how many trades were in your sample, and then how many winners, how many losers. Also, note the size and scope of the payout-payback cycles in this sample. What sorts of drawdowns do you see? How well do the winning streaks sustain? Think about how this trading setup would feel, and note any observations you might have that could help you filter out losers. Did the setup perform better in a trending market, in the mornings, on Wednesdays? Next, take a look at the risk-to-reward ratios the setup offers. What kind of follow-through was available in these plays? Would you make more money by setting a target level and exiting as that area is reached? Would it be better to use a more dynamic exit trigger such as a trailing stop? Once these tactical questions have been answered, and you have determined what it will take to make this setup work most efficiently for you...*write them down*. Lay out in detail how you plan to trade this particular strategy. This becomes your trading plan, and it is during this time that you will set the stage for profitability.

You need to answer in detail all these questions:

✔ Describe and define the setup. What does the market have to do to give you this edge?

✔ How does the market have to act to trigger your entry?

✔ What tactics and order types will you use to enter these trades?

✔ How will you determine where to set your stop loss order?

✔ What is your strategy for taking profit?

✔ How will you identify when you are in the transition zone from pay-out to payback?

✔ How will you identify when you are in the transition zone from pay-back to payout?

✔ How will you change your position management strategy after you have identified that you are trading within a payback cycle?

✔ How will you change your position management strategy after you have identified that you are trading within a payout cycle?

✔ What method will you use to find these setups?

✔ Will you trade this strategy in only one time frame?

✔ Will you trade this strategy to the short side as well as the long?

✔ How much money are you willing to lose in a normal drawdown before you stop trading?

✔ How much money are you willing to lose in a month before you stop trading?

✔ Define the failure you would have to see in order to stop trading this strategy.

Once you have answered these questions you should have a very complete and comprehensive trading plan. Having thought about and answered these questions before you place your first live trade, you will know how to handle just about every aspect of this particular strategy. This structure will act as a crutch during the more challenging periods in your trading. During a drawdown, you can look back and see if this losing period is within the levels of expected drawdown. When your trading is not working well, you can look at your rules and see if you are deviating from your plan. Most of the time the plan that traders come up with is a good one, but they just never see the performance they deserve because of their inability to follow that plan. This again is a facet of trader discipline that gets overlooked by many.

STICK TO YOUR TRADING PLAN!

I cannot count how many times traders have come to me for help saying, "I think I should be making money...I'm not sure what's wrong!" After looking over their trades and asking a few questions, it becomes apparent that their basic trading plan makes sense and has an inherent profitable expectancy! The flaw in their trading, the mistake that causes them to lose each and every month, is an inability to follow their own plan! One of my closest trader friends has a saying I have always liked. "Plan your trade, then trade your plan!" I have always been mystified at how hard it can be for traders to follow this simple adage. The reason for these breakdowns in discipline are most often rooted in fear. The fear of loss, the fear of missing a big move, or the worst fear of all...the fear of failure.

Fear of loss is conquered by learning to truly accept your level of risk in the markets. Taking ownership of the position sizing process proves that you are in total control of your risk assumption. By taking your position size down to a level that is comfortable, many traders can help to eliminate this trading fear.

Fear of missing out is conquered by learning where your money really comes from when trading. Money comes from predictability and risk management. Many traders mistake market movement for profit potential. If the market spikes without warning they look at the size of the move and begin to calculate the money they *could* have made in the move. But they forget to ask the most basic question. Why would they have taken the trade, and what would their plan have been? When I have worked with traders for a while, and they have advanced to a level where they are experiencing consistent profitability, they often ask me if it's time for them to add more markets to their trading screens. I ask them why? "Because I want to make more money" is the answer. If they can consistently make 5 units a month in the S&P, all they need to do to *double* their income is to double their position size! If it ain't broken, *don't fix it*! If you have a consistently profitable trading style, you are one of a very select elite in the trading world. Having finally achieved that success, why go off and try to fight that battle in another market? This would be like a gifted professional basketball player who switches to soccer after his basketball team wins a national championship! If you are making consistent money, just increase your unit size to increase your earning potential.

The final fear is the hardest one to beat. The fear of failure is a monkey on every beginning trader's back. Trading is a career built on *managing* failure. It is natural in the beginning to assume every loss is the direct result of your incompetence or stupidity. Traders tend to internalize and personalize their losses as they begin to trade. In addition, the pressure to pay the bills, support a family, or prove the naysayers wrong can cause you to trade with desperation. Each trade you take starts a destructive internal dialogue. "What if I lose on this trade?" "Oh, is this one going to fail?" "If this trade fails, how will I admit it to my family?" "Maybe I had better just get out...." It is astounding how some traders can talk themselves into an alternative reality moments after putting on a trade with supreme confidence. To defeat this demon is again an exercise in acceptance. You have to accept that each trade has the possibility for loss, and that each trade will do everything in its power to shake you out of your position. Having a clear trading plan and managing those positions with stop and limit orders can help take some of the emotion out of the equation. If you have the discipline to enter your orders and then *stick to them*, these broker-based orders will be there to take your loss for you, or to cash out of a winning position instantly and without emotion no matter what your personal feelings are at that moment.

CALCULATING YOUR ODDS

Now that you have a written trading plan and the discipline needed to trade your plan correctly, you are ready to begin the money management process. You need to calculate your odds and begin to project gain and loss potential for your plan. Let's take two hypothetical trading plans and see how this analysis process works.

Each trade has been tested on paper or with one contract to prove its value. Each test has a sample size of 30 trades in order to provide a better data set to analyze. The first trade strategy uses a multiday swing strategy with a profit objective of 2 or 3 to 1. The results for this test period in units are as follows:

−1	2.5	1.8	3	−1	−1.1	2	1.5	.8	−1
3	−1	2.5	1	−1	−1	3	−1	−1	−1
−1	−1	3	−1	−1	3	−1.3	2.3	.−1	−1

The profit after 30 trades is 12 units with a maximum experienced drawdown of 5 units. This gives a drawdown-to-profit ratio of better than 2 to 1, which is totally acceptable. This sample had 13 gainers and 17 losers for a win/loss ratio of 43 percent The average loss was −1.02, and the average gain was +2.26 for an experienced risk-to-reward ratio of 2.21 to 1.

What does this data tell us?

1. This trading plan has a positive expectancy.
2. It has a relatively low accuracy rate and a large experienced risk-to-reward ratio.
3. The drawdown was small enough relative to the reward experienced to be acceptable.
4. Thirty trades yielded 12 units of profit or .4 per trade. If the sample data holds true, for every $1000 risked, this strategy should yield $400 per trade over time. This is the edge this trade offers.

The next strategy is an intraday scalp strategy. It trades based off an overbought and/or oversold indicator, and seeks to capture a 1 to 1 profit. The results for its testing phase in units are as follows:

.8	−.5	1.2	1	−1	−.3	.8	1	−1	1.1
1	−1	1	1.1	.8	−1	.75	−1	1	.8
1	−1	.75	−1	1	1	−.6	1.2	−1	.5

The profit after 30 trades is 8.4 units with a maximum experienced drawdown of 2 units. This gives a drawdown-to-profit ratio of better than 4 to 1, which is outstanding. This sample had 19 gainers and 11 losers for a win/loss ratio of 63 percent. The average loss was −.85, and the average gain was +.94 for a experienced risk-to-reward ratio of 1.1 to 1.

What does this data tell us?

1. This trading plan has a positive expectancy.
2. It has a relatively high accuracy rate and a small experienced risk-to-reward ratio.
3. The drawdown was small enough relative to the reward experienced to be acceptable.
4. Thirty trades yielded 8.4 units of profit or .28 per trade. If the sample data holds true, for every $1000 risked, this strategy should yield $280 over time. This is the edge this trade offers.

SO, WHICH STRATEGY HAS THE STRONGER EDGE?

If we begin to contrast these two strategies we first know that both have a positive expectancy. If we trade either strategy going forward, we can expect to see a profit. On the surface the swing strategy seems better; it took in 12 units of profit and has a .4 per trade edge versus the .28 seen in the scalp strategy. *However*, if you look below the surface you will see some interesting possibilities. If you are willing to trade the swing strategy, then by default you are willing to take a 5-unit drawdown. Even though the scalp strategy only brought in 8.4 units, it had a maximum 2-unit drawdown. If you are willing to take a 5-unit drawdown, then you could trade the scalp strategy with 2.5 times more risk than the swing and still only expose yourself to a 5-unit drawdown.

What does all this mean? If you traded the swing strategy with $1000 risk your profit for the 30-trade sample would have been $12,000 with a $5000 drawdown. If you scaled up the scalp strategy and traded it with

$2500 on each trade then your profit for the 30-trade sample would have been $21,000 with a $5000 drawdown. Because of its small drawdown, the scalp strategy has *more* profit potential for the same level of risk as the swing strategy. So on the face of it, the scalp strategy should be the one to focus on. Once you have picked out a strategy based on your research, you can begin to play devil's advocate, as you try to find holes that the market will try to poke in your strategy. One of the downsides of the scalp strategy will be when it sees a greater than expected drawdown. If trading with the 1 to 2.5 risk ratio described above, each time the drawdown extends beyond 2, you will take a 2.5-unit loss. Thus if both strategies run into trouble and take two losses more than normal before the gains appear again, the first strategy would see a 7-unit loss, while the scalp strategy would experience a 10-unit drawdown. This reality is something to be considered when choosing what risk you want to take. It is very important to plan for the unlikely! For this reason I like to keep my size small enough that I could withstand twice the average drawdown and still have enough capital to trade comfortably. If you size your positions so you have the buying power to withstand a drawdown that is twice the norm, you will have the sticking power to weather a nasty losing streak. Rule No. 1 for any trader is to survive the loss and stay in the game! Many traders have cut short promising careers because they became greedy or hyperaggressive and took risks that finally caught up with them. The longer you trade the higher the chances that you will see the ultimate highs and lows of this cyclical business. If you accept this from the start and plan for the hurricanes of misery that will blow through your account from time to time, you ensure that you will be present and trading when the gains rain down, filling your account with a torrent of money!

So if you decide to implement the scalp strategy, the next step is to determine what the appropriate unit size should be. Your first choice is to set the maximum level of drawdown you wish to maintain. This is one area where the leverage that futures offer acts as an advantage. If you withstand a deep drawdown while trading stocks, your buying power will be greatly reduced. This will limit the position sizes you can take, and will further reduce your ability to work out of a drawdown. In a futures account, the margin requirements are so small, that it takes a much larger drawdown to force you to smaller position sizes. This is both a blessing and a curse. It can allow you to be more aggressive and withstand drawdowns that would seriously damage a stock trader's account; however, you can also take risks that can blow out your account and even leave you in debt to your broker. The care needed when setting your risk levels and a respect for the damage that leverage can cause you cannot be overemphasized.

If you are willing to take a 10 percent drawdown to your capital, then the next step is to look at the average stop and drawdown for the strategy under consideration. If the average stop for our scalping strategy is approximately $250, then our basic unit size in dollars is $250. If you then sustained a 2-unit drawdown, the losses would take $500 from your account. If you double this potential for loss as a safety measure, then you could conceivably see a $1000 loss per contract while trading this strategy. If you are willing to risk 10 percent of your account, then $10,000 would be the minimum account size required to trade this strategy.

WOULD YOU LIKE TO MAKE 67% A MONTH?

This is where so many games are played with the numbers. I'm sure all of you have seen grandiose claims of enormous returns available with this or that system and/or strategy. These numbers are easy to create because of the leverage that futures offer. Consider the scalping strategy we have been exploring. Technically it has a 2-unit drawdown, so if you take that literally and ignore the possibility of a drawdown outside the averages you could come up with these numbers. If the average loss is $250, then a 2-unit drawdown is $500. If your head-in-the-sand maximum drawdown is −2, then you could trade one contract with only $600 more than the margin requirement. Let's say this gives you a perfect-world number of $3000 needed for each contract. If you take this to the logical extreme, a $25,000 account could trade as many as eight contracts. If you take this high-wire level of risk and run it over the sample data we took, this strategy would have made approximately $16,800 or a 67 percent return! Sound familiar? Although technically possible, this level of risk is ludicrously dangerous. If there is one more stop than planned, if there is one snafu that causes a loss, the house of cards comes tumbling down, and you are left with nothing more than a fleeting memory of your money. Risk must be assumed with responsibility, and these levels need to be determined with cold calculating logic, not with the emotional greed of what is technically possible.

In order to bridge the gap from fantasy to reality, you have to begin by looking at the possibility for maximum drawdown. This gives you a basic idea of the potential for loss per losing streak. Next, you have to look at how many contracts are needed to scale size properly. Let's assume, in order to keep the stops near that average of $250 risk, that as many as three contracts need to be taken. This would make the $5000 number invalid, as $5000 would not be enough to cover the margin requirements for three contracts. If the margin requirement for each contract is $3000, a minimum of $9000 plus padding for the inevitable drawdown would be required before any trades are taken. If you feel that average drawdown level once doubled is enough of a margin of safety, then a $10,000 account would be required to trade this strategy. That initial $9000 becomes your working capital, and this is the account size you must maintain in order to be able to trade the number of contracts required. The remaining money is padding that will help you survive any drawdowns. Having established a realistic minimum capitalization to trade this strategy, you can begin to estimate its potential for profit.

Again, this all comes back to the essential balance between risk and reward. The larger the risks assumed, the larger the potential for profit or loss. If you press this strategy with maximum aggressiveness, you risk 2.5 percent of your account on every trade ($250 is 2.5 percent of $10,000). Since the strategy has a basic edge of .28, your edge for this trade will be $70 profit per trade over time. If the trade signals once or twice a day on average, then you can expect to see 30 trades a month. And 30 times $70 gives you a statistical expectancy of $2100 per month for every $10,000 you trade.

Working backward like this is an important part of the strategy-testing process. It gives you a realistic expectation for your setup and also helps you to define what capital is needed in order to realize your goals for income. In the above example, you would need a capital base of $40,000 in order to realize an income goal of $100,000 per year. But if you wish to trade at this level of extreme leverage, you must also accept the possibility that you could withstand an $8000 to $10,000 drawdown.

SIZE MATTERS

During the past several years I have come to know many traders from many walks of life. One of the fascinating lessons I have learned is that the difference between the trader who makes $150,000 per year and the trader who makes $1.5 million per year is not usually style, management technique, or trading brilliance, but rather consistency, discipline to stick to a trading plan, and the willingness to take an extremely large level of dollar risk per trade. The folks who see seven-figure incomes are willing to risk five figures every time they initiate a position. Having had the unique chance to talk to so many traders and analyze their trading styles, I have developed what I believe to be a pretty accurate rule of thumb. I call it "the 10k rule." Simply stated, it is this: "For every $100 risked per trade, a skilled professional speculator should see approximately $10,000 in reward per year." Take this concept and use it to reality-test your goals for income. Would you like to make $50,000 per year? Then you will need to risk approximately $500 per trade over the course of the next year. Would you like to make $100,000 per year? Then you will need to risk approximately $1000 per trade over the course of the next year. Let's look at some bigger numbers, since I'm sure everyone involved in this business hopes to bring in that seven-figure income someday. Would you like to make $1 million next year? Then be ready to risk $10,000 on your trades! And what about drawdowns? Imagine a $50,000 to $70,000 loss over the course of a rough week, with $100,000 in losses on a bad week from time to time. The ability to take large-dollar risks and still trade objectively is seldom if ever mentioned, but I believe it remains the major difference between the successful and super successful traders.

The concepts introduced in this chapter can be difficult to understand at first. But they are the foundation of any consistent trading system. In order to become a consistently profitable trader, you must fully understand how to correctly size your position, analyze and choose from a number of trading strategies, and appropriately choose what level of dollar risk your unit size should be. If you can properly analyze a trading strategy and can come up with your edge per trade in units, it simplifies the process dramatically. Determine what your unit size will be, then multiply that by your edge, and you'll have a fairly accurate prediction of the potential in any trading strategy.

During the trade strategy development, remember to stay with the profitability mind-set. Look for, analyze, and very carefully estimate your potential for loss first, then begin to think about profitability. There is a market saying, "Take care of losses, and the profits will take care of themselves." Truer words were never spoken. Anything you can do to reduce your average drawdown will dramatically impact your profitability over time. Know and accept what profit is realistic for your current level of risk. I have had many traders come to me in a depressed state of mind. They were disappointed with their trading income and felt there was something they were missing in order to fully realize their goals. As I analyzed their trading results, I could quickly see they had a valid plan with reasonable drawdowns and a positive expectancy. What they lacked was acceptance of reality. They were trading very well. If their profit was converted into units, their performance would have stood up well against many other professionals. But they believed that in order to make more money, they needed to trade more actively or to follow many more markets. In doing so, they changed their trading behavior so dramatically that they reduced or eliminated their edge, and actually slipped back to a negative expectation. For some strange reason (another trading paradox), it never occurred to them to simply increase their unit size (risk) in order to increase their income.

Once they understood the rule of 10, they went back to the style that had produced consistency in the past. They increased their dollar risk per trade and almost immediately began to post winning weeks and months again. Again, their self-imposed limitations had to do with acceptance. The business of trading suffers terribly from the "grass is greener" syndrome. Even seasoned professionals from time to time will forget what works for them and go looking for the holy grail when the real answers are staring them in the face.

CHAPTER 8

So, Why Aren't We All Rich?

> The game of speculation is the most uniformly fascinating game in the world. But it is not a game for the stupid, the mentally lazy, the person of inferior emotional balance, or the get-rich-quick adventurer. They will die poor.
>
> —*Jesse Livermore*

Over the past several years, I have seen traders fail in every possible way. Although every story is different, some incredible similarities exist. Almost every trading error has at its root a lack of acceptance of risk or an unrealistic expectation for profit. By far the most common error is a lack of respect for the market and its potential to do your account serious damage. The vast majority of wannabes come to the markets with no trading plan, and no real goal other than "to make a lot of money." They refuse to accept that this is an incredibly complex and difficult business. They begin to trade with a cavalier arrogance that feeds into every trick the market loves to pull. They take enormous risks, not because of any courage or risk tolerance, but rather because they simply do not understand what could happen if the market turns badly against their position. Because their risk levels are dangerously high, the reward (when they get lucky) can be enormous. Their short-term returns when they are experiencing a payout cycle will soundly trounce the professionals, so they feel smugly superior and continue with their high-risk behavior. Sooner or later these risks catch up with them, and they suffer devastating losses in the inevitable payback cycle. You *must* have a carefully developed trading plan if you are ever to succeed in this business. Look in any book that is written to help an individual wishing to start a small business, and you'll see a great deal written about creating a business plan. As a trader you *are* that small-business owner, and should spend time planning carefully how you intend to make your business thrive. I know of many traders with a great deal of experience who still spend an enormous amount of time and effort on their trading plan each year. They decide what their goals are, what strategies are performing well in the current market environment, and what types of position sizes they need to take in order to produce the level of income they desire. Your trading plan and the structure it provides can also prove very helpful as you deal with drawdowns and other trading setbacks. If your plan is well written, then you have thought out what setbacks are likely and how you will deal with them. Never forget that the payout-payback cycle will be your constant companion as you trade through the next year. This is a manic-depressive business, and the trader who best plans for and controls the depressive periods will have the most profit in the bank at the end of the year.

WHAT'S THE PLAN?

If the number one reason for failure is the lack of a cohesive trading plan, then the number two reason for trading failure has to be the inability to follow your plan. I could tell you story after story about traders I have known who had a reasonable trading plan with a profitable expectation. Yet for some reason they did not have the trust or discipline to stick to their plan. The market would always provide seductive opportunities for them to switch into "cowboy mode" and enter and/or manage their trades in a manner *specifically* discouraged by their trading plan. This would always damage their edge, and cause them to take losses that would leave them in a state of perpetual breakeven. When they were trading within a payout cycle, the euphoria of the winning streak led them to trade off plan in an attempt to sustain those euphoric feelings. When they were trading within a payback cycle, the depression and frustration of the losing streak would again lead them off plan as they tried to escape the negative feelings associated with losing. In another example of the contrary nature of markets, at the extremes of the payout-payback cycle when their plan would have helped them the most, they threw it out the window and traded by "feel." The third reason why traders fail is again linked to an inability to follow a plan. Traders who are prone to taking trades that are off plan consistently misdiagnose the weaknesses in their trading skill set. Because they're not following their plan, they cannot accurately determine whether their plan's edge has weakened due to a change in the market environment, or if their losses are simply due to the impulsive cowboy trades they have taken. They will take any adversity as a personal failure, and begin making adjustments to their trading strategies without knowing what is really to blame for their poor performance. If you are disciplined and stick to your trading plan, you will know that any period of poor performance can be blamed directly on the trading strategy your plan is based around. When you experience a period of drawdown that exceeds the normal payback cycle, you can focus on analyzing the strategy your plan is based around. Is your edge diminishing or gone due to a change in the economic environment? Is your edge being affected by a reduction in market volatility or follow-through? Or perhaps your edge is still intact, but you are trading in a period filled with anomalous market action. If you exercise discipline and trade your plan carefully, you will be able to determine *why* you are losing and be in a position to make the changes needed to get your performance back on track.

Most traders who wash out do so out of frustration and disgust after a long period of poor performance. Drawdowns are a natural part of the trading cycle, the way a strategy breathes money as the payout-payback cycle ebbs and flows. Managing drawdowns is first a function of your trading plan. As you research a new strategy, you develop a good feel of what the normal drawdowns should be. As long as your losing cycles stay within normal levels, you can continue to trade without stress. Once the drawdown begins to break beyond normal, then it's time to move into a diagnostic and stress management posture. This is contrary to human nature. When a drawdown gets extreme, your mind will be intensely focused on getting your money back. The first step to taking back what the market has stolen from you occurs when you figure out what has caused your losses. Anytime you feel desperate, *stop trading*! Anytime you feel a pressure to trade, or find yourself searching for patterns that are not in your trading plan, *stop trading*! Look for triggers in your personality to alert you when it's time to walk away. A few foolish errors made due to mental distress can take back the profit from several months with staggering ease. You must be ruthless whenever you realize that you are slipping away from your plan into a mode of desperation. Step one is to stop the bleeding and break away from your current self-destructive state. This is especially important if you are an intraday trader, because you can easily become mesmerized by the data flowing across your quote screen.

The best way to break out of such a mental trance is through physical action. Turn off your monitors, and go do something physically active that requires focus. Take a walk, play golf, juggle! As humorous as it may seem, I found juggling to be an important tool for me as I learned to trade. Keeping three balls in the air requires focus and physical awareness. When I started to feel that sense of desperation, that manic pressure to get even with the market, a few minutes of juggling would totally reset my mental state. By breaking the screen trace and truly taking my mind entirely off trading, I could free myself of the stress and frustration incurred by any previous trades for that day. I know other traders who use video games, crossword puzzles, or model building as their crutch to break the cycle of drawdown obsession and regain mental balance. So find some activity that you enjoy, which requires total concentration and focus, and see if that can't be your way to center yourself when emotions begin to run high. Stop the bleeding, get centered, and then begin to look for ways to get your money back!

THE DOCTOR'S PLIGHT

There is a passage from Mark Twain's *Life on the Mississippi* that has always struck me. Twain is describing his path to becoming a steamship pilot on the Mississippi. It is the same process all traders must go through to become truly objective and professional about their speculation. In order to most efficiently press your edge, you must let go of the thrill of winning and the despair of defeat. You must break the manic-depressive cycle the market projects; you must take your mind to a place of Zenlike calm. Receive and interpret the information the market gives you without bias and use that constant river of information to find the best directional indicators available to you at any given moment.

What Twain really is describing here is the achievement of mastery.

Now when I had mastered the language of this water and had come to know every trifling feature that bordered the great river as familiarly as I knew the letters of the alphabet, I had made a valuable acquisition. But I had lost something, too. I had lost something which could never be restored to me while I lived. All the grace, the beauty, the poetry had gone out of the majestic river! I still keep in mind a certain wonderful sunset which I witnessed when steamboating was new to me. A broad expanse of the river was turned to blood; in the middle distance the red hue brightened into gold, through which a solitary log came floating, black and conspicuous; in one place a long, slanting mark lay sparkling upon the water; in another the surface was broken by boiling, tumbling rings, that were as many-tinted as an opal; where the ruddy flush was faintest, was a smooth spot that was covered with graceful circles and radiating lines, ever so delicately traced; the shore on our left was densely wooded, and the somber shadow that fell from this forest was broken in one place by a long, ruffled trail that shone like silver; and high above the forest wall a clean-stemmed dead tree waved a single leafy bough that glowed like a flame in the unobstructed splendor that was flowing from the sun. There were graceful curves, reflected images, woody heights, soft distances; and over the whole scene, far and near, the dissolving lights drifted steadily, enriching it, every passing moment, with new marvels of coloring. I stood like one bewitched. I drank it in, in a speechless rapture. The world was new to me, and I had never seen anything like this at home. But as I have said, a day came when I began to cease from noting the glories and the charms which the moon and the sun and the twilight wrought upon the river's face; another day came when I ceased altogether to note them. Then, if that sunset scene had been repeated, I should have looked upon it without rapture, and should have commented upon it, inwardly, after this fashion: This sun means that we are going to have wind to-morrow; that floating log means that the river is rising, small thanks to it; that slanting mark on the water refers to a bluff reef which is going to kill somebody's steamboat one of these nights, if it keeps on stretching out like that; those tumbling "boils" show a dissolving bar and a changing channel there; the lines and circles in the slick water over yonder are a warning that that troublesome place is shoaling up dangerously; that silver streak in the shadow of the forest is the "break" from a new snag, and he has located himself in the very best place he could have found to fish for steamboats; that tall dead tree, with a single living branch, is not going to last long, and then how is a body ever going to get through this blind place at night without the friendly old landmark. No, the romance and the beauty were all gone from the river. All the value any feature of it had for me now was the amount of usefulness it could furnish toward compassing the safe piloting of a steamboat. Since those days, I have pitied doctors from my heart. What does the lovely flush in a beauty's cheek mean to a doctor but a "break" that ripples above some deadly disease? Are not all her visible charms sown thick with what are to him the signs and symbols of hidden decay? Does he ever see her beauty at all, or doesn't he simply view her professionally, and comment upon her unwholesome condition all to himself? And doesn't he sometimes wonder whether he has gained most or lost most by learning his trade?

It still gives me goose bumps to read that as it so perfectly describes the last step into mastery. When you truly see each trade as but a tiny piece of the pie, your emotional attachment to each trade's outcome nearly disappears. When you achieve this mental state, you will see your consistency and performance begin to reach mastery levels.

As you strive to achieve a mastery level, there are still many career-ending pitfalls to avoid. With a leverage that the futures markets offer, blowing out an account is a serious risk for the undisciplined trader. For every trader who liquidates an account and quits in disgust, there will be one or two traders whose trading careers will end in spectacular disaster. Blowing out an account can be financially devastating, as it is possible through leverage to lose more money than you actually had in your account. Just about every blowout could have been avoided if some semblance of a trading plan was in effect. Most accounts are blown out when traders choose not to use protective stop loss orders. These are the people who see trading losses as deep personal failures, rather than a natural part of the business. You can guarantee you will never blow out your account due to inaction by following one simple rule. Never allow a position to exist in your account unless there is a protective stop loss order in effect for that trade. In the world of trading which is full of paradoxes and rules based on balancing risk, this is one rule that is inviolate! You will never succeed as a trader if you violate this rule. (And, furthermore, you'd be quite lucky to survive your first 6 months.) The second cardinal sin that traders commit is averaging down into a losing trade. Adding to a position can be a useful tool within the structure of your trading plan, but the blowout trader is simply adding to positions in order to bring down the average cost of a position. This is done with the hope and prayer that sooner or later the market will bounce and trade can be covered at breakeven. This is the trading equivalent to the gamblers' Martingale system. In the Martingale system, you double your bet every time you lose in a game of chance. Mathematically, this seems like a perfect system but when real life rears its ugly head, you quickly realize that sooner or later you will hit a losing streak that will ruin you! This is exactly what happens to a trader who averages down. The market will often reward traders who average down with a bounce that allows them to extricate themselves from a poorly planned position. This is the reason why averaging down is such destructive behavior; the market will give you a false sense of success until finally it rips your trading account apart. So if golden rule number one is "Always use a protective stop loss order," golden rule number two would be "Never add to a losing position unless your plan specifically requires it."

DEALING WITH DISASTER

Disasters can also blow out a trading account. A disaster move is a large gap or volatility spike that causes you to take losses that greatly exceed your planned initial risk. Gaps, market spikes on news, and order entry errors can all cause uncontrolled losses for even the most disciplined trader. Some of these market events cannot be predicted or avoided, and are just some of the risks of doing business. However, there are certain envelopes of time surrounding important market events where these disasters seem to cluster. By avoiding trades during these high-risk periods, you can greatly reduce the risk of sustaining a disaster trade in your account. Any news that can change opinions can cause the market to sharply discount these new biases in an instant. Announcements by the Federal Reserve, crop reports, economic reports, currency decisions made by major governments, and option expiration days are all to be managed or avoided due to their disaster risk. In addition, I have seen many other traders take devastating losses as they participated in a runaway market situation. When you are employing a trend-following method, sometimes the trend can get out of control as euphoria or capitulation begins to exhibit itself. When the market is screaming in the right direction, it is easy to let the euphoria of accumulating profits convince you that the position just *has* to go a little bit farther. The more violent the euphoria or capitulation, the more violent the snapback is likely to be as the market finally reverses. When this reversal occurs, the market will be very thin, and slippage can be dramatic. To avoid these disaster-type losses, don't let greed get the better of you. When you are in a trade and you see signs of euphoria or capitulation, use those fast market conditions to take your exit into liquidity. If you look back at trades of this nature that went sour, nine times out of ten the market turned 5 minutes after you decided to continue holding for the big move.

If you are in a trade and experience one of these disaster scenarios, here are some tips to help you extricate yourself with the minimum possible damage to your account.

If the disaster is a gap, you can harness the natural tendency for gaps to fill. If a position gaps beyond the area where your protective stop loss order was placed, wait 5 minutes after the open, then place a new stop loss order a few ticks above the high for the day. If the market continues to squeeze, then your new stop loss order will be executed, and the loss will be taken. If the gap begins to fill, then your new stop loss order will keep you in the trade, and you will be able to exit your position as soon as the gap has filled back to support.

In the example shown in Figure 8.1, there was a clean pullback to support (1) that broke new highs and could have conceivably been held overnight. The next morning the market gaps down dramatically and setting a stop under the 5-minute low saves the trader from taking a much greater loss.

In the example in Figure 8.2, the initial trade is a short based off the false breakout-peek top around 884. The trade sells off beautifully, wiggles back to retest the 20-period exponential moving average (EMA), and again turns lower close in what looks like a new downtrend. The next morning, the price gaps up dramatically to open beyond the initial stop. The gap immediately fills, and an adjusted stop loss order set above the 5-minute high kept the trade open, turning what looks like a greater than expected loss into a profitable trade.

If you get caught in an intraday spike scenario, don't play games; use a market order to exit your position. If your protective stop loss order is

FIGURE 8.1

FIGURE 8.2

112

formatted as a stop market order, then this will happen automatically. And it is for this reason that all my protective stop loss orders are formatted as stop market orders. When such a spike occurs and the stop is triggered, you will be filled at the best price the market can offer at that moment in time.

In the example shown in Figure 8.3, the market was in a downtrend, and had offered several successful rally-to-resistance trades (1) and (2). The third rally to resistance (3) turned right at the 20-period EMA, and formed a hammer reversal candlestick. The trade set up and was looking great when "Saddam is dead" rumors rocked the market. This caused a dramatic spike, then a retrace as the market reacted to this news from the war in Iraq. Having a stop market order in effect would have given you the best possible fill in this spastic market environment.

If a trade is moving well into the profit, then be ready to act if that market begins to exhibit signs of euphoria or capitulation (high-volume, fast pace on the tape, wide bars, and highly volatile movement). Use these signals of a fast market as an opportunity to offer out your contracts into the euphoria, or bid your contracts into the capitulation. Euphoria and capitulation are both emotional events; there will be many emotionally driven traders frantically trying to take your contracts. As an objective nonemotional trader, you can see their foolish actions for what they are and are more than willing to let them assume the ever-increasing snapback risk as you take your profits.

The trade in the example in Figure 8.4 began as a buy off chart support (1). Support held, and the market began to rally. The rally soon accelerated out of control and began to exhibit strong signs of euphoria (2). The wide bars printed in the rally are uncharacteristic when compared to previous chart action. In addition, you can see the volume bloom (3) that formed as the euphoria peaked. Offering out into this euphoric action would have given you an exit between 884 and 886. Even though there was one last attempt by the market to break to new highs (4), with 20/20 hindsight you can see how an exit into euphoria would have given you a fill right near the high for the day.

Learning to avoid disaster when possible and manage it when it occurs is the last piece in the risk control puzzle. By entering trades when the odds are stacked in your favor and steadfastly refusing to fall into the markets traps that tempt you to engage in risky trading behavior, you set the stage for consistent profitability. So develop your plan, avoid trading when disaster risks are present, and keep yourself positioned in the line of least resistance. By doing so, you will be able to take whatever profit the market makes available to your chosen style for trading! Yes, Virginia, trading is *that* simple.

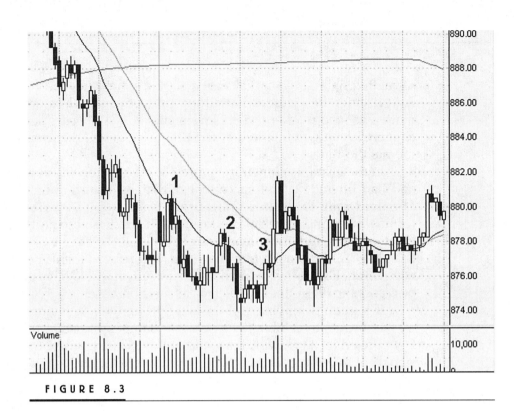

FIGURE 8.3

FIGURE 8.4

In order to best serve my consulting clients, I am always trying to define what makes me different, what makes me able to profit when so many others fail. I believe it is because I define my own reality as a trader. The market presents a unique experience for most of us. It offers total and complete freedom to create our own reality in which there are only two unalterable truths.

You cannot be right all the time; you can only trade within a set of probable outcomes.

You must capture more profit in dollars from your winning trades than you give back when your opinions are proved false.

Beyond this you have total freedom to create your own reality. You may choose to trade with the trend. You may choose to trade against the trend. You may choose to hold positions for long periods of time; you may choose to hold positions for short periods of time. You may choose to trade four to six times a month. You may choose to trade four to six times a day. The market will try repeatedly to define your reality for you, but the choice is yours whether you choose to accept this reality or create your own.

CONTROL YOUR OWN TRADING REALITY

By creating your own reality, you become detached from the crowd. Living outside the conventional wisdom, you are more objective and should be able to see the forest for the trees. This creates a constant stream of profitable situations that the rest of the trading world never knew existed. You create your own reality when the financial media is all talking about the strength and power of a particular market, and you see signs of euphoria into which to take profits and perhaps even initiate a short trade. You create your own reality when a friend gives you a trading tip and instead of following his or her advice, you initiate a trade in that market according to your own trading plan. You create your own reality when you see a peek top occur and define this as a bullish failure and therefore a shortable event. The rest of the trading world has had their reality defined for them, and will be long based on the simple pattern recognition principles that "A break to new highs is a bullish event." And it may indeed be, but the trader who lives and operates outside the market has the objectivity to see the breakout and then look inside that pattern to pick out the clues to its success or failure. The reality trader who lives outside the market has no personal investment in the success or failure of that particular breakout. The pattern simply offers the potential for a trading opportunity and the reality trader will let the market's actions define whether the trade is a short or a long (or even if it sets up at all!).

In my experience freeing your mind is entirely based on acceptance. You must accept the risk you assume in any trade, and believe deeply that the trade is but a tiny piece in the much larger puzzle of a profitable trading plan. That trade alone cannot make or break you, and therefore matters little. When I give a seminar, sometimes I will take a quarter, hide it in one of my hands, and tell different participants that they can have the quarter if they can choose correctly. When put on the spot they rarely hesitate and will choose quickly and decisively. This is because they don't have a fear of failure. They don't really care that much if they choose the wrong hand, because there is only a quarter at stake. If I go through the same exercise, but this time hide a $100 bill in one hand, everything changes! Now they feel a strong personal involvement. They take time to choose, try to look in my eyes and read my body language. They may even decide on one hand, then change their mind and select the other. There is nothing structurally different about this game. If there is a quarter, $100, or $1000 at stake, there is still a simple 50 percent probability of success. What changes is all internal. The seminar participants allow themselves to have their reality defined by the external motives of greed and fear.

If you take a moment to look back on your life and closely analyze your hero moments, I suspect in each you will find a situation where you had totally accepted whatever the risk or challenge was and had fully committed yourself. Usually, the clearest examples of this will come from sports success, such as coming back to win from what seemed an insurmountable point deficit, taking a high risk and/or high yield action (a "Hail Mary" pass). Or perhaps you performed a simple task with enormous pressure from an audience (making that game-winning free throw with everybody watching). Sports psychologists talk of unconscious competence, and that is exactly what this is. You detach from the world's external reality, where "I will be a hero if I make a field goal to win the Superbowl, or I will be a subject of ridicule if I miss" and create your own reality. In this high-performance reality the only thing that matters are the uprights, the ball, and your focus on the kick. You have done this task successfully a million times before in practice and in other games, so why is this time any different? Are the uprights of a different height or width? Is the ball a different size or weight? No, all is as it has been every other time; the only difference is that the external world is trying hard to force you to accept its reality, which is a reality of failure.

If external pressures such as the example above are difficult to handle, they are nothing compared to the pressure one puts on oneself. It has been my experience that nobody can be as hard on you as you yourself, and it is this internal pressure that a trader must overcome in order to reach his or her potential. Take the field goal example above and compare it to a scenario in which you must make one last simple 3-foot putt for birdie to card a new personal best. You are playing alone, and so there are no external pressures present. Nobody will even know if you make or miss the putt, yet in this situation so many of us would feel a level of pressure that would easily match or exceed the pressure of a game-winning field goal. In a team-based event, there are always reasons and excuses for failure. "The ball wasn't held well; there was a blocker I had to kick around." In a highly individual endeavor like golf or trading, there is nobody else to blame but yourself. So in order to perform at your best, don't allow your emotions to become the external reality of failure. Back away and create your own reality of success in which this is just another 3-foot tap-in. You know from experience that you rarely miss your putts at this distance, so you step up without fear, make a focused "yipless" stroke and succeed!

As a trader, you create your reality when you research an edge and define your trading plan for that strategy. This process is the equivalent to training for a sporting event. It is here you can objectively analyze what adversity may occur within this strategy, and how you will react when it occurs. The more carefully you build that reality, the more robust and stress free your trading will become. If your plan (your reality) accepts that for every three trades that you make one will be a loser, then after two winners in a row, how can you really be that shocked and frustrated that the third trade resolves itself with a loss? Sitting on the couch, reading this book, the answer is obvious. Sitting in front of your trading screen watching a $2000 gain for the day turn into a $1000 gain, most traders allow the market to dictate their reality and will pay an emotional and monetary price as a result.

For the majority of traders, the market dictates to them a reality of stress, frustration, and pain. This perfect hell is even endured by many consistently profitable traders. They are special people who can manage or even thrive off the stress and emotion involved. For the rest of us, this constant stress will take its toll and we will burn out after a few years. Ironically, this mental capitulation will occur just as a trader's skills move up to a much higher level, when they should be earning the biggest returns of their career. Instead they will be looking for another job or will be in the mental bunker trading for the weekend. If you are ever to achieve the great wealth and success that trading offers, you must be able to trade well over the course of a career. Do not allow the market, or any other person, to dictate your reality to you. You must create a market reality for yourself that will allow you to adapt and survive in this business long enough to fulfill your potential.

FREE YOUR MIND

Why am I different from you? How am I able to live outside the conventional wisdom and come to these realizations while so many must struggle to unlearn and create a new profitable reality for themselves?

You went to school.

In school you are trained and taught the right way to do things. In short your entire school experience is one of externally defined realities. It is focused on preparing children to function in an industrial society. This process does not reward creative thinking, critical thinking, or out-of-the-box problem solving. In fact willingness to question reality is often actively discouraged. Yet it is this ability to question reality and look for a better way (even if it breaks the rules) that has brought such wild success to an entire generation of computer innovators as the Internet and the information age bloomed. My education was guided by my parents, grandparents, and other mentors along the way. My grandfather was a teacher and taught me much of what I know about science. He and my mother taught me by practice and example to learn via the scientific method. I learned through experience and experimentation. The first step consisted of research and data gathering; the second step was to experiment and prove the concept. I would research a new concept by myself or with the help of others, then go about testing and questioning what I had just learned. By actively proving each piece of knowledge to myself (trust, but verify), I believe I internalized and retained the information in a way that many never experience. I have discovered by talking to others that many people were never able to take their education to this higher level of efficiency and competence until they were in college. Then, often for the first time, they were introduced to the concept of the scientific process. Having been lucky enough to have the gift of a trust-but-verify education facilitated by my family, I was put in a position at an early stage in life to begin my journey into the world of professional trading.

We have all seen the bumper sticker that says, "Question Authority." The trader's motto should be "Question Reality"! This is especially the case for trading education. When I work with my consulting clients, I try to give them an idea and then a way to prove the concept to themselves. By doing this, I can accelerate their learning curve, but in order for the lessons to stick, all traders must prove their validity for themselves. When clients try to put me on a pedestal or take my ideas as gospel, I immediately challenge them to question what I have just told them. If it is the truth, it can be independently verified easily by any who choose to try. Not only must you question the reality of conventional wisdom but you must also constantly question your own reality—your own trading plans. By doing so, you will keep adapting them to fit changing market conditions, and they will evolve over time as your skills and intuition build.

Free your mind.

CHAPTER 9

The Fog of War

You don't have to blow out the other fellow's light to let your own shine.

—*Bernard Baruch*

So this brings us to the beginning of the end! After discussions of the mathematics behind trading and the optimization of your edge, technical analysis and the art of chart reading, the science of position sizing, and managing the mental side of your trading life, the tools are before you. It's time to see how the rubber meets the road! It has been my experience that trading lessons which are backed by practical real-world examples act as the best lessons for my clients. These practical trading experiences seem to really resonate and have the best chance for retention. I always try to structure my presentations by beginning with information and ending with application.

The textbook-type presentation is great for learning concepts and tactics for trading. But it can be rather dry, so in this last chapter I hope to bring these ideas home to roost as I write about my trading for the next month. Hopefully, there will be some interesting situations during this time, and a few good payout-payback cycles for me to trade through. I want to focus this diary as much as I can on process, and what it's like to be a trader. In the previous chapters I have described my style for picking trades; hopefully, these descriptions will begin to come alive for you as you see the trades I choose to follow as the action unfolds. I hope through this trade summary to give you the chance to be a fly on the wall in my trading loft as I go about pressing my edge in the markets.

I work and trade from my home office. My office is separated from the rest of the house, which lets me close out the world and focus on my trading without outside distractions. Since much of the trading day is spent waiting for opportunity, I have a workout station with weights and machines right next to my desk. When the fidgety boredom sets in, these weights help burn off stress, and help me keep my sanity as I grind through a dull period in the market. My stereo is right at hand, with custom speakers to fit the acoustics of the room. All this equipment really helps me control my mental state. If I'm getting frustrated by a position, a few reps or some good music can really help me break out of a negative mind-set.

I choose to operate primarily in the S&P and Bond futures markets. I started my trading career as a stock trader, and these markets remain close to my heart. I spent a lot of time watching the stock indexes as I waited for the right moment to enter my equity trades. This helped me develop a good sense of market direction and timing as I was always trying to enter my stock trades just as the indexes changed trend. The majority of my positions in these markets are day trades. These short-duration swing trades off support or resistance keep me in tune with the market and leave me with plenty of time free to focus on my other endeavors while I wait for the bigger swings to develop. I find my day trades act as an indicator for the bigger time frame trend changes. When I have been trading to the long side in my smaller time frames and begin to see these long patterns weakening, I know a deeper time frame trend change is in the works. So not only do I pull income from my day trades but they allow me to more precisely enter and exit my deeper time frame positions.

When I began this journey, I started out as many do in the mystification stage of the trader's learning cycle. The bubble market was heating up the stock indexes, and I'm sure this is one of the reasons why I was attracted to the markets and began to learn about trading. I stumbled my way around for about 6 months before I found a book that helped me begin to build some understanding of what real trading was all about. Barry Rudd's *Stock Patterns for Day Trading* gave me a litany of chart patterns to look for. With this basic structure, the random nature of the markets began to resolve into a series of breakouts, corrections, and tests of support and resistance. I now had a vocabulary to work from. The momentum style of trading was in its heyday; breakouts, breakaway gaps, and other continuation patterns set up and flew. Even without a real trading plan and only the beginnings of discipline, I managed to stay a little bit above breakeven.

I found some Web sites filled with articles and links to other trading sites. The World Wide Web became my training partner as I surfed around sucking down every crumb of trading information I could find. I'm sure that it was on one of these sites that I discovered *Reminiscences of a Stock Operator* by Edwin Lefèvre, and *Trader Vic—Methods of a Wall Street Master* by Victor Sperandeo. These two books changed my mind-set and helped me discover the trading style I would develop over the next year and a half.

I was exposed to the concept of trading longer term for the first time through Sperandeo's book. As silly as it may sound, up to that point everything I had read was exclusively targeted around day trading. The direct access revolution had hit the equity trading world, and everybody was writing about it. For the first time, a trader working from a home office could have high-level access to the stock markets. No longer were you forced to work in New York City if you wished to become a stock trader. This opened the floodgates, and the independent retail day trader was born. Swing and position trading had been around forever, but day trading was the new big thing.

At this point, I had developed a reasonable skill set as a day trader. The problem was that my skills were all based around simple pattern recognition. I had not realized what being a trader truly meant. Trader Vic talked about economics—the deep-seated reasons behind market cyclicality. He also drew parallels between playing poker and trading. Something in those descriptions connected with me, and my outlook and philosophy were transformed. Instead of looking at charts and seeing patterns that predicted a probable outcome, I began to look at my charts and see the bars as the product of other traders taking action. I began to read their actions and trade against those opponents. With this simple change in mind-set, my trading was taken to a whole different level.

Then I read *Reminiscences of a Stock Operator*, and again my life as a trader changed. The book is ostensibly a work of fiction, but is based on the real-life experiences of a master trader. In the central character, Larry Livermore, I saw many of the successes as a trader I hoped to achieve someday. At this time in my life, I was grossly overtrading. I was taking my newfound skills and flogging them to death. Trying to be all things to all markets, I found myself quickly becoming burnt out by the intense focus and high-stress levels of trading 10 times a day in the smallest of time frames. I also noticed that I was becoming much better at identifying major trend changes. I would find a stock at a major support level, buy it and sell it 15 or 20 minutes later for what I considered a good profit. Three days later I would look back at a multipoint rally, and realize that I had been long a few levels off the lows! By my constant scalping I had missed many points of profit potential. I began to experiment with expanded time frames, and started to hold some trades overnight. Some of my largest gains came in the form of gaps or morning rallies in the stocks I had purchased the day before. As a day trader I would have a hard time getting filled in these sharp moves, but as a swing trader I was already in and captured every penny. Most importantly, I found myself avoiding the many whipsaws that had previously cost me money. With the bigger time frame came bigger stops, stops that were large enough to keep me in my trades while my trend worked itself out. My stress levels dropped dramatically, and my returns grew as my confidence increased. I had found my style!

BUILDING THE FOUNDATIONS

I was beginning a very exciting phase of my trading career. My trading skills and intuition were getting better, but I was still very much a "squiggle trader." I had more indicators on my charts than porcupines have needles! Most of my trading errors were the result of paralysis by overanalysis. I was trying to make every trade perfect. I did not understand and had not accepted the random nature of trading, and was totally ignorant of the payout-payback cycle. When I would begin to struggle, I would always go looking for my indicators to show me what I was doing wrong. There were some terribly depressive periods during this time when I felt like the biggest idiot to ever walk the face of the earth. I would often go back and read *Reminiscences* for inspiration. It seemed like every time I would reread this book, new passages would jump out at me. I had read the words before, but for some reason my brain wasn't ready to comprehend their true meaning. One such passage describes 4 years of money-less trading. Now this book was written in the years after the 1929 crash and described a different era for the stock markets. But I had never even considered the possibility that the market could be without edge or the kind of market in which "not even a skunk could make a scent." Once I opened my mind to that possibility, I began to see in my own trading the first signs of the payout-payback cycle. Listen to Livermore describe this period of frustration.

> It has always rankled in my mind that after I left Williamson & Brown's office the cream was off the market. We ran smack into a long moneyless period; four mighty lean years. There was not a penny to be made. As Billy Henriquez once said, "It was the kind of market in which not even a skunk could make a scent." It looked to me as though I was in Dutch with destiny. It might have been the plan of Providence to chasten me, but really I had not been filled with such pride as called for a fall. I had not committed any of those speculative sins which a trader must expiate on the debtor side of the account. I was not guilty of a typical sucker play. I left Williamson's and tried other brokers' offices. In every one of them I lost money. It served me right,

because I was trying to force the market into giving me what it didn't have to give to wit, opportunities for making money. I did not find any trouble in getting credit, because those who knew me had faith in me. You can get an idea of how strong their confidence was when I tell you that when I finally stopped trading on credit I owed well over one million dollars. The trouble was not that I had lost my grip but that during those four wretched years the opportunities for making money simply didn't exist.

Even though the book was written in the early 1900s, the trading errors described were the same as mine! Livermore tried to force the market into giving him trading opportunities, allowing his mind to see setups where there were none. Maintaining true objectivity had always been one of my biggest challenges, and this passage helped me realize the truth of Livermore's saying, "There is a time to be bullish, a time to be bearish, and a time to be fishing." As I began to more accurately identify the payback periods in the market, I began to accept that trading during payback periods would invite losses. My edge would be slim to none when the market was out of alignment with my style, and there was little I could do but wait for market alignment to return. Since all my time and energy up to that point had been focused on learning when *to* trade, it was very difficult for me to realize it was equally important to learn when *not to* trade!

Another passage really resonated for me as I was struggling with my day trading. The bubble in the stock market had burst, and things were changing all over. I was right about the overall direction for many of my stocks, but the market was becoming unstable in the smaller time frames and I was continually being whipsawed out of my positions. After triggering my stop, the stock would invariably head back in the direction of my original opinion. On one of my regular readings of *Reminiscences*, I realized that Livermore had followed a similar path. He started off trading in bucket shops, which were little more than gambling parlors that used market data as their gambling vehicle rather than sports events or games of chance. These bucket shops would allow him to place a bet on the direction of the stock as if he were purchasing it outright. However, these orders never made it to any exchange. The "House" was betting against him just as in a casino. Livermore was day trading in these bucket shops, and because no shares ever traded hands he could get instant fills with no potential for slippage or other market eccentricities. He was good at reading the market, and soon the bucket shop operators grew tired of losing to him. They banned him from their shops, and he was forced to go to New York and trade for real with the exchange itself. He struggled at first, then realized he had lost his day-trading edge because the realities of slippage and commissions were too great for him to overcome. His description of the move from day trader to swing/position trader really spoke to my situation at the time.

The first change I made in my play was in the matter of time. I couldn't wait for the sure thing to come along and then take a point or two out of it as I could in the bucket shops. I had to start much earlier if I wanted to catch the move in Fullerton's office. In other words, I had to study what was going to happen to anticipate stock movements. That sounds asininely commonplace, but you know what I mean. It was the change in my own attitude toward the game that was of supreme importance to me. It taught me, little by little, the essential difference between betting on fluctuations and anticipating inevitable advances and declines, between gambling and speculating.

I had to go further back than an hour in my studies of the market which was something I never would have learned to do in the biggest bucket shop in the world. I interested myself in trade reports, railroad earnings, and financial and commercial statistics. Of course I loved to trade heavily and they called me the Boy Plunger; but I also liked to study the moves. I never thought that anything was irksome if it helped me to trade more intelligently.

Studying my winning plays in Fullerton's office I discovered that although I often was 100 per cent right on the market that is, in my diagnosis of conditions and general trend—I was not making as much money as my market "rightness" entitled me to.

Why wasn't I?

There was as much to learn from partial victory as from defeat. For instance, I had been bullish from the very start of a bull market, and I had backed my opinion by buying stocks. An advance followed, as I had clearly foreseen. So far, all very well. But what else did I do? Why, I listened to the elder statesmen and curbed my youthful impetuousness. I made up my mind to be wise and play carefully, conservatively. Everybody knew that the way to do that was to take profits and buy back your stocks on reactions. And that is precisely what I did, or rather what I tried to do; for I often took profits and waited for a reaction that never came. And I saw my stock go kiting up ten points more and I sitting there with my four-point profit safe in my conservative pocket. They say you never grow poor taking profits. No, you don't. But neither do you grow rich taking a four-point profit in a bull market.

Where I should have made twenty thousand dollars I made two thousand. That was what my conservatism did for me.

I think it was a long step forward in my trading education when I realized at last that when old Mr. Partridge kept on telling the other customers, "Well, you know this is a bull market!" he really meant to tell them that the big money was not in the individual fluctuations but in the main movements that is, not in reading the tape but in sizing up the entire market and its trend.

And right here let me say one thing: After spending many years in Wall Street and after making and losing millions of dollars I want to tell you this: It never was my thinking that made the big money for me. It always was my sitting. Got that?

My sitting tight! It is no trick at all to be right on the market. You always find lots of early bulls in bull markets and early bears in bear markets. I've known many men who were right at exactly the right time, and began buying or selling stocks when prices were at the very level, which should show the greatest profit. And their experience invariably matched mine—that is, they made no real money out of it. Men who can both be right and sit tight are uncommon. I found it one of the hardest things to learn. But it is only after a stock operator has firmly grasped this that he can make big money. It is literally true that millions come easier to a trader after he knows how to trade than hundreds did in the days of his ignorance. The reason is that a man may see straight and clearly and yet become impatient or doubtful when the market takes its time about doing as he figured it must do. That is why so many men in Wall Street, who are not at all in the sucker class, not even in the third grade, nevertheless lose money.

The market does not beat them. They beat themselves, because though they have brains they cannot sit tight. Disregarding the big swing and trying to jump in and out was fatal to me. Nobody can catch all the fluctuations. In a bull market your game is to buy and hold until you believe that the bull market is near its end. To do this you must study general conditions and not tips or special factors affecting individual stocks. Then get out of all your stocks; get out for keeps! Wait until you see—or if you prefer, until you think you see the turn of the market—the beginning of a reversal of general conditions. You have to use your brains and your vision to do this; otherwise my advice would be as idiotic as to tell you to buy cheap and sell dear.

One of the most helpful things that anybody can learn is to give up trying to catch the last eighth or the first. These two are the most expensive eighths in the world. They have cost stock traders, in the aggregate, enough millions of dollars to build a concrete highway across the continent. Another thing I noticed in studying my plays in Fullerton's office after I began to trade less unintelligently was that my initial operations seldom showed me a loss. That naturally made me decide to start big. It gave me confidence in my own judgment before I allowed it to be vitiated by the advice of others or even by my own impatience at times. Without faith in his own judgment no man can go very far in this game. That is about all I have learned. . . . To study general conditions, to take a position and stick to it. I can wait without a twinge of impatience. I can see a setback without being shaken, knowing that it is only temporary. I have been short one hundred thousand shares and I have seen a big rally coming. I have figured and figured correctly—that such a rally as I felt was inevitable, and even wholesome, would make a difference of one million dollars in my paper profits. And I nevertheless have stood pat and seen half my paper profit wiped out, without once considering the advisability of covering my shorts to put them out again on the rally. I knew that if I did I might lose my position and with it the certainty of a big killing. It is the big swing in the markets that makes the big money for you.

Reading this created one of the biggest "A-ha!" moments of my career. This almost perfectly described my current situation....I was dealing with a changing market environment; I was finding my edge drying up at the day trade level; I found myself continually taking a tenth of the profit my market rightness entitled me to. Instead of focusing on 15- and 30-minute charts, I started to look at stocks from a daily or weekly perspective. I had to accept that this change in focus would dramatically reduce my trading frequency, and that in order to make the kind of money I wanted I would have to be willing to take more risk on each trade. As I began to position trade more and more often, I began to develop a deep trust in the order of the weekly charts. When day trading or swing trading, I had to accept that I would be whipsawed out of good positions fairly regularly. When position trading I found that the majority of my losses were taken because I was simply wrong on market direction. These were good losses as these stocks would often decline severely after my stop loss level was violated. There were very few stocks that were able to stop me out as market noise created a false whipsaw move. This gave me the trust and confidence I needed to take these trades with larger size. I have never had a problem taking a loss when the market proved me wrong. I don't hold a grudge or feel any lasting damage to my ego when my stop loss order saves me from taking a much larger loss. It does really get my goat though, when a stock whips me out in the noise and then proceeds to run in the direction of my original bias. It is in the frustration and anger that follow this kind of rip-off that my most costly mistakes have been made. So I found myself being drawn more and more to the position trades I trusted. More often than not, due to my accuracy and position size, I found I was making as much or more money on my one or two position trades in a given month as I did on 30 or more swing trades. I began to use my swing trading as a way to keep in touch with the markets, helping me to identify when it was time to enter or exit a deep time frame position.

EXPLORING OTHER MARKETS

As the bear market in stocks began to mature, it became much more difficult to find good trading opportunities. The volume dried out, and there was a general lack of trader participation that made my edge a lot thinner than it had been in the past. I knew my trading skills were universal, because they were built on the fundamentals of market movement. Supply and demand, support and resistance, and technical setup and failure were the building blocks of my style. These forces would exist in any market, so I began to explore my options and quickly discovered the futures markets. As I looked at the charts, I began to see some incredible trends. Especially in the nonfinancial futures markets, a pattern of quiet market and/or major trend seemed to be common. This fit very well with the way I liked to position trade. I also quickly fell in love with the liquidity available in the bond and S&P 500 market. Both vehicles had the depth I needed to avoid the missed fills and slippage that were becoming common as I day traded stocks. I knew my position trading in the equity markets could grow with me as my account grew. In the smaller time frames, I could see a distinct liquidity ceiling in stocks that would cap my earning potential. In the S&P 500 and T-bill market, I could see limitless liquidity as hundreds of contracts were easily available at any given point in time. These would become my day-trading markets.

The hardest thing for me as I made my transition to futures was to lose the position sizing power that the stock market gives you. Since the futures markets deal in a fixed lot size or contract, I had to change my style slightly in order to deliver the consistency of dollar risk that I believe is so important for success. Also, since the futures markets are hedging vehicles, they have an entirely different tone than the stock market. The stock market can easily become a one-way street as everybody competes for shares. Put the S&P 500 in the same situation, and you'll see plenty of contracts on the offer during the rise. These forces give you unparalleled liquidity for your entry and exit but also make these markets wiggle constantly. These constant wiggles, rinses, and traps make the futures markets the most emotionally charged I have ever traded. You *must* have the discipline to stick to your plan, or you are toast before you begin. This is why I harp constantly on discipline, risk management, and the necessity for a clear trading plan. I've built an unshakable faith over the years that no matter what the circumstances, the charts will always show you the way the market wants to move. I could cite many examples where chart action either kept me away from trades that would have ended in spectacular disaster, or helped me get positioned before a major news event sent the market flying. Each time the charts help you produce a gain or dodge a bullet it deepens your trust in your chart-reading ability. The ultimate example of the charts foretelling the future occurred for me on September 10, 2001. The market had felt weak to me the previous week, and Monday's action increased my bearish sentiment. I had several open shorts due to my opinion and used the setups offered on that Monday to increase my short exposure. I turned on CNBC the next morning and saw the coverage of the first airplane crash into the World Trade Center. At that point they were reporting it as a small plane accident, perhaps a single-engine Cessna that had gone out of control and crashed. The damage done to the building seemed out of proportion for a small aircraft, so I stopped focusing on my morning routine and started to watch the coverage. I was watching as the second plane crashed into the twin towers, and at that moment I knew this was no accident. My first thought was that terrorists had been able to hijack the landing systems that guide planes in on their final approach (think *Die Hard 2*). I could imagine that might take down one plane, but two? In addition, I could not imagine the pilots being unable to override the autopilot in time to correct their flight path. That left physical hijacking. In the wake of the embassy bombing and the attack on the *USS Cole*, this seemed like another escalation in terrorist activities against U.S. targets. I remember posting something to my clients that this was almost assuredly terrorism and was likely Bin Laden's big play. The news reporting had gone bonkers by this time, with reports of planes all over ready to attack the White House, the Capitol, etc. This media panic was reinforced when the Pentagon was struck soon afterward. When that plane went down, on a strike against a military target, I began to think about this as a precursor to an all-out war with multiple attacks coming in from many fronts. Some time in the swirl of coverage before the towers collapsed, I remembered that I had open positions! The markets had yet to open, and I quickly checked my account to make sure I had not forgotten about any open longs. I knew I was set to make a lot of money as the markets were guaranteed to open lower after a disaster such as this. Then the first tower collapsed. The only stock-related memory I have after that was feeling thankful that they closed down the markets. Had they opened for business as usual I believe we would have broken every record to the downside, such was the sense of mindless panic that morning.

In the days that followed before they reopened the stock market for business, I remember feeling very, very lucky to be short. I felt it was a dumb luck coincidence that the market had been bearishly biased on that Monday. Then I saw a news story on the Web that blew me away. "The SEC was investigating 'unusual' trading activity pre-September 11th." There had been a number of suspicious events in the days leading up to September 11th. Unusual short positions had been initiated against the airline stocks, and there were other stories of suspicious surges in short interest across the market. Just the way earnings news often leaks out and affects the price patterns in a stock before the actual news is reported, persons unknown knew attacks against the United States were pending and had begun to position themselves to profit when the actual events occurred. At that moment I felt both exhilarated and disgusted. Exhilarated because my trading style had *worked!* It had helped me identify the bearish pressures that existed in the market no matter what their source. Disgusted because I was about to see a profit that had been triggered by the actions of a subhuman group of fanatics who were willing to put months of time and effort into planning the murder of thousands of innocents. It was a bittersweet moment that deeply reinforced my belief that the charts rarely lie. Since that day I am much more willing to take trades based on chart action even if it is in contradiction with the conventional wisdom at the time, trusting in the tape to show me where the line of least resistance lies.

So, who knows what the next month's trading will look like. That's part of the fun. The only thing we know for certain is that next month won't be boring! I hope it will offer some good examples of the payout-payback cycle so this trading diary can give you a peek into the realities of trade management as you move from hero to zero and back again.

Week 1

JANUARY 13, 2003

First, some basics…I start by looking at a daily chart in order to determine my bias for the day. Then, I drop down to an intraday chart to more precisely enter and exit my trades. The charts in the figures that follow will be divided into formats. First, the daily chart as I describe what I'm seeing, and how I plan to approach that trading day. Next, I will post an intraday chart as I highlight the areas of interest for that day. These intraday charts will be of a 5-minute time period. On every chart, in every time frame, the only indicators will be a 20 EMA, 40 EMA, and 200 SMA.

So, with that in mind, let's get this thing started! The stock market has been in nightmare mode for the last 2 months. Any trend has been short-lived, and the only real trades that are performing consistently are the small scalps. This is a grinding market, one where you work to pay the bills rather than to build a fortune. The bigger swings are where the real money is made, but while you're waiting, there is still intraday opportunity that can keep a roof over your head. So with that in mind, I'm just scalping until I see some more consistent follow-through.

As always, I begin today by looking at my daily charts in deciding which market to focus on. The chart on the left is a daily chart of the S&P E-Mini, or ES. The chart on the right is a daily chart of the 10-year T-Bill ACE contract, or ZN. Both are electronically traded and extremely liquid.

As you can see in Figure 9.1, the S&P has been quite choppy and chaotic recently. It has been congested the last couple of days and may either be topping out or basing for a break. The chart pattern is quite unclear, so I plan to focus on the bonds as their daily chart has been quite orderly. You can see how the market has topped off, formed a lower high, and is currently selling back toward an area of chart support. I will be watching the bonds today for a test of support and a possible trend change.

I was busy in the morning, so missed the gap down off support which would have been an excellent entry. (See Figure 9.2.) The first wiggle did not pull back far enough for my taste, but when the second wiggle pulled back to moving average as well as chart support (1), I took my first entry long. The support wasn't strong enough to turn the bonds, and my stop loss order was hit for a quick loss. Unfortunately, after the whip got me the bonds rallied sharply. The next opportunity came as the market tested the 200 SMA at extension around 112.240. This could have been a sell signal as

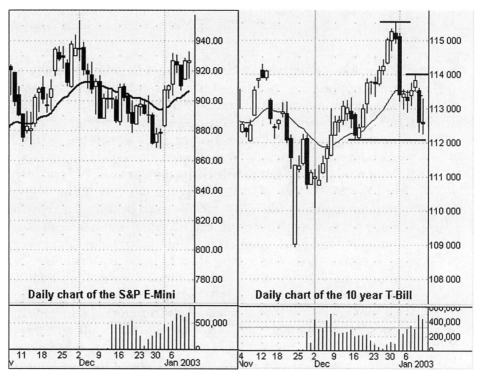

F I G U R E   9 . 1

F I G U R E   9 . 2

the market tested resistance after an extended run. I chose to pass on this short opportunity, because of my bullish bias formed from the daily perspective. If my original opinion was correct and the market was reacting off of daily support, then shorting would be to fight the trend. The decision to pass saved me from another quick stop as the 200 SMA was broken without much difficulty. At that point the market was overbought and due for a rest. After a multicandle correction, price tested not only the 200 SMA but the 20 EMA as well. It was at this support (2) that I took my second trade to the long side. This trade worked beautifully, showing me a profit from the moment I received my fill. Since I'm just scalping these futures today for the quick easy gain, I offered out below the previous high and was easily filled. The market then rolled over, forming a lower high and moved back to test the 20 EMA. Since a lower high had been formed, I believe there would be some bearish momentum, and wanted to see a deeper correction and a retest of the support level from trade (2) before considering another long. Price continued to fall and soon tested chart support. It then formed a peek bottom as price broke below the previous swing low, then quickly reversed. It was after this confirmation that I entered my third long for the day (3). This trade struggled a bit. After the initial bounce off support, it based and then broke out to form a new high for the day. Since my trading plan is to capture a small move off support or resistance, I again offered out into the buying surge and was easily filled. At this point the market began to trade in a choppy manner, without forming the clear swings I want to see. I had a pleasantly profitable day; my two winners easily taking care of the loss from my first trade. The market looks like it was moving into congestion, so I called it a day.

Scorecard:

Correctly identified daily trend? YES
Traded with the intraday trend? YES
Avoided at least one stop? YES
Ended the day profitably? YES

JANUARY 14, 2003

The S&P 500 continues to be a mess on its daily chart. I will continue to focus on the bonds since they have a clean reversal off the daily support I indicated yesterday.

(As a side note, you can see clearly in Figure 9.3 the action of a futures contract as it becomes the "front month." There is almost no data through-

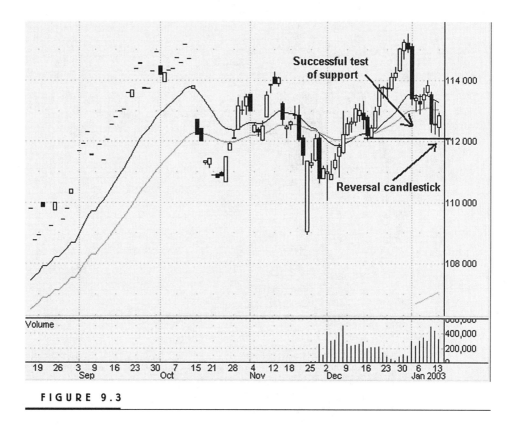

FIGURE 9.3

out September and October, and then a few spread trades begin to create price data in November. The volume then explodes as the rollover occurs in the beginning of December.)

With the reversal candlestick printed yesterday, I will continue to watch the bonds for long opportunities.

In the morning there was a quick up-thrust, with one nice pullback to the 20 MA. (See Figure 9.4.) I didn't log in early enough to catch that move, so I bought the next pullback to support (1) around 113.040. The trade failed to bounce after four bars, and I took advantage of a small upspike to exit at breakeven. This proved to be the proper action as the market then broke down as it looked for an area of support that could truly bounce it. It finally bounced around 113, but did so without any clear support or particularly juicy buy signal. I took this as a sign that the market was changing trend. In my view, if the market were truly strong it would have continued higher off the first test of the 20 MA.

So with this opinion, I began to look for a short opportunity. After the bounce off the 113 level ran out of momentum, the bonds began to

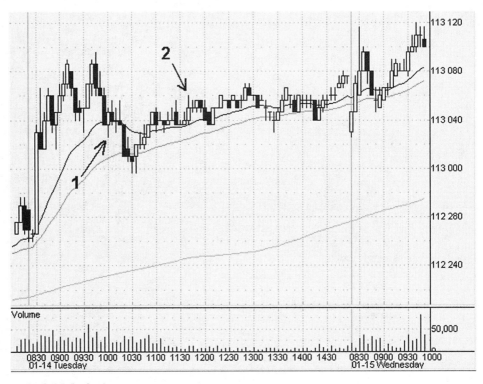

FIGURE 9.4

base. There were several small attempts to break out above this base, but the bullish momentum was short-lived. After one of these attempts, the market pulled back to the 20 MA, and then made another attempt at a breakout. As this breakout failed I took a short position off this peek top (2). Again my trade did little for me, drifting down to the lows of the base, then quickly reversing. Since I am entering trades as the market is extended *against* the trend as I see it, I should see quick and positive action after my entry. When a trade chips and chops, I go into a much more defensive mode and will probably scratch the trade if the market gives me an excuse. After my second trade retested the lows of the base and failed to break, I moved my stop to break even. Within minutes, the price had returned to my entry point, and I took my second scratch for the day.

At this point, it felt to me like a payback day was now identified. I had two careful entries that were appropriate for my trading plan. They both refused to perform, and left me with nothing as the breakeven stops were triggered. Since I believe so deeply in the concept of the payout-payback cycle, I figured that a so-so morning was an indication that a bad afternoon was likely to follow. I decided to skip the rest of the day, and see what tomorrow would bring.

In retrospect, this was exactly the correct choice. The market did little but base into the close. I saw one trade in hindsight I might have taken, but even though it would have been moderately profitable it would have been an agonizing hold. Contrast that with the easy gains seen in the previous day.

Scorecard:

Correctly identified daily trend? YES
Traded with the intraday trend? YES
Avoided at least one stop? NO
Ended the day profitably? NO

JANUARY 15, 2003

I have been doing reasonably well, and was feeling very much in sync with the bonds. The S&P 500 continues to act in a disturbed manner. As I'm trading stocks with the folks I'm teaching, the S&P 500 has surprised me several times over the last few days. Why trade a market when you're out of sync with its action, especially when the bonds are acting so orderly? A trader is always seeking the market that is most closely aligned to his or her trading style. So for me, this will be another day to focus on the bonds.

As you can see from the daily chart in Figure 9.5, the bonds have rallied cleanly off their test of support and are now trading in an area of 20 EMA resistance. Today is likely to be a transition day as the market deals with resistance. My plan is to focus on long opportunities during the morning, then back away and wait for a possible short entry in the afternoon.

The morning began bullishly as I suspected. (See Figure 9.6.) Normally when you watch a stock or futures contract intraday as it tests a level of daily support and/or resistance, you will observe a trampoline effect. Since the bonds are rallying into an area of daily resistance, you can expect to see a bullish morning, then a transition zone, and finally a reversal into the close. This was the scenario I hoped for going into the day. As it happened, I got my first long opportunity (1) off a pullback to the 20 MA. This produced an easy retest of the highs for the scalp exit. The market continued to chop against the 20 MA support, and then formed what looked to me like a euphoric top. Because of my daily bias for a turnaround day, this euphoria now put me into a bearish mind-set. I began to look for confirmation of the top, either in a double top or lower high off the first pullback. A lower high formed (2) within 30 minutes after the euphoria's top tick. At this

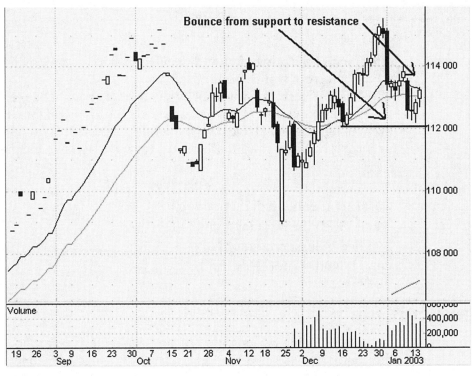

Bounce from support to resistance

114 000

112 000

110 000

108 000

Volume

400,000

200,000

19 26 3 9 16 23 30 7 15 21 28 4 12 18 25 2 9 16 23 30 6 13
        Sep   Oct   Nov   Dec   Jan 2003

F I G U R E   9 . 5

2

113 200

113 160

113 120

3

1

113 080

113 040

Volume

50,000

1400 1430 0830 0900 0930 1000 1030 1100 1130 1200 1230 1300 1330 1400 1430 0830 0900
           01-15 Wednesday   01-16 Thursday

F I G U R E   9 . 6

point a deeper time frame trade sets up. The bond market has rallied from a daily support level into a zone of resistance caused by the 20 EMA. We have two intraday confirmations of resistance (euphoric last gasp of the uptrend, and a lower high). Therefore a potential trend change at a daily level is likely. Entry on these deeper time frame trades is also simpler as a few ticks will not make or break your risk-to-reward ratio for the trade. Having seen what is likely to be the high for the day, a stop set a few ticks above the day's high should protect adequately in case resistance fails.

Interesting to note that shortly after the deeper time frame short setup occurred, a bullish scalp pattern presented itself (3). Even within the context of a daily trend change, there was still enough bullish energy to bounce the bonds off the 20 MA support levels! This shows the fractal nature of the markets. Traders can be operating profitably both long and short at the same time in the same market!

Scorecard:

Correctly identified daily trend (change)? YES
Traded with the intraday trend? YES
Avoided at least one stop? NO
Ended the day profitably? YES

JANUARY 16, 2003

This day begins with a clear rally to resistance on the daily chart. (See Figure 9.7.) The reversal candlestick formed yesterday should attract sellers to help drive the market lower.

My goal for today is to scalp to the short side as I wait for the daily trade to follow through. If the market drops sharply today I might consider covering, but in any case, I will be flat before noon because the Philadelphia Fed numbers will be released, and these usually cause violent whipsaws in the market. This external force also has the power to ruin chart patterns. The chart patterns form and have indicative value because they are tracking the supply and demand forces within a market. Add an important news item to the mix and the market may begin to discount forces that didn't exist the day before. Since these forces are new, they are absent from your charts, so the charts will tend to give you false signals until some time has passed after the news announcement. After the Fed numbers are posted, I will stay away from the market unless a blindingly obvious scalp presents itself.

I was on the phone with one of my consulting clients this morning, so missed the early morning rally to the 200 SMA resistance level. (See

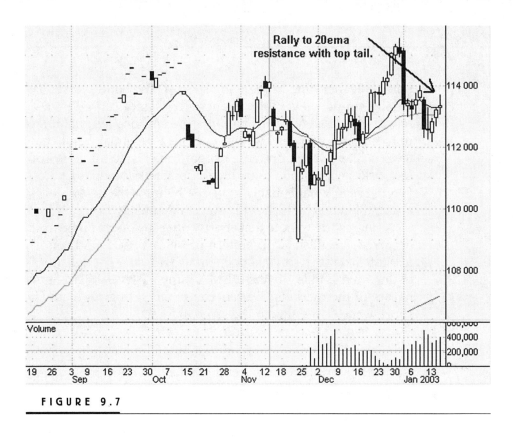

Rally to 20ema resistance with top tail.

FIGURE 9.7

Figure 9.8.) The market continued to fall and gave me another opportunity to get short (1) against the 20 EMA around 10:45. The resistance held, and price rolled over for an easy scalp. The market then broke the new lows by the smallest of margins and reversed (2). This peek bottom is a valid pattern for me to take as scalp long. I chose to pass, as this trade would be against my daily bias, and I don't expect to see a reversal today. To scalp against the trend is to row against the tide and will just exhaust your capital.

By passing on the peek bottom, I missed a stop as the price broke to new lows. The Philadelphia Fed numbers were due out within 10 minutes as well, so the sharp selling into 112.20 offered an easy exit for the daily based swing trade.

After the numbers, the market sharply reversed and rallied without any significant wiggles back to test the 200 SMA. This pullback gave me the opportunity to get long against the 20 EMA (3). The follow-through came fairly easily for the scalp exit. Taking this trade required me to be open-minded as my original expectation for the day was bearish in its entirety. However, the Fed numbers have shocked the market out of its bearish trend. By remaining detached and picky, I opened up the opportunity for more trade during that session.

FIGURE 9.8

Scorecard:

Correctly identified daily trend? YES
Traded with the intraday trend? YES
Avoided at least one stop? YES
Ended the day profitably? YES

JANUARY 17, 2003

No trading for me today, since this is the third Friday of the month. Options expire today, and that brings all kinds of chaotic forces into the markets. As I was learning my craft, I tried and tried to make sense out of these expiration days. I have never been good at reading them, and they just cost me money so I avoid them like the plague. Go back through your trading logs, and I strongly suspect you will find that you are a net loser on options expiration Friday! So instead of trading when the odds are against you, use this as an excuse for a 3-day weekend, and spend the money you would have lost relaxing and rejuvenating your spirits for the next week of trading.

Week 2

JANUARY 21, 2003

The bonds have now rallied back up to test an area of moving average resistance around 114. (See Figure 9.9.) I will be watching for shorts early in the morning as this resistance is tested, then will be ready to switch long if it can be broken. The S&P has finally fought its way out of the range and has fallen to an area of chart support. It has an inside range day to confirm this support, so I will be watching for long setup as the market reverses. The bonds and the S&P tend to trade inversely to one another. When the stocks are strong, the bonds tend to be weak. So, with the bonds at resistance, and the S&P 500 at support, there is double confirmation that both are ready to change trend.

The bonds gapped up and flew up through the 114 resistance level. (See Figure 9.10.) It then formed a spastic, unstable top (1), which I passed on because I felt my stop might be too easily tagged in such an unstable market environment. If this was indeed the top, then we were at a point of daily trend change. There would be plenty of room to the downside left for

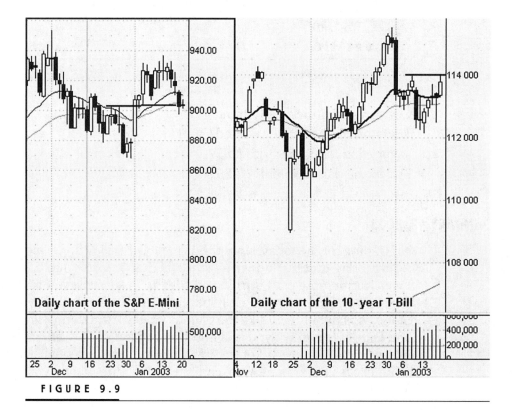

FIGURE 9.9

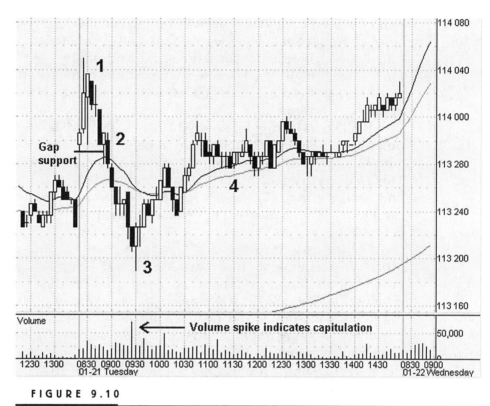

FIGURE 9.10

me to nab off a safer setup. The market fell quickly to test gap support as well as the 20 EMA. I went long as this support reversed the market (2), and was quickly stopped as the bounce failed and new lows were formed. In retrospect, since my daily opinion was for a bearish reversal off 114, this trade was too aggressive and fought the trend. If I am to take a counter trend trade, it needs to be a bounce play only off a major selling wave that takes the market into oversold territory. This exact scenario presented itself 30 minutes later as the market continued to sell. A little after 9:30, the selling reached a feverish pitch and a large volume spike indicated that short-term capitulation had occurred. I now had an appropriate bounce scenario (3) and opened a trade to the long side. By waiting this time until a proper setup presented itself, the trade was a success. Because my plan was to capture a simple bounce, I covered into moving average resistance around 113.250. The market continued higher, and topped off for a possible rally to resistance around the 113.28 level. I passed on this trade because it did not seem clear enough for me, and so avoided a stop as its wiggle was short-lived and new highs were quickly formed. As this wave of buying ran into the resistance offered by the 114 level, a top was formed and a pullback to support (4) was printed. I passed on this long pattern, which I believed would fail due to the overhead daily resistance at 114. I began to stalk it for a failure and went short as the setup surge failed and began to form a lower high. The trade moved a little way for me, then began to gyrate. It never came near my target, and stopped me for my second loss of the day.

While I was struggling with the bonds, the S&P 500 was also being unkind. See (Figure 9.11.) Since my daily opinion was for support and a bullish reversal, I went long (1) off the first peek bottom of the day. This resulted in a stop as the market continued lower, and I took a second shot at a long (2) when I saw a volume bloom and Doji reversal candlestick. This trade tried to reverse for me, but also was stopped out before long.

Having just finished out last week with a nice payout, this Monday was looking like payback central. Having been slapped around pretty thoroughly, I backed away to let the dust (and my emotions) settle. The market was obviously not working itself out according to my daily opinion. It was time for me to objectively reassess the trend. My two long opportunities in the morning were appropriate and not impulsively taken. So I saw the morning action, not as a mistake, the market is simply proving my opinion wrong. So, if I'm wrong about a bullish reversal for the day, I'll eat lunch, regroup, and come back looking for shorts in the afternoon. A short opportunity presented itself (3) as the market rallied to form a peek top around 1:15. I went short off this pattern, and finally was able to bank a profit as I covered the short into the previous swing low. I was then ready and waiting to go short on any flag or pullback offered in the afternoon. The market laughed in my face and continued to drift lower without ever offering me a chance to enter.

Having had such a nice payout last week, I knew the chances were getting higher for a period of payback. This day still caught me unawares as both the bonds and S&P 500 went the wrong way against my daily opinion. I was tired at the end of this day, happy that I was able to turn things around for a profitable third trade in the S&P, but wondering if a bigger payback cycle was about to begin after last week's success.

Scorecard:

Correctly identified daily trend? NO
Traded with the intraday trend? NO
Avoided at least one stop? YES
Ended the day profitably? NO

FIGURE 9.11

JANUARY 22, 2003

Having experienced a nice payout cycle, then getting slapped with a pay-back day on Monday, I came into today's session with great caution. If a more complex payback cycle is beginning, then I'm going to see a lot of stops for my patterns. It's time to protect my gains from the prior week, and be ultra picky about the trades that I take going forward. Looking at my daily charts (See Figure 9.12), I get further reinforcement of my cautious stance. Both have broken away from potential reversal zones; they are extended but look as if they will continue in the direction of the trend. I'm going to be watching for long trades in the bonds and shorts for the S&P 500.

The bonds gapped up and rallied strongly out of the gate. (See Figure 9.13.) They offered a good countertrend pattern as they topped with double Dojis. Since I think I'm in a payback cycle, I'm sticking rigidly to my daily opinion and will be ultra picky about the trades I take. My daily opinion says go long in the bonds, so I passed on this short which obviously would have worked. My first trade was taken (1) as the first pullback found support at the 20 EMA. This trade showed

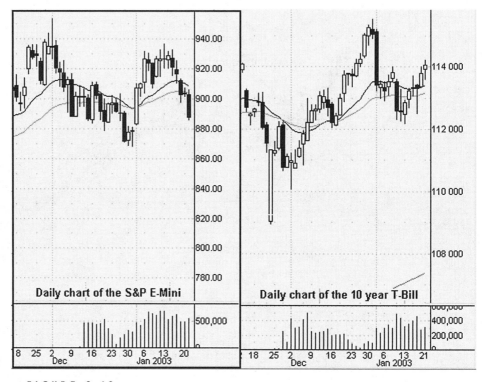

FIGURE 9.12

me some profit, but then fell back down to stop me out as it broke the new lows. The first trade of the day, and I'm down already. More confirmation that payback is upon me. The next long opportunity that offered itself was a peek bottom (2) as the market wiggled and jiggled down to test the 40 EMA. This trade was slow, but eventually followed through to my target near the previous high at 114.120. There was another pullback to the 20 EMA midday, but I passed on this long since the correction was only formed by two bars of selling. I feel sure now that I'm dealing with a payback period. I want any pullback that I take to be deep and extended so that I have stronger bounce potential driving my trade. The two-bar pullback bounced a little, but quickly failed to form a lower high. This pullback eventually found support and moved higher, but the support was not in an easily identifiable area, and price was below the moving averages. I stayed away until just before the close, when a buying surge took the market to a new high for the day. After the high was formed, a five-bar pullback 20 EMA occurred. Finally, this was the clarity I had been seeking. I went long off

FIGURE 9.13

this moving average support (3) and covered for a profit as the market made new highs.

The S&P 500 also had a rough day as it remained range bound until just before the close. (See Figure 9.14.) There was a valid peek bottom (1) in the morning that would have worked, but again I was trading defensively and was not about to take the first trade of the day directly in conflict with my daily opinion (which was bearish). The S&P then began to roll gently within a range. Having defined the highs (2) and lows (1) during the morning session, the market began to ping-pong from low to high again. There was a short opportunity (3) as the market retested the range highs, but I chose to pass on the setup. I have never been comfortable trading in ranges. My accuracy is poor, and my feel is iffy at best. I am very good when a market is overbought and/or oversold or trending, and have found through painful experience that I am much better off waiting on the sidelines until the market fits *my* style rather than trying to be all things to all markets. So I passed on the short at range highs, and was rewarded for my patience as the market bounced to form a clean swing back to a lower high (4). Now, this is my kind of pattern, and it was exactly what I had been waiting for. I went short off this lower high, and soon thereafter covered for profit as the market tested support around 882. Happy to have found the one trade that fit my style, I ended the day with one shot, one kill.

The action of the last two days shows a pretty typical example of the transition from payout to payback markets. Very rarely will you see the change coming; instead it will blindside you as it did for me on Monday. Because the payback usually comes without warning, you should not blame yourself for the losses incurred. Instead, grade your trade management by how well you perform over the next few days as the payout cycle matures. Had I been unaware of the payout-payback cycle, I would have had another rotten day today. I was trading very defensively, and even though I missed a couple of trades that would have proved profitable, I also missed a couple of trades that would have cost me money. By being picky and managing the day with the knowledge that the payback cycle was trying to get me, I ended the day feeling good about the trades I took and showing black in my P&L.

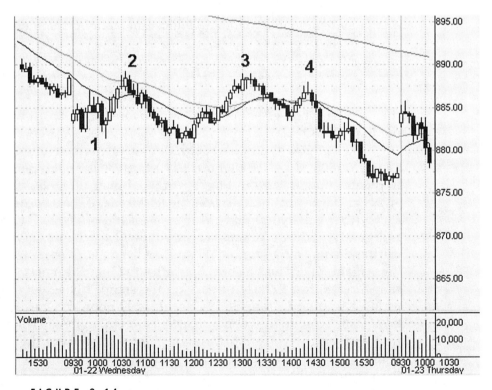

FIGURE 9.14

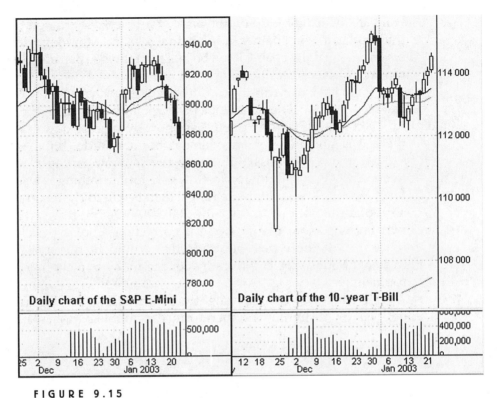

FIGURE 9.15

Scorecard:

Correctly identified daily trend? YES
Traded with the intraday trend? YES
Avoided at least one stop? YES
Ended the day profitably? YES

JANUARY 23, 2003

OK, there is no question now . . . the payback cycle is in full swing! The market gave me my easy profits last week, and now is trying to take them back. My daily charts are becoming grossly overextended. (See Figure 9.15.) The momentum is likely to push them further into extension, but you know a violent snapback is lurking. You're kind of stuck in a "damned if you do, damned if you don't" scenario. If you go with the daily trend, you open yourself up to enormous snapback risk, but if you fade the trend and look for the reversal, you risk standing in front of a freight train. The risk-sensitive hairs are all standing up on the back of my neck, so if I don't find a single trade today it won't bother me a bit. I'm going into this day without any real bias from my daily charts. I will be looking for extension and double or peek tops or bottoms to scalp against.

If we start off with the 5-minute intraday chart for the S&P 500, you can see a graphical depiction of a payback market. (See Figure 9.16.) It gaps up, then sells off swiftly to retest support from yesterday. At this point (1), there was potential for an oversold bounce trade, but I was not very excited about this possibility since the moving averages were so close overhead. After that, there was a whole lot of nothing. The market went from highs to lows within the range, then began to chop higher. There was a bit of a pullback just under the 200 SMA (2), but it was disorderly and was nothing more than a two-bar correction. Looking back with 20/20 hindsight, the only possible trade that would fit my style was the first oversold bounce scalp. No trades for me today in a choppy market environment.

The bonds were only slightly better today. (See Figure 9.17.) They gapped down slightly and then formed a double bottom (1), which I took

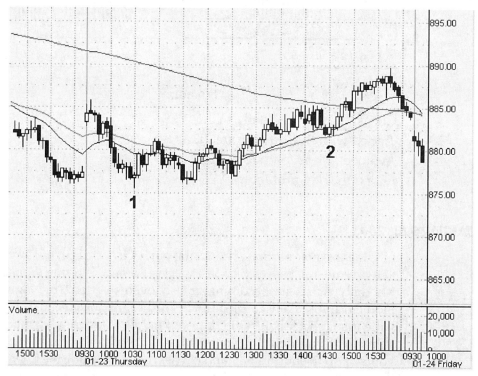

FIGURE 9.16

long. I closed this trade for a few ticks profit as it bounced up to test the overhanging moving average resistance. The rally off the double bottom eventually took the market to a new high for the day. I bought the first pullback after that breakout (2) and was quickly rewarded with a stop for my troubles. After that, the market did little but dodge around chaotically so I stayed away. Then finally, just before the close, the bonds fell to test 200 SMA support (3). It bounced and then fell back to retest the lows forming a micro double bottom. I took this as confirmation of support and initiated a long position. The market staggered off support and delivered only a tick or two of profit.

Yuck! What a baloney day, and what a great opportunity to lose money! This is exactly what a payback market looks and feels like. It's like lifting dead weight. You can work so hard to pick the perfect entry, and the market will only sluggishly respond. I feel a little foolish for having taken three trades in the bonds. On a day such as this, that feels to me like overtrading. I did not find one trade worth taking in the S&P 500, so that makes me feel a little bit better about my trade management. After a week with only a stop or two, this week has been a grind as I deal with this payback cycle. I was able to quickly identify the payback, and that saved me from

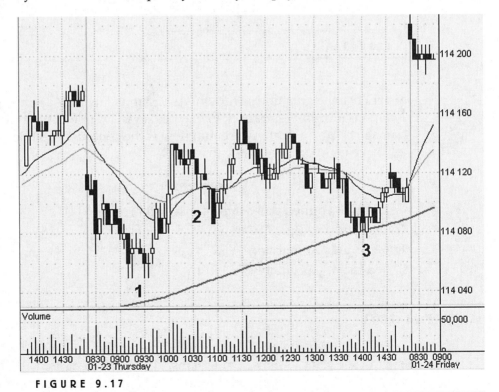

FIGURE 9.17

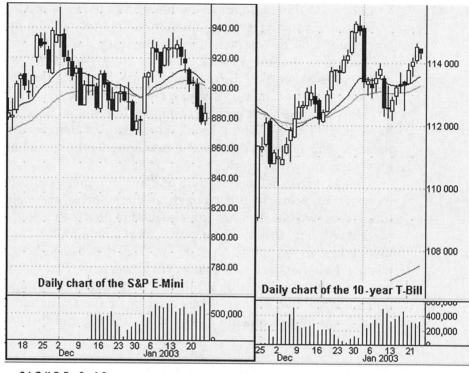

Daily chart of the S&P E-Mini

Daily chart of the 10-year T-Bill

FIGURE 9.18

experiencing a greater drawdown. As it stands, my infinitesimal gain from today's trading takes me back to the breakeven point for the week. The only damage being done to my account now is the commissions I have incurred as I have churned my money this week.

Scorecard:

Correctly identified daily trend (or lack thereof!)? YES
Traded with the intraday trend? YES
Avoided at least one stop? YES
Ended the day profitably? BARELY

JANUARY 24, 2003

TGIF! It's Friday after a tough week, where all I have to show for my labors is a bill for commissions. I'm looking at the daily charts, and again have very little of the opinion. (See Figure 9.18.) I can see an argument that these inside range bars are continuation patterns, and will take the price further into extension. On the other hand, we are so very extended and due for a correction, so these may just be messy reversals. Having had such an awful payback environment yesterday, I'm going to approach this day without much of a bias. I will be watching my 5-minute chart for signs of the trend, and will trade whatever I see.

The bonds gapped up and then really began to rally hard. (See Figure 9.19.) They continued to move higher and higher, until finally the volume bloomed and two top tails presented themselves (1). I took that as a euphoric topping pattern, and went short for a scalp back to moving average support. Since the euphoric move offered no wiggles for entry, I knew many traders would have missed the rally. They would all be stalking the pullback as they tried to dull the pain of missing out on the euphoric upthrust. As the bonds pulled back to test the 20 EMA, I put in a limit order to bid at the moving average for twice my size. This order, if filled, would cover my short for a profit, and initiate a long position off moving average support at the same time. The price did indeed fall to fill my bid, and so I flipped my position

FIGURE 9.19

from long to short. I was low tick on the pullback as the market bounced off the 20 EMA. I covered this trade for profit as the highs were retested. At this point I'm thinking, "Hmm, the trend has been decent today." Add to this the fact that I am two for two after several days of lackluster action, and I am beginning to wonder if my payback cycle has ended. The bonds continued to rally aggressively, and then formed one final pullback to the 20 EMA. I passed on this pullback trade even though it was a valid pattern because of the extension in the market. I knew there were plenty of bulls with profits to be taken, and that any excuse would bring in sharp selling. By passing on this trade I avoided a stop as the market did indeed find an excuse and began to sell off. After a sharp drop, it wiggled back to test the 20 EMA (3) and began to form a base. Seeing the sharp selling after an extended up move, I felt that the market had topped. I saw this base as a continuation pattern, and went short as the lows of the base were broken. The market fell off a cliff, and I exited into the 114.200 level as the selling became extreme and volume began to bloom.

While I was finding success with the bond futures, a day of total frustration appeared in the S&P 500. (See Figure 9.20.) The day started off with a sustained wave of selling. After finally bottoming out, it began to form a bear flag as it drifted along, waiting for the 20 EMA to catch up. I was waiting for that test of moving average resistance (1) in order to go short. My trade never set up as the S&Ps rolled over and began to do their falling anvil impression. I was doomed to sit and watch as the profits which should have been mine passed me by. Again the market bounced (2) and began to flag back to the 20 EMA. Again, I was waiting, no slavering to get short. But no! I was denied as the price kept falling without touching the moving average. The market then presented me with one of the most classic trap scenarios. Having correctly predicted the trend, I was totally unable to get short and get my money. My frustration levels were high, and when those emotions are present all you want to do is get even with the market. This is the worst possible thing you can do, as it distorts your observational skills as you look for a trade, *any trade* . . . to get you on board the trade. I've seen traders in this state throw away every rule and tactic that made them profitable, shooting from the hip in total cowboy mode as they tried to reduce the pain to their ego. Having missed an enormous move to the downside, the market finally tested the 20 EMA (3). At this point with the market so oversold, the chances for follow-through were dim. Yet I know that many traders were shouting, "Ah-ha, I've got you this time!" as they gleefully went short against the 20 EMA. Having fallen into this trap more times than I care to admit during my early years, I accepted the fact that I had missed the selloff. The market went dead sideways after

FIGURE 9.20

the moving average test, rinsing stop levels again and again before falling just a couple of points to retest the lows. As disgusting as it was to have missed the entire selloff, I avoided the sucker play (3), so did no damage to my capital. As a trader, my job is to develop the best trading plan I can— a plan that fits with my strengths and skills as a trader. Once that plan is carefully authored, my job is to trade within its structure without deviating from the rules it lays out. Number 1, this keeps my trading consistent, so my edge is efficiently applied. Number 2, and most importantly, staying with a plan allows me to accurately troubleshoot my trading when things go awry. If you are sticking to the plan, and are losing money beyond what should be a normal drawdown, then it's time to reassess your trading strategy. Since you stuck with the plan, you know it's the plan's fault when you lose, and can then troubleshoot and tweak your strategy as you adapt to a changing market environment. If you fail to follow a plan or have no plan to begin with, you will never know whether your losses are caused by a flawed strategy, trade mismanagement, improper risk control, or mental errors. You will be stabbing around in the dark without any diagnostic tools at your disposal. Your profit or loss will be more dependent on luck than skill or experience.

So the week ends on a high note! The challenge of the payback cycle was well met, and the drawdown experience was extremely minimal. By getting myself back to breakeven yesterday, I was able to put every penny of my bond profits in the bank. I had no hole to dig myself out of, so my three for three day in the bonds made my week! This is something you'll see over and over throughout your trading career. You will experience periods of boredom as you tread water, and wait for more favorable market conditions to return. Then often without warning, a win streak will reappear to deliver your profit for the entire week. The majority of your gains in a given year will be banked off a surprisingly small number of winning days. Like the doctor's oath, your first priority is to "do no harm" to your trading account. If you trade carefully and defensively, your drawdowns will be radically minimized. Then, when the market offers you a series of successful trades, that chunk of profit will take your equity well over the top!

This is the action we observe for this week's trading. A rotten first day, with continued rottenness successfully avoided, then a return to profitability. I close the week out with the hope that today's stopless action indicates a return of the payout cycle for next week!

Scorecard:

Correctly identified daily trend (or lack thereof!)? YES

Traded with the intraday trend? YES

Avoided at least one stop? YES

Ended the day profitably? YES

Week 3

JANUARY 27, 2003

Nothing like a Monday after a relaxing weekend to get you back in a stress-free and objective state! I'm feeling great this morning, and like what I see in the daily charts. The S&P 500 is now becoming ridiculously extended, having basically sold off now for 8 days in a row without a significant wiggle. The bonds have done much the same thing to the upside, and the two charts in Figure 9.21 show clearly the inverse relationship these two futures contracts have to one another. As we are so extended, I would expect to see a reversal day and the beginnings of a bounce in today's session. I am excited to see the S&P 500 trending again, as it had spent quite a long time basing without offering much opportunity. The bonds were left with a bit of a topping tail on Friday, so I would suspect they are due for some profit taking as a correction forms.

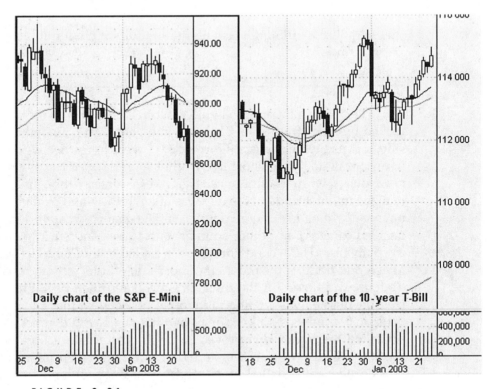

FIGURE 9.21

FIGURE 9.22

The bonds gapped up slightly, then fell off a cliff as the markets were rocked by news from Iraq. They became very overextended to the downside, and as the first reversal formed (1) I went long. (See Figure 9.22.) The bounce was small and short-lived, and I soon stopped out as price broke to new lows. The market bounced again, of course without me this time. I realized my first trade of the day was taken into a valid exhaustion pattern, but was fighting my overall daily bias. The result? An almost instant loss. I decided to avoid any other countertrend trades and stick to trading with my daily bias. The second bounce soon rallied to the 20 EMA (2), and I took my second trade of the day to the short side off this rally to resistance. The trade moved down off the resistance level, and then began to stall. I realized the market was waiting for another news event that was scheduled to begin in 5 minutes. Not knowing how that news would affect the market, I scratched the trade. This proved to be the correct decision as the market quickly rallied on the news, and I would have taken another loss. This news-driven rally stalled at 200 SMA resistance (3), and I took my final trade for the day. Finally, after what felt like a blundering morning I had some decent follow-through for my trade. Feeling confused and out of sync, I decided to let the bonds finish the session by themselves. I had squeaked out a profit for the day and just didn't feel like continuing. This day's action was different from a normal payback day where patterns simply fail. The chaotic movement today was caused by news events and so support and resistance levels had much less power to turn the trend.

An equally strange day was unfolding for me in the S&P. (See Figure 9.23.) The morning was a triangle-shaped mess of totally chaotic action. Then the news hit and the price plummeted. I was successful, however, in playing the bounce off this bottom (1), which I think in retrospect proves a point. My capitulation play in the bonds was a long *against* my bearish daily bias. This trade gave almost nothing before failing badly as it rushed back to my stop.

This first trade in the S&P 500 was the exact same price pattern. A sharp drop followed by signs of reversal. But unlike the bonds, this pattern was taken in the direction of my daily bias! I don't think it is a coincidence that this one was successful. The daily trend is a powerful ally, and I got sucked into fighting it when I traded the bonds against my daily bias. In the afternoon, the S&P 500 began to drift back down and I was watching

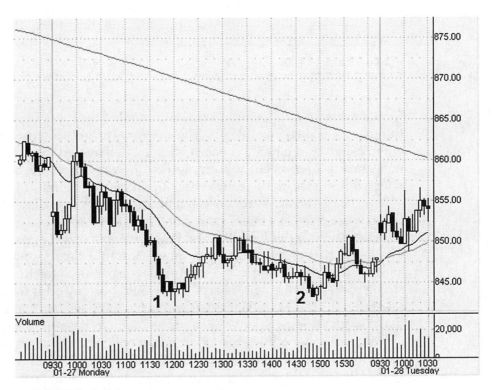

FIGURE 9.23

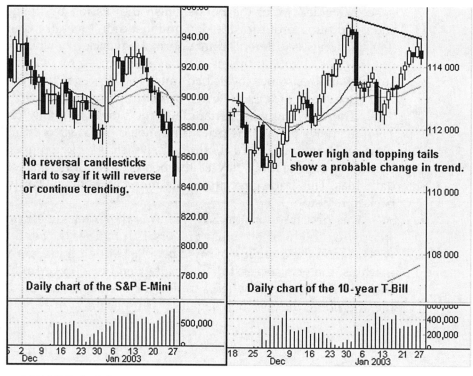

No reversal candlesticks
Hard to say if it will reverse
or continue trending.

Daily chart of the S&P E-Mini

Lower high and topping tails
show a probable change in trend.

Daily chart of the 10-year T-Bill

FIGURE 9.24

for a double bottom to form. I had put in a bid and was busy with other things as I waited for my fill. The price never got down to the level I wanted, and by the time I checked back in I had missed the trade. On what had already been a fairly crummy day, it was especially frustrating to watch this missed trade resume back up to retest the highs of the range.

So I had a bit of a letdown as I came into the day expecting a lot. Instead the day was more of a mishmash with the first S&P trade being the best. On a brighter note, it did look like my daily opinion for the bonds was correct. The daily chart of the bonds chart now showed a clear topping pattern. I chose to pass on a swing to the short side here because I felt the bonds were strong enough on the daily chart that it would hurt my odds for bearish follow-through. The S&P 500 was left with a big daily sell bar, and I didn't feel that intraday higher low was strong enough to base a swing trade on. Having made some mistakes today, and wondering about a news risk for tomorrow, I plan to trade only bonds tomorrow as I think their daily reversal candle will deliver a decent downtrend for day trade shorts.

Scorecard:

Correctly identified daily trend (or lack thereof!)? YES
Traded with the intraday trend? NO
Avoided at least one stop? YES
Ended the day profitably? BARELY

JANUARY 28, 2003

We begin this day with a beautiful daily bond reversal. There is a possible lower high on the chart, and two topping tails confirm the changing trend. (See Figure 9.24.) Contrast this clarity with the daily chart of the S&P 500. It is terribly extended to the downside, so a reversal is logical as the market tries to correct from an oversold situation. However, the daily chart has no trigger for this trend change. There are no particular bottoming tails, no Dojis, or hammers to give traders an excuse to buy. Because I have such clarity in the bonds, and yesterday was such an iffy day, I'm just going to focus on trading the bonds to the short side today.

The sharp morning move to the downside confirms my daily opinion for a bearish day in the bonds. (See Figure 9.25.) I was looking for an excuse to get short and saw a clean rally to the 20 EMA (1) with a nice reversal candlestick. I went short at this level and was almost immediately stopped. This countertrend rally continued for quite a while after my loss was taken. Then a violent spike to the downside formed as some economic numbers were released. Price became very extended to the downside once again, but remembering my lesson from yesterday I passed on the bounce trade. This decision was quickly rewarded as the price kept going lower, and I would have taken a second stop. The price then rallied to resistance (2) at the 20 EMA. This pattern fit my plan, so I entered the trade and closed it for a profit soon thereafter. The rest of the day was choppy and unpredictable, so I had no further trades.

Scorecard:

Correctly identified daily trend? YES
Traded with the intraday trend? YES
Avoided at least one stop? YES
Ended the day profitably? YES

FIGURE 9.25

JANUARY 29, 2003

Today the daily charts present an interesting conflict. (See Figure 9.26.) The S&P 500, which is very extended, has formed an inside range bar, which acts as a reversal indicator. However, the bonds have pulled back to the 20 EMA support level, and closed with a reversal candlestick. This leaves a swing-type pullback to support for the daily trader to ponder. Now the bonds and the S&P tend to trade inversely to one another. If the bonds are up, the S&P is probably down. So here we are presented with two daily buy patterns. . . . Which can we trust? This is a tough question, but I'm going to go with a bullish bias for the S&P, and I suspect therefore the bias will be bearish for the bonds. The S&P is just so extended, I can't imagine that it won't bounce at least back to chart resistance around 870. The bonds were extended, but have had 2 days to release some of this pressure. So it is for that reason that I move into this day with a bullish S&P bias.

Yikes, what a day. (See Figure 9.27.) The market gapped lower, and then began to cycle against the 200 SMA resistance level. I wanted to wait for that range to break, and then would begin to look for pullbacks in the

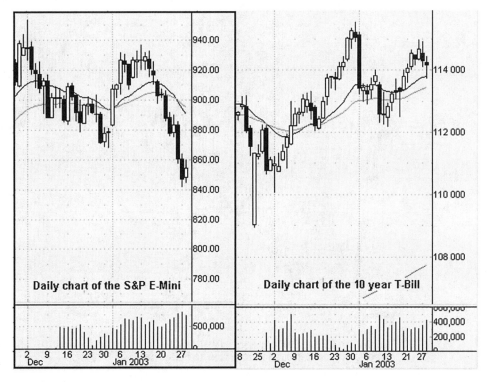

FIGURE 9.26

direction in my daily trend. Midday the range and 200 SMA resistance area were broken, and then price fell back to test the 20 SMA support level (1). I had my setup, and was happy to see the market break out and begin to run. I exited into resistance, and then watched as the price went almost 5 points beyond my exit! That's OK. I took some money out of the market on that pullback, but more importantly stuck to my plan from start to finish. Obviously a powerful uptrend was beginning as the bounce developed. I stood by to wait for the next pullback. It came later in the afternoon (2) as price fell to test support at the 20 EMA. It killed me to see this, as the Fed was about to announce the results of its meeting. This news always provokes a strong reaction from the market so it's very dangerous to trade during this time. You can see the spikes and explosion of volume that resulted after the Fed news was released. I definitely avoided a stop there by passing on the pullback to support. The rally continued, but I never got a pullback to enter against. When the price finally tested the 20 EMA, it did so late in the day and I doubted very much whether there would be any bounce. So, passing on that final pullback allowed me to avoid yet another stop. But the day left a bad taste in my mouth as I had correctly called trend

FIGURE 9.27

change, but was unable to participate fully in the rally. This is the price you pay emotionally for following your trading plan. Sometimes it burns your ego badly because you stayed with your discipline and missed big moves as a result. But, by sticking to your plan you are pressing your edge in a consistent manner, so you have consistent results. Your brain will never allow you to forget a day like today, however, where your style let you down. At the same time, your brain lets you easily forget all the stops you avoided and the elegant entries and exits your plan has delivered in the past. This selective memory causes more damage to traders' returns than does anything else. A classic example would be for me to take the pain and frustration of missing out today and project it onto tomorrow's trading. Having just seen a big trend day, the market is very likely to print nothing but chop tomorrow. So if I trade in that chop with a mind-set of making up for lost ground, I will probably get killed. The market is ever so much more powerful than you are, and any attempts to manufacture profitable trades will end in disaster. You just have to keep pressing your edge, taking those trades which offer you a positive expectancy. Unless you damage your edge through trading error, the odds will keep you well in the black.

The bonds had an equally frustrating day. (See Figure 9.28.) They were congested and choppy through most of the morning. There were a couple of possible shorts against the 20 EMA, but they were not clear enough for me to take. Finally, the market dropped sharply away from its 20 EMA to test support at the previous day's low (1). It then formed a hammer reversal candlestick, and I went long for my first trade of the day. My plan was for a straightforward bounce to resistance, which I got in short order. From a pattern standpoint, any day of the week but today I would have gone short as the price rallied into the 20 EMA (2). But again, the Fed was about to announce, and I did not want to take a trade with massive news risk attached. As luck would have it, the Fed announcement took the market lower off resistance. I was left to watch two good patterns in the S&P 500 and bonds go without me.

So this ends a frustrating day. On a positive note, I had two shots, two kills, no stops. So even though my ego is bruised, my trading style did deliver me a profitable and stopless day. This has been one of those weeks where you feel like you're off your game. I have not had a day yet where I felt 100 percent on. Yet, even though I feel like I haven't traded well, my account has remained in the black. It is interesting to note the emotional contrast. If you

FIGURE 9.28

165

had asked me how I did this week I would have replied, "lousy." Yet to my surprise, I'm up a little more than two units, and it's only Wednesday. Your mind will play many tricks on you as you go about your trading. This is why I feel so strongly that having the structure of a clear trading plan is crucial to success. I am experiencing plenty of negative emotions this week, but I have my plan as the crutch that keeps me profitable in spite of myself!

Scorecard:

Correctly identified daily trend? YES
Traded with the intraday trend? YES
Avoided at least one stop? YES
Ended the day profitably? YES

JANUARY 30, 2003

This continues to be a weird week. (See Figure 9.29.) The daily chart of the S&P 500 has a very wide range bullish engulfing bar. This should provoke

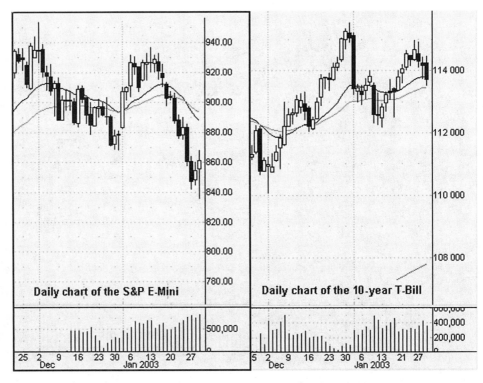

FIGURE 9.29

a nice reaction to the upside. But we still have conflict as the bonds continue to trade in an area of moving average support. I'm really not sure what to think here. That wild bar for the S&P disturbs me a little; the pullback in the bonds looks a lot cleaner to my eyes. I think I'm going to let the morning pass and try to identify and ride the intraday trend. If the bonds reverse and can confirm an uptrend intraday, I think a swing to the upside would be warranted.

The morning yielded a sharp selloff and reversal for the bonds. (See Figure 9.30.) This reversal finally became euphoric (1) as the price moved up to test an area of chart resistance from the previous day's trading. Since the intraday trend had not confirmed yet to my eyes, I was willing to take a countertrend short as the euphoria waned. My goal for this trade was a test of the 20 MA support level. If this test was successful, I felt that would be the support needed for my swing, so when it tagged the 20 EMA (2), I covered my short and took contracts for swing and day trade positions. These were two different trades with two different plans entered at the same point. For my day trade, I wanted to see a test of the 200 SMA and put my stop under

FIGURE 9.30

the 5-minute swing low. For my swing trade, I wanted to see a retest of the daily swing highs, and put my stop under the daily low. My day trade worked out well, and feeling flushed, I think from the confirmation of my previous entry, I bought the next pullback chart and 20 EMA support (3). This was an impulsive entry and did not have the extension I normally require of a pullback trade. With only a one-bar correction, it did not have the snapback potential that my first pullback trade contained. The low quality of this pick was confirmed as the market rallied back to test the 200 SMA and then failed to take out my stop. Whether I'm getting tired after a tough week or just feeling invincible because I think the daily trend is on my side, it doesn't really matter. After a foolish choice such as this, it is time to stop trading. I end the day up a couple of ticks on my pair of day trades, but am happy to see my swing looking healthy as the bonds closed strongly.

I'm not sure where my brain was today, but it wasn't in my trading loft! The S&P 500 opened, started out very choppy and congested, then printed a multi-bar selloff from range highs to lows. (See Figure 9.31.) A near textbook rally to retest the breakdown then formed (1) as price moved up to test 20 EMA resistance level.

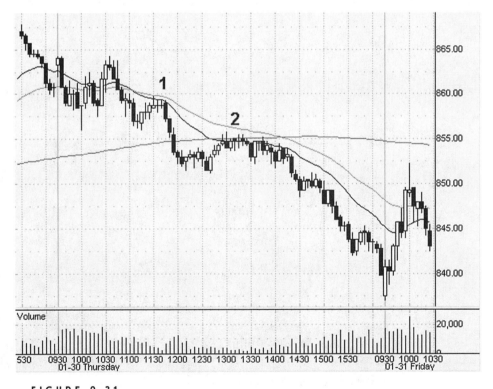

FIGURE 9.31

This looks like a painfully obvious short setup as I write this after-hours. It didn't wiggle much and would have worked beautifully. Somehow though, I just didn't see it. After that wave of selling had exhausted itself, it began to rally until it finally tested an area of moving average resistance (2) where both the 200 SMA and 20 EMA had converged. I took this test of resistance as an excuse to get short, and then when it just went sideways convinced myself to deviate from the plan and scratch the trade. The market then kicked me upside the head as it fell like a rock reminding me yet again to plan my trade and *trade my plan*!

So after having my first real bonehead day in some time, I need to back off and be ready to trade properly tomorrow. It's time to distance myself from the market and regain my objectivity. I allowed my mind to see what it wanted to see today, and as usual it lied like a rug. Tonight is a night to go out and catch some recharging R&R.

Scorecard:

Correctly identified daily trend? YES

Traded with the intraday trend? YES

Avoided at least one stop? NO

Ended the day profitably? BARELY

JANUARY 31, 2003

Yesterday's meltdown in the S&P after the previous day's bullish engulfing bar is quite disturbing. That bullish candlestick should have provoked strong buying response from any bulls watching the market. This action coupled with the nice swing buy setup on the daily bond chart tells me the stock market wants to move sharply lower. (See Figure 9.32.) If I'm right, then my swing long in the bonds is going to be a very good one. As the stock market falls, money should move toward the bond market helping to drive price above the previous swing high. I will be watching the bonds for bullish patterns and the S&P 500 for bearish patterns during this Friday session. I have had a comfortably profitable week, in spite of my foolish errors yesterday, so I see my job today as more of maintaining my gains than trying to hit something out of the park.

Another totally backwards day from the S&P 500! On a day where I thought we would see bearish follow-through, we instead see a gap and snap! (See Figure 9.33.) There were two potential longs that I saw as the price pullback in the neighborhood of the 20 EMA (1) and (2). Both of these trades were going against my daily opinion, and I felt fairly comfortable

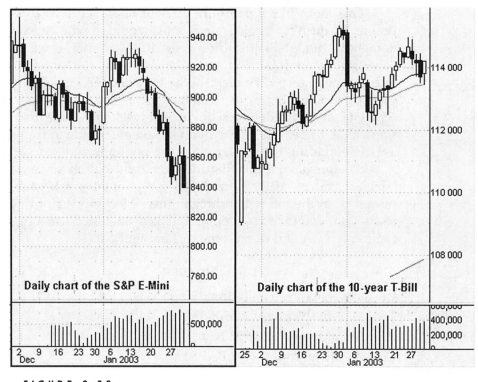

FIGURE 9.32

going long but hesitated to go into cowboy mode after blowing it yesterday. I decided instead to pass and ended up the day without taking a trade in the S&P E-Minis.

The day was little different for me in the bond market. (See Figure 9.34.) What a freak show! There was a potential bounce trade as the market tested the 200 SMA, but there were fast market conditions during this time so fills were difficult and risk was high. The price continued to oscillate wildly until finally it sold off into an area of previous price support (1). At this point I expected a bounce back to the 20 EMA, so took that as my first trade for the day. This trade went just as expected, and I took my profits as the moving average resistance was tested. The price continued slightly higher, then continued to triangulate into the close. This congested action didn't produce any more day trades, so I ended the session with a one-shot, one-kill trade.

If we drop down in time frame to a 30-minute chart for the bonds, we can get a good read on where the swing trade stands. You can see the downtrend that led into the daily support level around 113.160. (See Figure

FIGURE 9.33

9.35.) As this daily support was tested, the 30-minute chart saw a sharp increase in volume (1) and a beautiful hammer reversal candlestick. Our rally then began until eventually the 20 EMA was tested (2) and then broken. Price continued to move higher and on the 31st began to form a symmetrical triangle (3) with the 20 EMA acting as support. You can see how the volatility is coiling, gathering bullish power each time it tests the 20 EMA. With luck, this triangle will come to a head and break out on Monday. Having built such a pretty volatility coil, the market is likely to use that energy to break from this triangle and form a sharp price thrust. So far the price action continues to confirm this swing long, so I will hold it over the weekend in anticipation of a bullish triangle break on Monday.

Another week ended! I banked some nice profits this week in spite of a difficult environment and several trading errors. My swing looks good for Monday, and I'm happy to have shaken off yesterday's blunder in order to close out with a profit today. The continuation pattern (symmetrical triangle) in the bonds reinforces my opinion that the stock market is about to sell off rather dramatically again. Those poor investors! It is dur-

F I G U R E   9 . 3 4

F I G U R E   9 . 3 5

ing times like these that I am reminded of how powerful an edge it is to be an agile short-term trader. An impending price decline to me is an opportunity to be short and make money, rather than another disaster in the making for those in the "buy and hope" camps.

Scorecard:

Correctly identified daily trend? YES
Traded with the intraday trend? YES
Avoided at least one stop? NO
Ended the day profitably? YES

Week 4

FEBRUARY 3, 2003

This week started off on a sour note. The daily of the S&P E-Mini and the 10-year T-bills looks awful! (See Figure 9.36.) The S&P is beginning another choppy base as the up day/down day chaos begins to form. The bonds are little better, but after those nice swing patterns set up to the long side, it did little but triangulate. I am feeling very uninspired by what I see. I will be looking for long trades in the bonds as I'm hoping for that triangle to break out to the outside. I really don't have any feel for the S&P at this point, so only take a trade there if it's really choice. After starting out this month so well, I can begin to feel the struggle of a payback cycle looming. Mistakes, trades that don't work all that well…these are usually signals of transition from payout to payback. Time for me to be a bit more cautious as I try to keep my profits from my successes over the last couple of weeks.

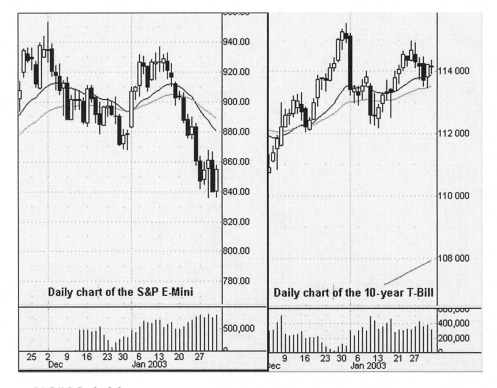

Daily chart of the S&P E-Mini

Daily chart of the 10-year T-Bill

FIGURE 9.36

Ugh! Instead of a breakout from the triangle, the bonds gapped down in a most unpleasant manner! The morning offered little as the price just wobbled within its range. (See Figure 9.37.) The gap was most unexpected for me, so I'm beginning to think my bullish daily bias may be incorrect. I began to look for short opportunities intraday and saw a valid rally to the 20 EMA and 200 SMA (1). This opportunity occurred just before economic numbers were scheduled for release, so I stood aside and was happy as a vicious spike/drop occurred. The selling finally found short-term support and they rallied back to resistance (2) at the 20 EMA. This was the first worthy move that I had seen so far, so I went short. The price may have gone my way one tick, but then flipped on a dime and stopped me out.

So, I start today with a bullish bias, see that dashed as a surprise gap takes us lower out of the open, and adding insult to injury my first trade is an almost instant stop. I'm feeling like a turtle who just wants to tuck his head back into his shell and wait for a better day to dawn. I smell payback in the worst way, and perhaps you can see it yourself as you begin to gauge the flow of my trading over the last month. I started out strong with

FIGURE 9.37

good tests of support and resistance. The price swings were clean, there were few spikes, and many of the trades were no-brainers. It was very simple: Enter at support or resistance, then ride the trend change to a profit. Now things are getting complicated. We see gaps and congested spiky action, resistance levels getting blown out like my first trade today, and generally bad follow-through. Has my style changed? Am I doing something wrong that is causing the difficulties? Whenever you reach a rough period in your trading, you always need to step back and objectively look at your trading logs. Did you stick to your plan? If the answer is yes, then your difficulties are probably caused by the misalignment of the payback cycle. You really can't do anything to fix your trading in a payback. In my experience it is much better to identify and accept the period of adversity. Once identified, you can reduce your risk and aggressiveness during this payback phase to minimize the losses your style may deliver.

The day continued to be choppy and weird. You could have shorted against the 200 SMA, but it would have been a painful hold and you might have been rinsed out before the actual selloff occurred. So I figured that was a stop avoided, and kept watching for a clean setup. Finally there was a clean rally to the 20 EMA (3), which gave me the short setup I had been looking for. The follow-through was lackluster at best, and I ended up with a teeny profit to start the week with a loss for the day.

While the bonds were hacking and gasping their way through the session, the S&Ps were not faring much better. (See Figure 9.38.) They rallied, then crashed back through moving average support levels without a pause. At this point I was just through getting slapped around by the bonds, so passed on the pullback trade (1) around 2:00. After that rally tested the high of the day, a sharp selloff occurred and I was stalking the next rally to resistance for a short. The setup was clean (2) but delivered nothing, and I eventually scratched it to avoid the close. At this point I'm feeling certain that a new payback cycle has begun. I will approach my trading tomorrow with the utmost caution, and be willing to let anything but the best trades pass me by as I go into a strongly defensive posture.

My swing trade in the bonds also fared badly on this payback day. Instead of breaking up out of its near-perfect triangle, it gapped down viciously! If we go back to the 30-minute chart (see Figure 9.39), you can see how quickly the price slammed back down the trade near my entry point (1). This gap came as a shock to me, but I was sticking to my plan, so did not allow this sell spike to shake me out of my position. I still had a powerful ally in the 200 SMA, which lurked just below my entry point. I wanted to see this support tested before I made any decisions about trailing stops or exiting the position. Sure enough, price soon tested the 200 SMA (2) and immediately tailed higher to form a hammer. When the ham-

FIGURE 9.38

mer's high was broken, I trailed my protective stop loss order to a few ticks below that hammer's low. Then the numbers came out, and my stop was taken. I ended up taking a loss on the trade as my exit was slightly below my entry point.

So this has to be the worst day so far in this diary! The swing trade stopped out for a loss, my day trades in the bonds were not profitable, and my single S&P trade was nothing more than a scratch! The payback cycle is in full swing; it's time to take a day off. The chances are very high after today's misery that I will continue losing for a couple of days. I find my personal payback cycle usually lasts 2 to 4 days. So if I can identify the beginning as I believe I have done today, I can avoid 1 or 2 days of low odds trading before I'm likely to begin my transition back to payout. Understanding the payout-payback cycle helps relieve an enormous amount of stress and frustration on a day like today. In years past, after a wretched failure day such as this, I would have spent the entire evening pouring over my charts in a vain attempt to figure out what I did wrong. I would be building up stress and anger, which would carry over into the next day's trading. Because of the nature of the payback cycle, this day

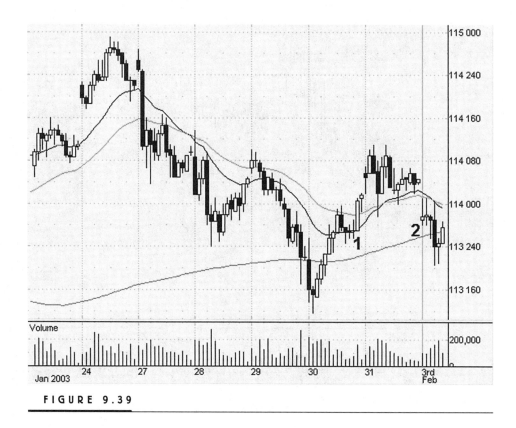

FIGURE 9.39

would probably also be a loser which would further increase my funk. Beginning the third day out of the payback cycle with an ever-increasing drawdown and emotional upheaval, I would tend to make my biggest and most blatantly stupid trading errors. After the fact, I would realize my blunders and back away from the market to lick my wounds. By following this cycle of loss and frustration, I would neatly maximize the drawdown inherent in the payback cycle, then back away from the market just as the richest days of the payout cycle began to show themselves. After seeing several days where all my setups had wonderful follow-through, I would begin trading again. But by missing the first few days of the payout cycle, I would only have a few days of success before conditions flipped, and the whole payback/drawdown period began again. It took me a very long time to discover the payback-payout cycle and to realize how badly I was managing it. I was trading more actively as I tried to fix my trading during the payback cycle, thus increasing my loss during the drawdown phase. Then, due to my mental fatigue and frustration, I would withdraw at precisely the moment the market offered its richest trading opportunities. When I began to invert this behavior, I saw a dramatic decrease in my drawdowns, and my trading moved up to a whole new level!

Scorecard:

Correctly identified daily trend? NO
Traded with the intraday trend? YES
Avoided at least one stop? YES
Ended the day profitably? NO

FEBRUARY 4, 2003

Had a great day off today, released all the stress and frustration from yesterday's losing. I'm stopping back in to take a look at the day with hindsight's perspective to see if my choice to bail was a good one after all. Since I wasn't going to trade today, I didn't bother to look at the daily charts or form any opinions, so I went straight to my 5-minute charts.

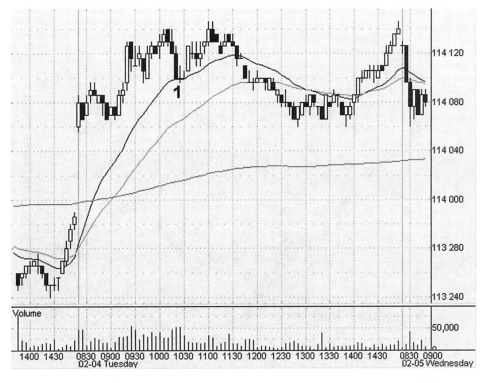

FIGURE 9.40

My first peek at the bonds tells me everything I need to know. (See Figure 9.40.) After the gap down yesterday the market gapped up as violently today. The action was not trending, and looks quite spiky and chaotic. The only trade I see that would have worked is the test of the 20 EMA (1) around 10:30. But even that had an unclear reversal pattern as it printed an inside range candlestick with a topping tail. I can easily see myself thinking that topping tail is an indication that the 20 EMA is about to be broken. I'm guessing that I would have passed on this trade had I been here watching it. So this chart acts as nice confirmation for my decision to ignore the markets and have fun today.

A look at the 5-minute chart for the S&P E-Mini also confirms my choice to jump ship. (See Figure 9.41.) The first trade I see is a rally to resistance (1) around 11:45. If I had been watching, I'm sure I would have taken this trade. It delivered almost nothing before breaking the 20 EMA resistance so would have cost me money as the trade stopped out. The only other trade that I might have considered was the messy double top that was printed around 2:45. But this is only a so-so pattern, and

FIGURE 9.41

after the morning loss I bet that I would have passed. The real shock for this day came after the closing bell. Cisco had an earnings report, and the market was waiting in breathless anticipation for those numbers to be announced. In the flurry of action that resulted as traders tried to play off the news, somebody made an expensive error. Instead of sending a market order to buy 60 or 600 contracts, a slip of the finger sent the order in at *6000 contracts!* This market order completely overwhelmed the sell side liquidity, which was already thin in anticipation of Cisco's earnings. This foul-up resulted in a massive price spike that took the ES up *100 points* and back again in a matter of seconds! In the blink of an eye, the price had rallied to take out the last major weekly swing high. The exchange finally decided to break all trades that had taken place above 860, but even so this was a disastrous price spike for anyone who had held a smaller time frame trade overnight. This death spike reminds us that there is always a hidden element of risk in any market. No matter how careful your risk management, no matter how many stop loss orders you set, there is always the chance for something bizarre to reach in and make a grab for your money. This is why trading must be viewed as a business. The capital you use for your trading should be money you are willing to lose in its entirety. This is risk capital, and with skilled risk management you should never have a disastrous loss, but to deny its possibility is to live with your head in the sand.

Even though I did not execute one trade, I feel like today was a complete success. I had a nice day of rest away from the market and avoided one stop at minimum. For my way of thinking, that puts me up one unit for the day. The loss I avoided is money in my pocket the next time I post a winning trade. For every stop I avoid, I have one unit fewer in my drawdown to make up as I begin to win again. Since today's action confirmed the presence of a payback cycle, the odds are highest for 2 days more of sloppy action. I will watch the market tomorrow, but will only trade if the pattern looks perfect. With any luck, this will be a short payback cycle. If that is the case, then tomorrow should be a transition day with the payout returning for Thursday's and Friday's sessions.

Scorecard:

Correctly identified daily trend (or lack thereof!)? YES
Traded with the intraday trend? NO TRADES
Avoided at least one stop? FOR SURE
Ended the day profitably? NO TRADES

FEBRUARY 5, 2003

The daily charts continue to offer mixed messages. The S&P is now a bloody mess as it ping-pongs from the highs back to the lows of the range. The bonds are a little better, as they have continued to hold their moving average support. (See Figure 9.42.) It looks now like I was wiggled out of my swing trade. That burns me a little, but how could I have predicted a gap down/gap up whipsaw? I did the right thing when the continuation pattern offered by the triangle failed. That was the best odds-based decision. This time it just didn't work out in my favor. So my bias going into this day is avoid the S&P and watch for long opportunities in the bonds.

Again, my correct identification of a payback cycle keeps me out of a strange day with plenty of opportunities for loss and frustration in the S&P. (See Figure 9.43.) The first setup that I saw (1) was a pullback to support at the 20 EMA. This pullback occurred below the 200 SMA, so I passed due to that overhanging resistance level. The next possibility was also a pullback (2) as price tested the 20 MA after the double top at the 855 area. Again, I passed since this would be a pullback below a double top that

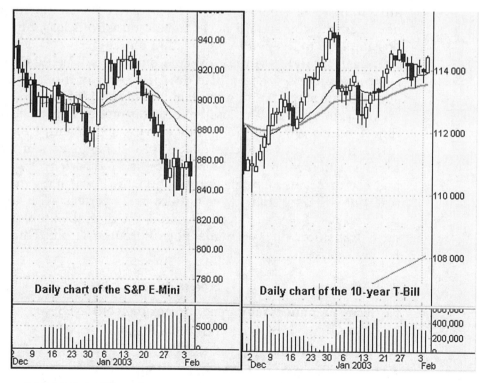

Daily chart of the S&P E-Mini

Daily chart of the 10-year T-Bill

FIGURE 9.42

FIGURE 9.43

should be a bearish pattern. The price continued to act contrary to my opinions, and the final insult would have been the Doji at the 200 SMA (3). Had I gone long off that otherwise valid pattern I would have been stopped almost instantly. Another great day to avoid trading as the payback cycle works its way through the market.

The bonds were only slightly better today. (See Figure 9.44.) There were some strong price swings that offered opportunity if I was able to capture them, but they did not turn in the areas of support or resistance that I was following. I took my first trade of the day (1) as price sold off sharply into the 200 SMA and a small hammer candlestick was printed. This gave me an easy rally from that moving average support to moving average resistance at the 20 EMA. I exited into that target level, then sat back and watched the market rally maniacally. It then fell like a brick to retest the 200 SMA. I could have taken this (2) long again for a bounce, but the violence and instability shown by the previous move and sudden reversal kept me on the sidelines. I was watching for a rally to the 20 EMA resistance level, but the price continued to remain unstable as it rallied through the 20 EMA, then pivoted and fell back down to break down

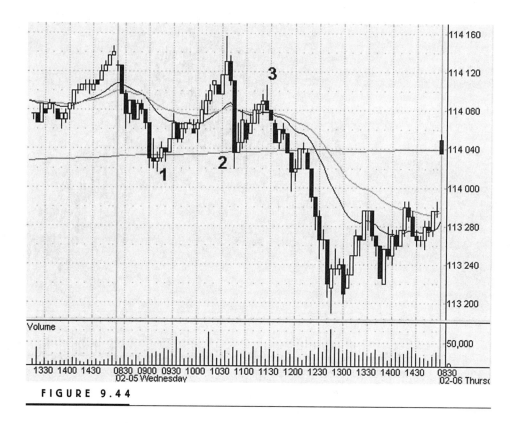

FIGURE 9.44

through new lows. With one winning trade on the books, I was happy to ignore the might have beens and to just run away from that day with my small profit.

So this has been day 3 of a fairly classic payback cycle. My personal tendency is to see a return to a payout environment on the fourth or fifth day of my payback cycle. So, with this in mind I will be more aggressive tomorrow as I try to take advantage of the first couple of days in the payout cycle. These are often the richest and can make the difference between an ordinary or extremely profitable month. Because of this tendency, it's worth sticking my neck out a little bit more as the payback cycle begins to wane.

Scorecard:

Correctly identified daily trend? YES
Traded with the intraday trend? YES
Avoided at least one stop? FOR SURE
Ended the day profitably? YES

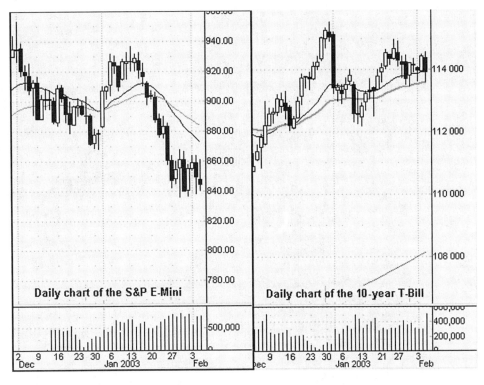

Daily chart of the S&P E-Mini

Daily chart of the 10-year T-Bill

FEBRUARY 6, 2003

Even though I know the chances are good for me to begin moving back toward a payout cycle, I really don't like what I see on the daily charts of the bonds or S&P 500. (See Figure 9.45.) Both are congested and choppy, without any of the extension that can give you a safer, more accurate prediction for the day's bias. Even so, I will keep an open mind and see what the market can offer. I'm happy with the week so far. I have dealt with what could have been a nasty losing streak, and am only down a little on the week due to commissions. My job during the payback cycle is to keep losses to a minimum, and I have done so. Now it's time to get back into a payout environment and make some money again!

The S&P 500 opened, rallied to the 20 EMA in a blink, then tanked. (See Figure 9.46.) I took my first trade (1) as the 20 EMA was tested for the first time. It gave me a couple points, then flipped back up toward the moving average. I bailed as the reversal began, taking a small gain and then watched it mush around for the rest of the day. Based on that

FIGURE 9.46

trendless action, I felt that this was one last payback day, so went back into the bunker. There was a possible long as price retested below for the day (2), but the market felt fast and unstable at that point, so I passed.

My day in the bonds was equally lackluster. There was a nice price thrust and the beginnings of a bull flag in the morning, but it never tested the 20 EMA. (See Figure 9.47.) After a series of chip-chop moves, the market finally tested the 20 EMA and I went long (1). This trade immediately began to form topping tails, and I took this as a bad sign. The price was not even able to retest the high for the day, so I scratched this trade for a minuscule gain. The rest of the day was nothing more than basing chop, so I stayed away.

So the lame market action continues. My prediction that today was the end of the payback was obviously proved false. I would still call today's action to be part of a payback style market. This being the case, I am now 4 days into this most recent payback cycle. The odds continued to be high for a return to a more profitable payout environment, so I will continue to maintain a more aggressive posture going into Friday's session. I was a bit lucky today, as there weren't many valid setups for my style of

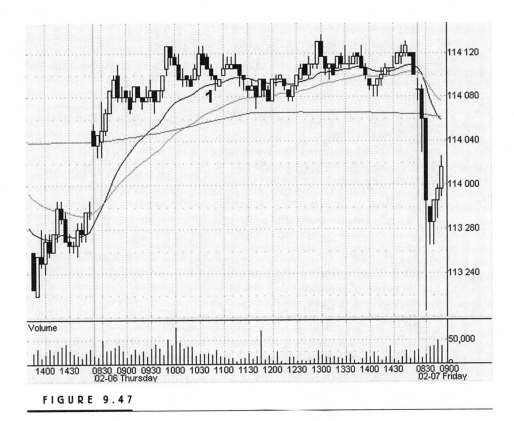

FIGURE 9.47

trading. Had there been more valid setups, I would have been in there, slugging for everyone. These transition days moving out of the payback cycle are where I take my biggest losses. I'm willing to step it up in the face of adversity because I know from experience that even though I may step it up and get smoked, if I maintain my aggressiveness I will bank some serious green as the payout cycle returns.

Scorecard:

Correctly identified daily trend? YES
Traded with the intraday trend? YES
Avoided at least one stop? PROBABLY
Ended the day profitably? BARELY

FEBRUARY 7, 2003

Okay, TGIF!!! I have one last day to save this otherwise pathetic week. One look at the daily charts shows why this week has been so difficult.

(See Figure 9.48.) I am a trend trader. I like to buy pullbacks to support and sell rallies to resistance. This entire week has been nothing but a sideways base, no trend, nothing but a ping-pong match between the range highs and lows. At this point I'm up about half a unit, and feeling happy to see any black ink. I know that the next payout cycle is lurking, and I am hoping that maybe today is the day for a change in the market's weather.

Bah! Humbug! The market continues to trade in a most choppy manner. (See Figure 9.49.) This is offering little opportunity to my style of trading. The S&P 500 shows this clearly today. The market is definitely trading in a downtrend and after a violent morning move to the downside, it finally bounces and trades back toward the 20 EMA (1). This was not a clean test, as there was a wiggle and a higher low on the 5-minute chart before the 20 EMA was tested. For this reason, I passed on the trade and then watched the price turn away from the 20 EMA and sell off for the rest of the day. It offered me no setups, so I was forced to sit, then watch it sell without taking part in the bearish trend. This is a classic situation where traders begin to commit errors. Traders wait for their setup, and seeing none begin to manufacture short entries in their mind. They are so afraid to miss out on a potential selloff that they throw their plan out the window and begin to trade from the hip. These fear-based trades (fear of missing out) never work that well, and can cause you to lose on a day when your directional opinion is correct. Nothing will tweak your psyche more than taking two or three short trades on a day like Friday and still close out with a loss! I have been there, done that, own the T-shirt, and I'll never do it again! I'm sticking to my plan, as it has served me well for a long, long time now.

Ugh! An equally nasty day in the bonds (see Figure 9.50) . . . after a massive spike to the downside, price began to rally until it finally formed a topping tail at the 200 SMA (1). I went short off test and was rewarded with a quick stop for my troubles. I was rather surprised to see the 200 SMA broken, so began to look for long opportunities. I bought the next pullback to the 200 SMA support level (2), and sat for what seemed like an eternity as I waited for it to bottom out and finally rally. I closed this trade into resistance from the previous day around 114.120. With this one trade, I made my week! Up until this point I had been treading water during a most unpleasant payback cycle. But now, at the last second I finally pulled out a decent trade, and so ended my week up a little more than one unit. It is rather unusual for me to see 5 days of chaotic payback action. I am beginning to move beyond my envelope of 2 to 4 days of payback before the cycle shifts. I'm surprised the daily base has lasted this long. It must be

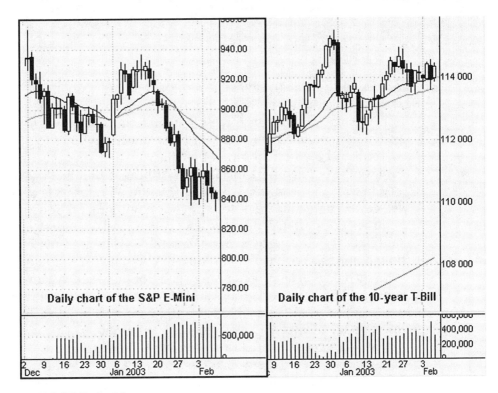

Daily chart of the S&P E-Mini

Daily chart of the 10-year T-Bill

FIGURE 9.48

FIGURE 9.49

because of the war troubles in Iraq, the terrible economic news, and the rampant uncertainty in the equity markets. Nobody has the visibility they need to step in and buy for the longer term. They are all just scalping against each other as they wait for these uncertain times to pass.

So I end my first month of this diary on a down note. I had hoped to see a complete payout-payback cycle within the month, but it seems I will need to wait one more week. I plan to continue to chronicle my trades until we see the transition back to a payout environment. You can see how I identified the shift in conditions, and began to play defense as I waited for conditions to change to a more favorable trending environment. Even though things were choppy and mixed, I was able to keep my drawdowns very small, and even posted a small gain for the week. Again, trading is all about outperformance. I would suspect many traders are sitting on a nasty loss for this week. I was able to totally eliminate any loss for this trying time and even banked a few C notes for my troubles. This management of the payback cycle is crucial to consistent success as a trader. Accepting that these cycles exist can be difficult as many traders wish to be all things to all markets. But if you reach a level of maturity as a trader, you will stop

FIGURE 9.50

butting heads with the payback cycle. Instead, you just knuckle down and play defense. Your drawdowns will be much smaller and your gains larger and more consistent as you will be able to exploit the profit potential of the payout cycle to its max.

Scorecard:

Correctly identified daily trend? YES
Traded with the intraday trend? YES
Avoided at least one stop? PROBABLY
Ended the day profitably? YES

Week 5

FEBRUARY 10, 2003

Well, let's see what this week brings. After experiencing a payback period last week, the first few days of this week should be the transition back to payout. The cycles that are normally driven by the trend-chop-trend tendency of the markets are being scrambled a bit by the news-driven environment. The overhanging uncertainty in the politico-economic swirl surrounding the Iraqi and South Korean conflicts seems to be causing the payback cycle to last a bit longer than is normal.

As I look over my daily charts (see Figure 9.51), it seems we have finally seen a breakdown out of the base for the S&P 500. The bonds are stuck in a base of their own, and even though the overall trend there seems to be clearly upward, I don't think the existing pattern will drive the contract as cleanly as the S&P breakdown. I will be focusing on the ES today to the short side.

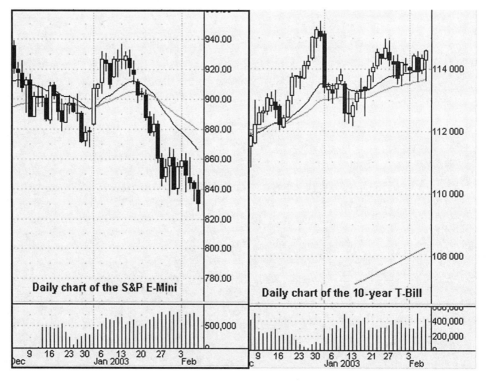

FIGURE 9.51

The S&P started selling off during the morning session as I expected. (See Figure 9.52.) It then bottomed (1), forming a clean 5-minute reversal candlestick. I was watching eagerly for this pivot to produce a rally to the moving averages for me to short. It never got there, so I continued to stand by as the price fell to a new low for the day. This breakdown (2) was very short-lived. Bottom tails quickly formed as the faders "caught the knife" and absorbed all the selling pressure. As this action occurred I began to rethink my bearish bias for the day. If the price was unable to break down, I had a potential peek bottom staring me in the face. As I was contemplating this possibility, there was another price spike to the downside. The price broke down below the previous tail's low by one tick, then immediately reversed. This was the confirmation I needed, so I initiated a long based on this peek reversal action (2). The market immediately bounced, and I took profits into the 20 EMA. I then sat back and watched in chagrin that the market pressed through the moving average resistance and exploded to test the 200 SMA. Then the market began to chop in a most congested manner. I had a humorous experience later that afternoon as I took a short trade (3)

FIGURE 9.52

against the 20 EMA resistance level. I mentioned to my clients that I thought the market was about to sell off having formed a lower high and then a low momentum bounce off of range lows to the 20 EMA resistance level. One of them asked me if this trade was based on the head-and-shoulders pattern that had formed as the 200 SMA was tested. I was staring at the exact same chart, but had completely failed to see the previous range as a head and shoulders! Once he mentioned it, it became obvious as the chart in Figure 9.52 shows, but the experience was a reminder about how subjective trading really is. I was short based on a rally to resistance off of range support, using my style to help me determine the line of least resistance. And he was looking at a broader price pattern that had formed during the lunchtime doldrums. Both of our opinions looked correct at the time but were developed from entirely different views of price action. This is why the markets will always offer opportunity. There are so many different people who can have wildly differing views about the same chart action. These differences in opinion are what keep the markets active and liquid. The only market that is devoid of opportunity is a dull market without participation. As long as there are active traders, there is money to be made! My second trade for the day off this lower high ended with a slight loss. The price fell away from my entry point, then retested the 20 EMA forming a topping tail. I trailed my stop, and my contracts were quickly taken from me as that resistance level was broken. So, by keeping my objective I was able to change my bias and grab profits to the long side in the morning. Then my second trade was taken after a complex top was formed. Even though it squeezed me out for a loss, it was a good pattern and one I would take again. Good trade, bad outcome!

Without a strong opinion based on the daily charts for the bonds, I was in a wait-and-see mode for the day. The bonds gapped down to open right at their 200 SMA, and, in retrospect, an aggressive buy against that support was probably the best trade for the day. However, I'm not really a gap trader so this pattern didn't fit within my trading plan. After a smooth rally to fill the gap, the price hit resistance and then rolled over. It sold off to the 20 EMA, which acted as support. In my view, the bonds should have fallen sharply away from this area of gap resistance. They were quite extended to the upside, and I saw this moving average support as a sign that the market wished to move higher. I took a long position as price moved up off support (1) and only saw a tiny move in my direction before the price reversed and I was stopped. The price then sold off as smoothly as it had rallied. This was rather surprising to me, especially as it sold through the 200 SMA support level without showing any signs of slowing. It then broke below the opening bars low and began to form bottoming tails. (See Figure 9.53.) The peek bottom is probably one of the most powerful intraday patterns in my repertoire, so when the price (2) broke down, then quickly reversed to form a second bottom tail I went long in reaction to this peek bottom. Again, a near perfect price pattern yields only a tiny paper profit before turning to stop me out. Guess the payback cycle is not yet complete!

Sheez! The day started out so nicely with a good change in bias and profitable long setup in the S&P. But three stops later, the day ends with a loss. All the stops were taken on good patterns. I'm not finding fault in my execution as I analyze after the close, so this must just be an extension of the payback cycle. The classic symptoms of a payout cycle after all are mystifying stops taken off seemingly perfect patterns. When you know in your heart that you took the right trade, but still the market fails to reward you, you just have to accept that you're in a payback cycle. Many newer traders begin to look internally for the reasons why they are losing. It is easy to find fault with yourself, rather than understanding the fundamental nature of market alignment and/or misalign-

FIGURE 9.53

ment that causes the payout-payback cycle to occur. Trading off support and resistance offers a strong edge and just plain works! There are times, however, when the market doesn't respect support and resistance levels that you believe are important. Look at the bonds today. They printed a giant rally, then declined, and to my eye, only two support or resistance levels were respected. The first was the 200 SMA off the gap open. The second was the gap fill resistance around 114.16 so that price retested the area of Friday's close. Other than that, every conceivable test of support or resistance that I see was either a complete failure or a mediocre reversal at best. For a support and resistance trader, and especially a trader who tries to follow the trend, this kind of action will never yield a consistently profitable result. This was a classic payback day. So, the bottom line here is a mental one. When you start to feel shocked and confused by the stops you are taking, step back and objectively analyze your entry decisions. If they were not impulsively taken outside your trading plan, then you're probably just experiencing a payback day. Don't sweat it; don't blame yourself. Just work to identify, as quickly as possible, if the day is a payback; then stop the bleeding! Get back on defense as you wait for the market to swing back into alignment with your style.

There is a fundamental level of cyclicality inherent in any trading style; our daily charts act as a good illustration of this today. (See Figure 9.54.) Last month the bonds were trending and providing most of my profit. During this time the S&P 500 was basing in a random and choppy manner. Now these roles are reversed, and the S&P 500 daily shows that extended move to the downside with a hammer-type reversal candlestick. The bonds are now chopping within a random base. Just as I focused on the bonds while they were trending, it looks like now is the time to ignore the bonds and focus on the S&P to the long side as this hammer is likely to attract bullish attention.

I began the day with a bullish expectation for the S&P 500. The market opened, thrust higher, then fell back to the 20 EMA to form a hammer candlestick which quickly reversed the intraday trend. Much to my chagrin, I missed this long! Once I saw support coming in, I entered a limit order to buy. The market quickly moved away from my limit price, and I was never filled. In trading, there are always ramifications for every choice you make. I chose to enter with limit orders, thus locking in the price at which I'm willing to take the trade. Because I'm using limit orders, I never experience slippage on my entries; however, the downside is that once in a while I will miss the trade. I believe over time this control over slippage on entry will more than pay for any lost opportunity.

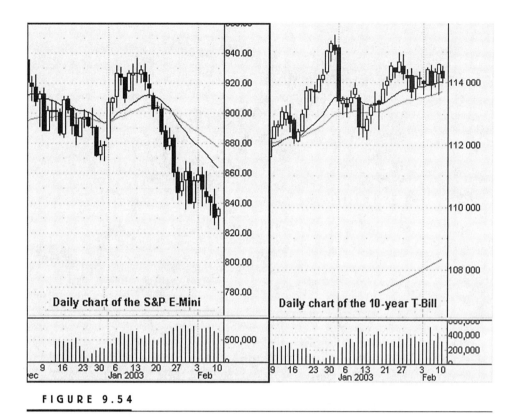

Daily chart of the S&P E-Mini

Daily chart of the 10-year T-Bill

FIGURE 9.54

The market ran up off the 20 EMA back to test the highs for the day. (See Figure 9.55.) It then formed a near perfect double top (1), and I quickly reacted by taking a short position. Harnessing the sentiment behind my saying, "That which should go up . . . *should go up!*" I figured that the failure of the market to break new highs would deliver a selling spike back to 20 EMA support. This was precisely what happened, and I covered into the support offered by the 20 EMA. The market paused only for a moment at this support, then continued to sell. It sold steadily for almost an hour without one significant wiggle. I was waiting for a long trade as the 200 SMA was tested. The price just missed the 200 SMA and began to bounce. It then wobbled and fell back down to test the 200 SMA. In addition, it formed a peek bottom (2), which was all the confirmation I needed to get long. Again, I was looking for a simple bounce from the support offered by the 200 SMA to the resistance levels of the now declining 20 EMA. This objective was quickly reached, and the price even continued a bit higher before turning as the sellers regained control. Again the market became oversold as the

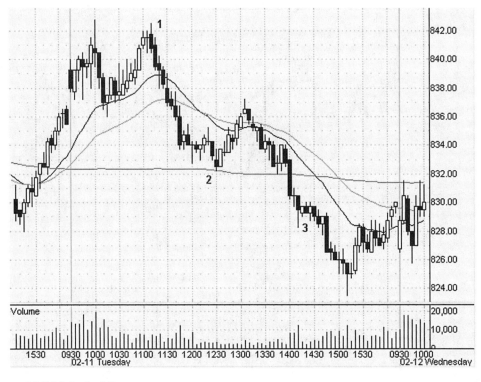

FIGURE 9.55

selling pressure pushed it lower and lower without a wiggle. I was target-ing the major swing low at 828 for another bounce-type trade. Once sup-port was tested, I figured the market was good for a bounce back toward the 200 SMA and 20 EMA. In a replay of my second trade, the first bounce occurred just above support. I waited for the perfect entry, and was rewarded by a true test of support (3) 15 minutes later. Again I had my peek bottom as a 5-minute hammer candlestick formed! I went long at this point, and never saw more than a few ticks of profit as support was broken and the price continued to crater. This final trade shows exactly what a good stop looks like. My opinion was proved wrong as there was never any bounce off support. My choice of stop levels (set a few ticks under the ham-mer candlestick's low) was then confirmed by the market as the selling con-tinued for many points beyond my stop. My protective stop loss order did its job here, acting as my insurance policy against uncontrolled loss.

Since I was in the middle of a fairly significant payback cycle and had little directional opinion about the bonds, I chose to stay out of the bond market for the day. Even though I was sure about this choice, I still watched the action as I tried to confirm my decision.

The bonds opened and spent the first 2 hours of the session in a choppy base. (See Figure 9.56.) There was a violent rally to the 200 SMA resistance area (1), but the market was acting thin and unstable, so I suspect I would have had a difficult time being filled. The price then broke out to new highs, and pulled back to retest the 20 EMA, 40 EMA, and 200 SMA support levels. Had I been trading bonds, I know I would have bought into this strong support level and would have been rewarded with a quick stop for my troubles. The price continued to trade in an unstable manner, rushing back up to test the moving averages (3) but without any real setups that I would have taken. So my payback cycle is still in full effect for the bonds. By choosing to withdraw from this day, I avoided frustration and at minimum one stop. As I look back on this most recent payback cycle, I'm happy at how I have managed it. Damage has been kept to a minimum; stress and frustration are under control. I

FIGURE 9.56

am just in a holding pattern as I wait for conditions to shift back into my favor. I am starting to wonder about the length of this payback cycle. Normally, I can expect to see a 3- to 4-day payback cycle, then the action will shift back into a more favorable payout mode. I am now well beyond those parameters, and this payback is feeling like an anomalous news or war-driven period of chop. In a normal payout-payback cycle, I become very aggressive after 3 or 4 days of payback. I know the odds are increasing dramatically for a shift back to a payout environment. I want to maximize the profit potential of the first few days of order. Now that the window has passed, I feel it is time to go back into a more conservative mode as I wait for the war jitters to work themselves out. It feels obvious to me that there are external events which are disturbing the normal cycles that I have counted on in the past. I have never traded through a period of war, having started trading after the Gulf War. I expect to see a continuation of the payback until the news out of the United Nations is able to mollify the market participants.

I feel quite happy about this day's trading. I avoided frustration and loss in the bonds, and banked two out of three in a much more orderly S&P 500. The payback is now moving outside the normal duration envelope, so my hackles are raised, and I plan to be a bit more conservative for the rest of this week.

Scorecard:

Correctly identified daily trend? YES
Traded with the intraday trend? YES
Avoided at least one stop? YES
Ended the day profitably? YES

FEBRUARY 12, 2003

Yuck! Nothing but a choppy environment is left on the daily after yesterday's action. (See Figure 9.57.) The S&P 500 has a setup and flush pattern showing, so it's more likely to see a continued downside. However, it's extended, so any selling will be prone to spikes and short squeezes which raise the risk level for bearish setups. The bonds continue to do little but base. The daily 20 EMA has been holding, and if I was forced to guess, I'd say they will break higher in the next 2 days. I have to say I'm entirely uninspired by these daily charts, really debating if I want to trade at all today. Guess I will just watch and see if something out of the ordinary shows itself.

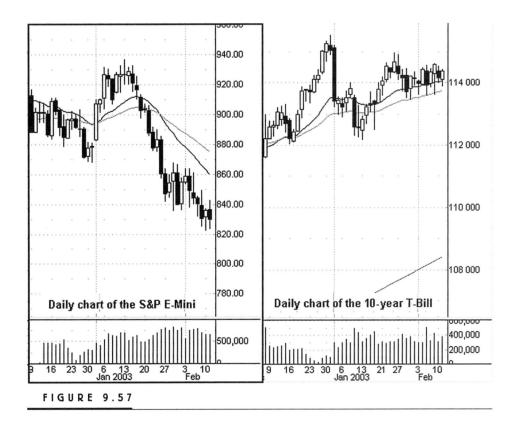

FIGURE 9.57

The first hour of the day in the S&P 500 confirms my apathy. (See Figure 9.58.) Showing little but an unstable spiking environment (1), I decide to stay away for now. At approximately 11:45 A.M., there is a clean rally to the 20 EMA as well as chart resistance (2). This is the best setup I've seen today, so I've initiated a short position against resistance. I am quickly rinsed out of my short as the price squeezes higher to break resistance, grabs a few stops, and falls back in the direction of the trend. OK! That's it for me. I was careful to wait for what I thought was the best pattern of the day. It immediately rinsed and ran in the direction of my opinion. The evilness index seems to be high today as we continue in the payback cycle. I feel no incentive to throw good money after bad, so close out my order entry screens and ignore the rest of the day.

As I look back, I see two other trades I would have considered. The double bottom long (3), which would have rinsed me before running back to my target area at the 20 EMA. Then the rally to the 20 EMA (4), which *also* would have rinsed me before trending as I thought it would! The other day I talked about good stops. For some reason, it has never both-

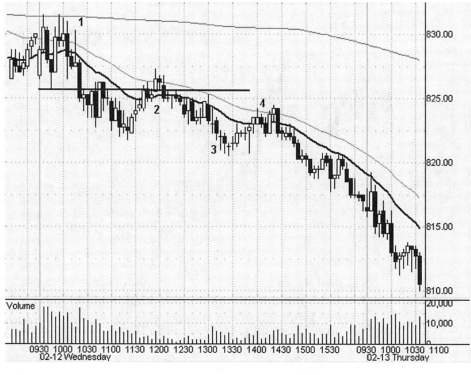

FIGURE 9.58

ered me when the market proves my opinion false. If I think the market is going up and instead it goes down, the loss I take never eats at my ego. I can see how much money my stop saved me, and I'm ready to move on to the next trade. A rinse, or rip off stop, is a loss that consistently gets my goat, and sends me over the edge into anger and frustration. A rinse occurs when you enter against support or resistance, and there is a manipulative stop running move which blips in the wrong direction just far enough to stop you out before screaming back in its original direction. In the S&P 500 today, we saw three rinse and runs in a row! On each test of support or resistance, the market head faked, then stopped everybody out before making the money move. Had I continued to trade after my first rinse, I would have ended the day right about the market direction for all three trades, but would have nothing but three stops to show for it! I would have been seething all evening, and would have to work very hard not to carry that anger into the next trading day. I avoided two out of three of the traps set for me in today's session. The first loss pains me a little since the market did indeed sell away from that resistance. However, I felt relieved and happy to see the next two trades also pull a classic rinse and run without me on board! This payback cycle is beginning to get more and more vicious.

I was never even tempted by the bonds today. They gapped out fairly strongly at the open, then filled the gap. (See Figure 9.59.) This support (1) eventually held, but the price went into chaotic gyrations before the intraday trend was able to shift. There was a nice lower high (2), which is a pattern I normally would trade except for the fact that today the 20 EMA was just below. This offered a very limited profit potential for the trade, one that would not justify the risk I would assume in entering. The market continued to flip-flop, and formed a triangle (3) that eventually broke into the close. I might have taken small profit out of it had I been watching, but at this point I had already taken my stop in the S&P 500 and had chosen to bail for the day. Even if I had a superman fill into that triangle, it still would not have provided enough profit potential to overcome my S&P 500 loss.

The payback continues to get uglier and uglier. I'm hoping that this action means it's all coming to a head. I'm happy with my trading so far this week, but am getting disgusted with the lack of opportunity. The last

FIGURE 9.59

couple of days have felt like a waste of my time. Usually when I start to slip into this "Why bother, the market stinks" mind-set, the end of the pay-back is close at hand. My emotions, like a capitulation bar, will usually convince me to take a vacation 2 days before the biggest payout day of the month! I have learned this lesson the hard way, and now will usually decide to take time off at the end of a sustained winning streak. That way, I conveniently miss the next payback cycle, and come back refreshed and ready to trade just as payout begins again.

Scorecard:

Correctly identified daily trend? YES
Traded with the intraday trend? YES
Avoided at least one stop? YES
Ended the day profitably? NO

FEBRUARY 13, 2003

I'm starting to feel a lot more optimistic this morning as I look at my daily charts. (See Figure 9.60.) In both the bonds and the S&P 500 we finally have extension! The bonds are moving back up for a potential breakout or dou-ble top, the S&P 500 becoming quite extended on the downside and is moving into an area of gap support off the October lows. I have been wait-ing for months for this test of support and will be watching for an oppor-tunity to initiate a swing trade to the long side.

If we take a look at a daily chart of the SPY in Figure 9.61 (which is the S&P 500 index proxy that trades as a stock), we can look back over several months to see where the gap support lies. After the violent bullish engulfing bar of October 10, 2002, the price gapped up dramatically the following day. After several months of flip-flop basing, we are finally correcting to a point where this gap support may be tested. I believe this support level to be sig-nificant and will expect it to provoke a powerful bounce off any successful test. The market closed just shy of support yesterday, so I will be watching for the test during today's session. I believe I will be able to pick the bottom within 6 points, so will use an arbitrary stop for my swing trade.

I felt the bonds would continue to rally as they were drawn up for the double top test off the daily chart. (See Figure 9.62.) They printed their first test of the 20 EMA support level around 9:35 A.M. (1). I went long at this point and what followed illustrates clearly the need to stick to your trading plan. The price rallied slightly, then pulled back to test my stop. It came within two ticks of my stop, and then reversed. Had I chickened out, I would have

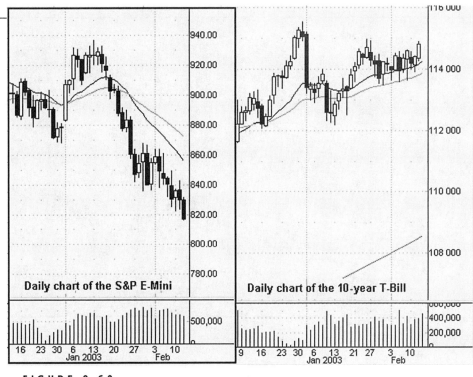

FIGURE 9.60

guaranteed a loss for the trade, and would have felt like an idiot when it began to immediately move back to the range high. Once it hit the highs for the range, it began to roll over yet again. At this point I had been in the trade close to 2 hours without any significant profit. I scratched the trade, anticipating a sharp breakdown below 115, then got to sit and watch as a powerful rally ensued. I got a chance to buy the first pullback (3), which immediately began to base. I ended up scratching this trade as well for a few ticks of profit as it broke above the 115.160 level. So it was a bit of a frustrating day, but even so I was two for two on the day. The profits were awfully small, but they were profits nonetheless. The day felt much more orderly than any action I had seen so far this week. Add to this my negative mind-set after the rinse day yesterday, and it sure seems like the next payback cycle is starting! (I find it fascinating that even after years of trading, I can still use my emotions and moods as a contrary indicator!)

My day in the S&P 500 was very much like the bonds. (See Figure 9.63.) The morning selloff was smooth and orderly, but did not offer me any test of the 20 EMA. Finally, I had my chance to enter (1) off the first test of moving average resistance. The market pushed away from the 20 EMA, and then began to chop. Remembering the rinses of the previous day, I took the profit I had at this point, and waited for the next tradable setup.

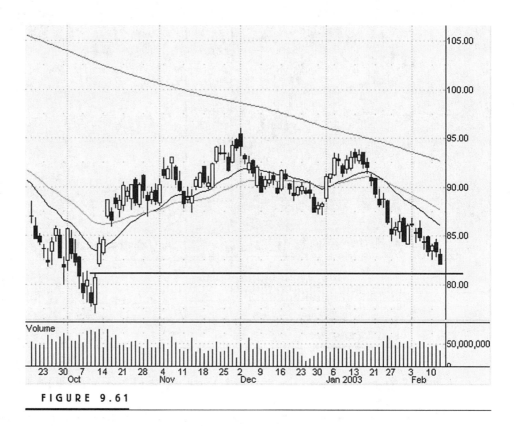

FIGURE 9.61

The market continued lower, and during lunchtime began to trade in my target zone of daily gap support. It rallied to test the 20 EMA, but because I felt the market was in an area of important support I was not interested in going short. Instead, I waited for the selling to retest the lows in the hopes that a double bottom would form. Not only did my double bottom form but to sweeten the pattern it was a peek double bottom (2)! I opened my swing trade to the long side, and set my stop an arbitrary 6 points lower. The market then responded to support as a maniacal rally/short squeeze began. The market basically exploded, only forming one minor wiggle before testing the 200 SMA (3). At this point, a massive volume spike was formed, and I knew a more significant wiggle was likely to follow. Even though this was a swing trade, the intraday euphoria was incredibly obvious, at least to me. I was physically aching to take profits. I just could not let that powerful exit signal go by, so I took my profit into the 200 SMA. I still wished to be long, as I believe the daily reversal was good for 1 or 2 days of follow-through. I saw an area of chart support working near the highs of the previous wiggle above 815. I put in a bid just

FIGURE 9.62

above that level to buy back my contracts for the overnight swing (4). I was quickly hit, and the price rallied to close near the highs for the day. So, just like last week I seem to be pulling it out of the bag near week's end. Although the swing trade isn't closed yet, it looks perfect and my open paper profits have taken me well into the black for the week.

This week so far has highlighted the manic-depressive nature of trading. I ended the day yesterday discouraged and angry, down on the week and feeling chastised by the market. Then all of a sudden, today the payback cycle seems to have ended, and the transition back to payout has begun. Had I followed my emotions, I would have taken the day off in disgust and missed my swing trade entry. How classic a payout-payback–cycle error that would have been! Going to bed tonight with a stopless day and a nice open swing!

Scorecard:

Correctly identified daily trend? YES
Traded with the intraday trend? YES

FIGURE 9.63

Avoided at least one stop? YES
Ended the day profitably? OH, YES

FEBRUARY 14, 2003

Again, we see a very intriguing daily situation. (See Figure 9.64.) The S&Ps have pivoted cleanly off of their daily gap support from way back in October. The bonds broke briefly to a new high, then reversed to leave a topping tail in the beginning of a double top pattern on the daily. The pay-out cycle seems to be building; let's see what this day can bring!

What a roller coaster! The day started out as a continuation of the base near highs from yesterday's euphoria. (See Figure 9.65.) I was happy to hold in anticipation of a breakout until I saw the false breakout (1) around 10:15 A.M. As I was watching the tape, I saw significant fading pressure as the price broke to new highs. That which should go up, should go up, and this certainly looked like a failure. I exited my swing, with the willingness to reenter if a setup showed itself. The fade did indeed take the

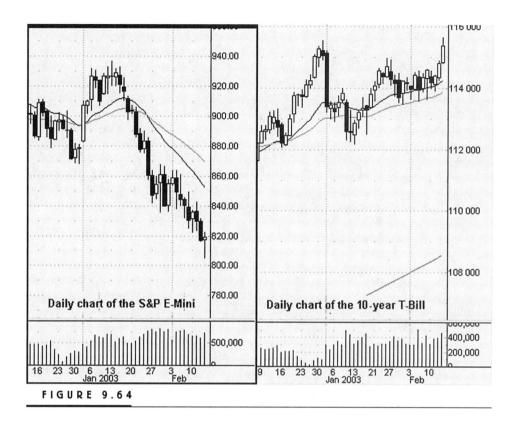

Daily chart of the S&P E-Mini

Daily chart of the 10-year T-Bill

FIGURE 9.64

price back down to test the 200 SMA, but then another euphoric blastoff occurred! Just as quickly, it topped off and began to sell like there was no tomorrow. This has been quite an amazing week. We have gone from steady selling to euphoria, then more euphoria and now capitulation! As the price fell into the 815 support level I had used to reenter in yesterday's session, it began to turn. I took a little bit of a gamble, and reentered my swing to the long side (2). The price then squeezed all day long to close up near its highs. So even though I got out a little too early and missed the morning's euphoric spike, I was back in my swing with a nice open profit.

While the S&P 500 was bouncing around like a 5-year old after consuming a liter of soda, the bonds were out gallivanting around in their own right. (See Figure 9.66.) After a congested base, they sold off sharply into the 200 SMA. I took a long into this support level (1) and was quickly stopped as the price continued to hemorrhage. The bonds are one of the deepest and most stable markets you could imagine, and when they begin to spike and print giant death bars like that, I stand aside. I am most accurate in a quieter trending environment; pullbacks and report or resistance tests are my forte. When the market begins to flip-flop with a more

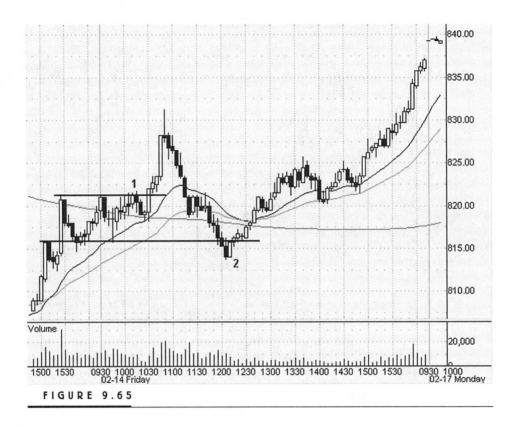

FIGURE 9.65

momentum-driven mind-set, my accuracy begins to falter. So once the bonds set that tone for the day, I knew it was time to step aside.

The environment remains mixed; my swing is the only bright spot as it continues to provide me with profit. This certainly feels like the beginning of a transition market as we move back into the payout cycle. If things are shifting back to normal after this longer than expected payback, then a 1-to-2-day transition period is usually the norm for me. We have Monday off due to Patriot's Day, so this would put me into the beginning of a nice winning streak on Tuesday or Wednesday of next week. I'm looking forward to that immensely, not only because it will put me back into a winning environment but also because it will be a stereotypical end to a payback cycle. My goal for this trading log has always been to show how a style is traded through the good market/bad market phases of the payout-payback cycle: make money during the payout and manage the adversity of the payback. Keep drawdowns small when a losing environment presents itself and then move quickly back into the black when winning trades begin to show themselves again. This week has acted as a good example. It began rather pathetically,

FIGURE 9.66

and I was down for the week going into Thursday. Then the swing opportunity presented itself, as well as the so-so intraday trades that ended up mildly probable. In one fell swoop, you go from misery and drawdown to black ink and new equity highs. That is the manic-depressive cycle of a professional trader. You have to have incredible strength of self, and a willingness to keep your chin up as the market heaps abuse upon you. It is so very easy to fall into the trap the markets will set, allowing your emotions to dictate your behaviors. Instead, pros know that their job is to press the edge their style makes available, playing the odds they know are stacked in their favor. Trading is the business of taking risks, so there will be bumps in the road but a trust in your edge will help you get through these periods of adversity and back into the glory of the win streak.

Scorecard:

Correctly identified daily trend? YES
Traded with the intraday trend? YES
Avoided at least one stop? PROBABLY
Ended the day profitably? YES

Week 6

FEBRUARY 18, 2003

After what feels like eons of chop, we are finally seeing a real daily swing. (See Figure 9.67.) The S&P 500 has pivoted off support and has printed a follow-through day. The 20 EMA lurks just above at 850. Because of the tendency for market swings to follow the pattern of pivot day, follow-through day, exit into resistance day, I will be out of my S&P swing by the end of trading today. My hope is to exit as the 20 EMA is tested, but if the market falls short of that target I will still exit based on the time factor of the swing. The bonds have topped out and are pulling back toward the 20 EMA as well as chart support from the chaotic base. I will be watching for a swing reversal as the price tests this support zone. So I have a bit of a dual bias for both markets today. I am bullish on the S&P until 850 is tested, then I expect the bears to take control again as resistance is tested. I am bearish on the bonds until they test support after which I expect the bulls to come out and play.

The bonds started out weak as I expected, but never gave me an adequate pullback to the 20 EMA in order to get short. (See Figure 9.68.) There was then a very sharp selloff around 9:45 with a markedly increased surge of volume. This capitulation action was my first hint of confirmation that the 20 EMA from the daily was going to act as support. I wasn't quite ready to go long for a swing yet, but as the bonds formed a 5-minute double bottom (1), I liked the thought of a scalp back toward the 20 EMA. This bounce from the double bottom quickly gave me my scalp profit as the 20 EMA was tested. Then, the price moved up into an area of chart resistance as price retested the breakdown (2). I took this as a test of resistance and went short. The price did indeed fall away from resistance, but it missed my target area. Because this was simply a scalp off of resistance, I was unwilling to let the trade go back above my breakeven point. As I realized the price was coming back to get me, I scratched the trade at my entry point. The price then rallied to break above the area I identified as chart resistance. It then began to form a base (3), which was the confirmation I had needed for my swing. When the base's high was broken, the swing long went into effect. Ultimately, the base ended up with a false breakout and a flush move before the trend was able to regain control. But my stop below the day's low left me plenty of room on this minor whipsaw. I had one final scalp opportunity (4) as the bonds corrected back to test the 20 EMA before continuing higher to close at a new high for the day. So I guess my analysis on Friday was correct; this is the beginning of a new payout cycle! There was plenty of movement today, and the trend remained orderly with lower highs and lower lows,

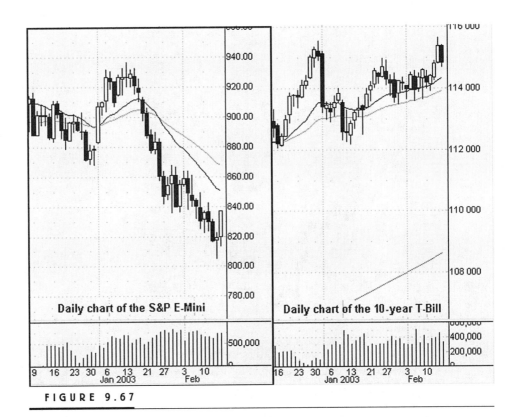

FIGURE 9.67

then a double bottom, and finally a series of higher highs and higher lows moving into the close. When the market is clean, my trend-following style does very well. Today's market was aligned to my style of support and resistance trading. The basing chop had vanished for today, and you can see how that translated into a stopless profitable day!

The S&Ps gapped up nicely this morning and continued to rally until they challenged the daily 20 MA resistance area around 850. (See Figure 9.69.) At this point, my target for the swing long had been reached. I took my profits into the 850 zone (1) and began to look for short opportunities as I believed the trend would change. There was a valid long pattern (2) as the price formed a bull flag to test the 20 EMA, but I passed because my daily resistance area had been tested and I suspected that the trend was changing. In retrospect, this long would have offered an easy scalp back toward the day's highs, but this did not bother me since I knew I was holding my discipline by sticking to my plan. I kept waiting patiently for a short setup worth taking, but one never appeared. The market kept basing until it finally degenerated into a large volatility whip into the close.

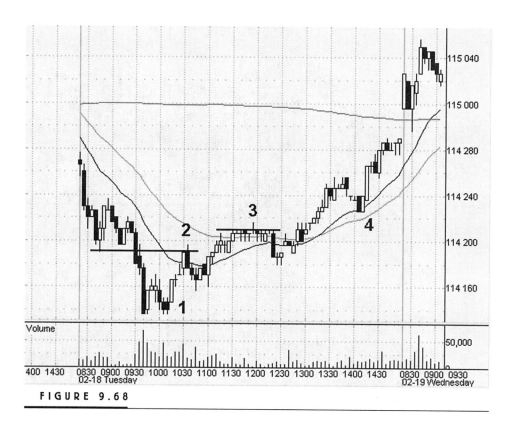

FIGURE 9.68

So the payout cycle has returned with a vengeance! It is beginning to look like the extra length of the last payback cycle is going to deliver us an extra juicy payout in reward for our patience. The S&P long swing was closed at target levels, making up for the drawdown incurred from any stops taken in the payback cycle. The successful scalps took me back into the black, and now I'm poised to begin pushing equity to new highs as the week unfolds. I'm so glad to have extended this log as I waited for the transition from payback to payout. It has been a very classic cycle. If you can take one thing away from this book, I would hope it is the understanding of how important loss prevention is to overall performance as a trader. For many of my consulting clients, the concept of market alignment acts as a key that opens many doors. They are finally able to give up their struggle to be all things to all markets, and instead begin to learn how to bob and weave as they try to avoid losses during periods of market misalignment. I have seen a number of consistent losers post their first profitable month by simply embracing this shift in mind-set.

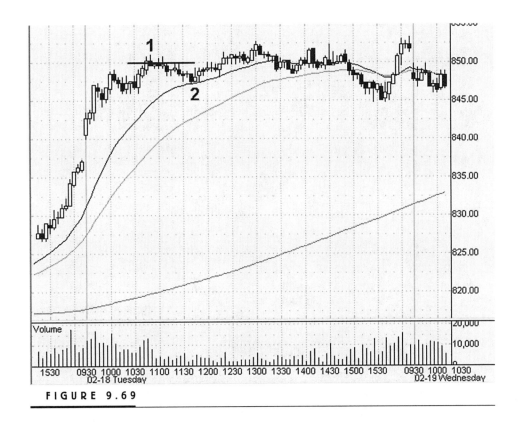

FIGURE 9.69

Scorecard:

Correctly identified daily trend? YES
Traded with the intraday trend? YES
Avoided at least one stop? YES
Ended the day profitably? YES

FEBRUARY 19, 2003

Again, we see a nicely swinging market for both the bonds and the S&P (Figure 9.70). The bonds have a beautiful pullback to 20 EMA support, which portends well for the swing. The S&P 500 has rallied to resistance, but has yet to form a reversal candlestick. I think today will be a day for rallies to resistance in the S&P, and pullbacks to support in the bonds.

The S&Ps were quite strange today. They gapped down away from the daily 20 EMA and sold off as I expected. However, the selloff was a

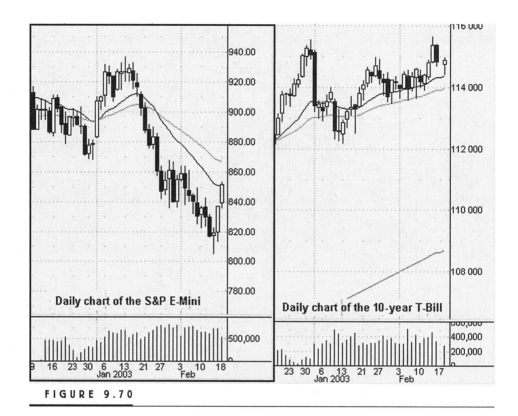

FIGURE 9.70

very tight channel-bound retracement. There were a few opportunities, but on the whole the action felt very muddy (Figure 9.71). After the opening range break, the market continued to chop. It finally blipped up to test the 20 EMA (1) in what looks like a blindingly obvious short. At the time, I was watching for a rally to resistance, but just didn't see this as an opportunity. This trade shows how the mind can sometimes ignore the obvious. I was presented with a second chance (2) as another rally to 20 EMA occurred. This time I was ready, and took the scalp as the market formed a topping tail at resistance. After the noontime doldrums, the market began to accelerate its selling. I wanted very much to buy a test of the 200 SMA for a bounce as I thought the market was getting very oversold. The first attempt missed the 200 SMA, so I kept stalking. The price then rolled over and formed a peek bottom (3). I jumped on this opportunity, and saw the market climb just a few ticks in the right direction before dropping hard to take out the low of the day and therefore my stop. I ended my day with a one-win, one-loss result for the S&P.

This was also a funky day for the bonds. Again, there was a nice trend but it just didn't offer many wiggles for me to capitalize on. (See Figure

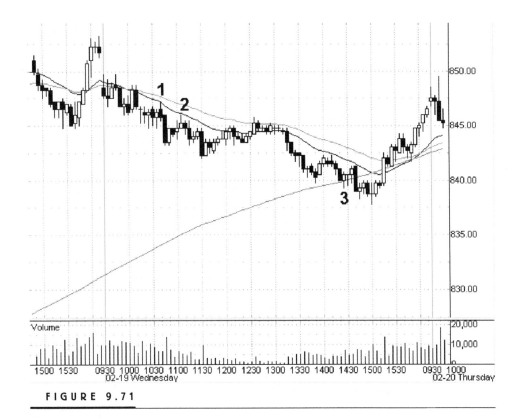

FIGURE 9.71

9.72.) Midday, there were two nearly identical pullbacks to the 20 EMA support level (1) and (2). I snagged the first one and missed the next as I was downstairs eating lunch. After those two paltry pullbacks, there was never another setup that I wanted. So, I ended the day with a one-shot, one-kill trade.

As I looked at my economic calendar, I realize with disappointment that tomorrow's session was going to be a huge news day. Core PPI, initial claims, and trade balance information would hit the market at 8:30 A.M. Leading indicators were due at 10:00 A.M., and the Philadelphia Fed was scheduled for noon. Any of these numbers have the potential to spark wild volatility in the bond market. When I initiated my swing, I was hoping to exit it into a retest of the last major swing high. Instead, due to tomorrow's number schedule, I realized I needed to find an exit point during today's trading. I looked back on my 30-minute chart, and found an area of gap resistance around 115.100. (See Figure 9.73.) I decided to amend my target due to the news risk, and offered out just below gap resistance. The morning rally terminated right in this zone of resistance, then corrected, and

FIGURE 9.72

was trying to break new highs as the closing bell rang. I was able to exit my swing into the first test of the 115.100 level, which put me flat for any uncontrolled volatility triggered by the numbers tomorrow morning.

After yesterday's easy profitability, I suppose I was due for a bit of a digestion day. However, I was expecting more profit potential from my intraday scalps. The hero for me today was the swing, so even though there weren't many intraday pullbacks I still was able to participate in the rally.

Scorecard:

Correctly identified daily trend? YES
Traded with the intraday trend? YES
Avoided at least one stop? YES
Ended the day profitably? YES

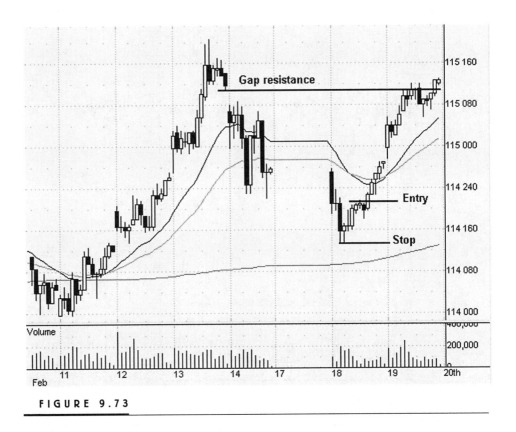

FIGURE 9.73

FEBRUARY 20, 2003

I really don't know what to expect for today. With all the different news events scheduled for this morning, the only thing I know for sure is that there will be wild spikes of volatile action. Just simply looking at the daily, I'd say the bonds will continue higher as they try to retest the last daily swing high (Figure 9.74). The S&P is wobbling around its daily 20 EMA. It put in a bit of a bottom tail yesterday, so this may be the beginning of a base for the 20 EMA breaks for just a slow rollover off resistance. It's too early to tell, so I believe I will focus today on the bonds because they have a cleaner daily. Since I think today is likely to be spiky, I'm going to give myself a one-stop rule for each market. I will trade as I see fit until I take a stop, then will shut down for the day in that market.

As I suspected, the S&P 500's 5-minute chart is a mess. (See Figure 9.75.) Late in the afternoon, it prints one bear flag (1). It looked too good to

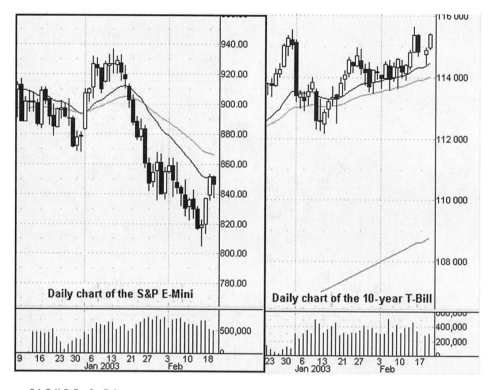

FIGURE 9.74

pass up, so I took a short, which quickly stopped me out before it ran back toward the lows. Having patiently waited all day for my trade, this stop triggers my one-stop rule and I ignore the rest of the day's action.

The bonds waggle violently in the morning (see Figure 9.76), then give me a nice orderly bull flag (1) to the 20 EMA. This jigs and jags, but ends up paying me in the end. After the noontime confusion that surrounds the Philadelphia Fed numbers, another pullback to the 20 EMA (2) helps me to finish the day profitably and keep my winning streak intact.

So the day ends in a so-so fashion with two winners and one loser. This wraps up my week, as tomorrow is the third Friday of the month—options expiration day. As options traders square themselves in anticipation of expiration day, they often dip into the stock market to offset positions. This brings a level of supply and demand to the market that didn't exist yesterday and will be gone on Monday. These supply and demand forces come out of left field, and therefore will blindside you

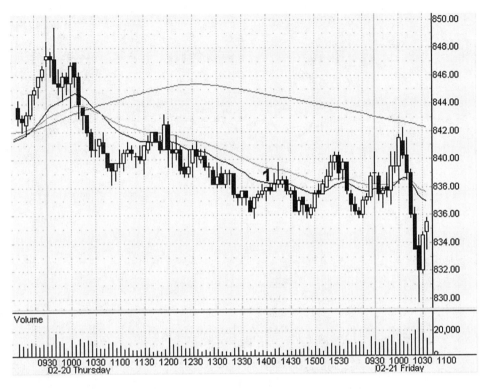

FIGURE 9.75

again and again if you're trying to trade as I do using historical support and resistance levels. It took me a while to realize that I was a net loser on options expiration Friday. But since then, I haven't traded expirations at all, and this decision has saved me a great deal of money.

Scorecard:

Correctly identified daily trend? YES
Traded with the intraday trend? YES
Avoided at least one stop? YES
Ended the day profitably? YES

FEBRUARY 21, 2003

Today was such a typical options expiration day that I thought I would include the 5-minute charts to illustrate my point. (See Figure 9.77.)

FIGURE 9.76

First, you can see how the bonds opened up with several spiky bars, then sold off sharply. If you had taken a long at the 200 SMA (1), you most likely would have been stopped out before the eventual reversal. The rally back to the 20 EMA (2) was fast and vicious. Exhibiting all the tendencies of a thin market, you may or may not have been able to get short and stay in the trade. Even if you avoided the stop, there was one nasty spike back toward the last swing high to deal with before the price eventually moved lower. Then, a long off the second test of the 200 SMA (3) would also have shown you a few ticks of profit before slamming back down to take out your stop.

The S&P 500 was even more evil (Figure 9.78). The first test of the 20 EMA (1) after a break above yesterday's swing high around 840 would have quickly stopped you as the price dove. If you had sold the first test on the chart and 20 EMA resistance (2), you would have also taken an instant stop. The uptrend then began to establish itself, but of the three pullbacks the market had (3), the only one that actually tested the 20 EMA would have resulted in another stop.

FIGURE 9.77

This was a typical action for an options expiration day. The market posts moves that make you just scratch your head and say, "Huh?" These are the blindside maneuvers that are seen consistently on expiration Friday due to the external supply and demand forces coming in from the options markets. The edge that I normally can count on is gone for this day, so I stand aside and just revel in all the stops I missed!

Scorecard:

Correctly identified daily trend (or lack thereof)? YES
Traded with the intraday trend? NO TRADES
Avoided at least one stop? TONS
Ended the day profitably? FLAT

Thus ends the peek over my shoulder for the last month or so. It has been an extremely challenging market driven by war, news, and economic surprises. However, during this time I experienced the easy profit-rich

FIGURE 9.78

environment of a payout cycle, as well as the challenging, almost antago-
nistic environment of the payback. I hope you could "feel" how the tone
of the market changed as things shifted from payout to payback and back
again. There were both winning and losing swing trades, and you can see
how I scalped the intraday trend while I waited for the daily to offer a multiday swing entry. The reason I devoted so much time and space to this
trading log is because I believe strongly that profitability comes from your
risk management *process* rather than any secrets of trade selection. You can
see how simplistic my trading style is: identify the trend, look for rallies to
resistance or pullbacks to support, enter on confirmation of support, and
try to surf the bounce. Yes, trading really is this simple!

I don't think it matters what patterns or indicators you use. It has
been my experience that just about everybody can find a viable edge in the
markets. But so very few are able to take the next step. Develop a clear
trading plan, then *execute* that plan to most efficiently press your edge.
They will abandon a perfectly valid strategy because they mistake a nor-

mal payback cycle for a complete breakdown in the strategy's usefulness. They will vary their aggressiveness and position size based on how they feel, *not* their odds for the next trade. At best, your edge as a trader is quite small. It doesn't take much in terms of error to reduce or eliminate that edge entirely over the course of weeks or months. Trading is quite a lot like parachute jumping. If you are ultra careful as you pack your parachute and inspect your rigging, you can make hundreds of jumps without incident. But there is little room for error. If you decide to cut corners and there is a problem, your fun can come to an abrupt and tragic end. In the same vein, you *must* respect the destructive power of a market. *Never* take a trade without first having identified a level to place your protective stop loss order. *Never* have any trade open without an active stop loss order to protect you when things go awry.

Know that this is an incredibly manic-depressive business. You will experience periods of great euphoria just before the payback cycle beats you around the head and shoulders. You will experience periods of "why me" depression and disgust just before the biggest payout cycle you have ever seen makes itself available. By accepting the inevitability of the payout-payback cycle and the emotional upheaval it can produce, you can begin to step aside and detach your mind from these emotional swirls. By understanding the process of payout-payback you can rise above it and release the stress and misery that so many traders deal with on a daily basis. I can help nudge you toward the right path, but it is you who must have the discipline to follow it. Believe me though, it is worth it. I hope that each and every one of you can rise above the stress and trade with peace and conviction. It is an indescribably wonderful (and profitable) place to be!

GLOSSARY

> Markets are the same now as they were 5 or 10 years ago because they keep changing—just like they did then....
>
> —*Ed Seykota*

Ascending triangle A continuation pattern in which a period of consolidation forms that trades within a horizontal level of resistance, and an ascending level of support.

Bar chart *See* Open, High, Low, Close chart.

Base *See* Consolidation.

Bear flag A channel-bound correction that drifts up against the trend.

Blow-off A violent high-volatility move to the upside used to define the final move into euphoria.

Bottoming tail The term used to describe a candlestick that has a large bottom side wick, indicating that the price sold off and then bounced.

Bounce The act of reversal from a level of support or resistance. Usually refers to a quick, high-volatility pivot.

Bounce trade A trading strategy that targets the initial move away from an area of support or resistance and will exit once a snapback has occurred. Usually synonymous with Scalp.

Breakaway gap A strongly trending move that begins with a gap in the direction of the trend that fails to fill within the first 30 minutes of trading.

Breakdown The act of price breaking below a level of support, the setup of a pennant (base near lows), or pattern based on a break of support.

Breakeven The level at which a trade will move from profit to loss, often used for trailing stops.

Breakout The act of price breaking above a level of resistance, the setup of a pennant (base near highs), or pattern based on a break of resistance.

Bull flag A channel-bound correction that drifts down against the trend.

Candlestick chart A Japanese form of charting price information which fills in the spaces between a bar's opening and closing prices, which eases the identification of price patterns and market reversals.

Capitulation A term describing a market process in which a period of high-volume panic selling occurs, often resulting in a reversal.

Chaos A period of markedly random and volatile price movement.

Chart reading The craft of predicting probable price movement through analysis of price and volume information displayed in graphic form.

Close A term used to describe the last price traded for the period under study.

Congestion *See* Consolidation.

Consistency A word that acts both to describe sustained profitability as well as sticking with a particular strategy for a period of time.

Consolidation A period of quiet market action in which there is no real movement either up or down.

Continuation pattern A price pattern that predicts a probable resumption of the trend.

Descending triangle A continuation pattern in which a period of consolidation forms that trades within a horizontal level of support and a descending level of resistance.

Discipline An all-encompassing word that describes the ability to stick to a trading plan, no matter what emotional upheaval the market inflicts.

Doji The term used to describe a candlestick whose opening and closing prices are more or less the same.

Double bottom A reversal pattern in which price retests and bounces off the support offered by a previous swing low.

Double top A reversal pattern in which price retests and bounces down away from the resistance offered by a previous swing high.

Downtrend A sustained bearish environment in which the market forms a series of lower highs and lower lows.

Edge *See* Positive expectancy.

Elliott wave theory Developed in the late 1930s by Ralph Nelson Elliott during a period of convalescence. It defines a market tendency to trend with a "5 by 3" wave count. The market will tend to form five price waves in the direction of the overall trend, and then build three countertrend waves as the correction forms. This theory can be used to identify areas of probable trend change, and to quantify the risk of failure for pullback setups.

Euphoria A term describing a market process in which a period of high-volume panic buying occurs, often resulting in a reversal.

Exponential moving average (EMA) A technical indicator that is derived by weighting a simple moving average with recent price data so that it responds more quickly to recent changes in price.

Faders Traders who employ a countertrend strategy that seeks to profit by the failure of traditional setups.

False setup *See* Trap setup.

Fire and forget A term from the military used to refer to self-guiding ordinance; a trade with OCO orders active that requires no active management from the trader.

First higher low Describes the first swing low that forms above the prior swing low in an established downtrend; the first signs of a change in trend.

First lower high Describes the first swing high that forms below the prior swing high in an established uptrend; the first signs of a change in trend.

Gap An opening price that is higher or lower than the previous day's close.

Gap and flush Used to describe a day when price gaps up, then quickly falls away from the levels of the gap opening.

Gap and snap Used to describe a day when price gaps down, then quickly rallies up off the levels of the gap opening.

Gap fill Used to describe a price move back toward the previous day's close after a gap-type opening.

Gap trap A gap-based shock event in which a market that has closed near its highs or lows gaps in the opposite direction the following day and breaks the previous day's high or low.

Hammer Term most commonly used to describe a candlestick that opens, sells off, then reverses to close above its opening price. Can also be used to describe a bearish reversal candlestick that opens, rallies strongly, then reverses to close below its opening price.

High A term used to describe the highest price traded for the period under study.

Higher high A price move in an established uptrend that breaks above the previous swing high.

Higher low A price move in an uptrend that establishes a swing low whose extreme low is higher than the previous swing low.

Inside range bar A price bar whose extreme high and low are entirely contained within the previous day's bar.

Limit order An order to buy or sell contracts that indicates you're unwilling to transact business that price beyond the limit level.

Liquidity pool An area where many orders to buy or sell have been clustered; the usual profits objective of a fading type setup.

Low A term used to describe the lowest price traded for the period under study.

Lower high A price move in a downtrend that establishes a swing high whose extreme high is lower than the previous swing high.

Lower low A price move in an established downtrend that breaks below the previous swing low.

Market order An order to buy or sell contracts that indicates you're willing to take whatever price the market makes available for your entry.

Mental game Used to describe the process by which a trader manages emotions and responses to trading successes or failures in order to reduce or eliminate trading errors.

Minimum Profit Objective (MPO) The level at which the reward assumed justifies the risk assumed at the outset of the trade.

Momentum trading Trading style that seeks to capture the profit potential offered by crashing or runaway markets.

Moving Average (MA) *See* Simple moving average (SMA).

One Cancels Other (OCO) order Pairs an order to sell with an order to buy. When one side of the pairing is filled, the other open order is canceled. OCO is most commonly used to link a protective stop loss order with an order to take profits, allowing a trade to resolve itself unattended.

Open A term used to describe the first price traded for the period under study.

Open, High, Low, Close (OHLC) chart The most common way for price information to be charted. Each price bar's height is determined by the extremes in price that the market experienced during the time of the bar's duration. A small horizontal tick is then placed at the level of the open and close for the time period the bar represents.

Payback cycle A term used to describe a period of sustained strategy failure due to market misalignment.

Payout cycle A term used to describe a period of sustained strategy success due to market alignment.

Peek bottom A derivative of the double bottom pattern where price retests an important swing low, then after a false breakdown quickly reverses.

Peek top A derivative of the double top pattern where price retests an important swing high, then after a false breakout quickly reverses.

Pennant A channel-bound correction through time as price bases near highs or lows.

Pivot A term used to define a V-type reversal.

Play *See* Setup.

Positive expectancy The knowledge proved through research that a particular price pattern or market behavior offers an acceptable level of predictability and risk to reward to provide a consistently profitable outcome over time.

Price rejection Used to describe a price move that attempts to rally or decline and is quickly rejected by a hidden pool of buyers and/or sellers.

Price target *See* Profit objective.

Price thrust Used to describe a strong directional move, usually in the direction of a trend.

Profit objective The predetermined price at which profits will be taken.

Ramp A violent move in price to the upside.

Resistance An area of price where there are more sellers than buyers.

Reversal candlestick A term used to describe a candlestick that indicates a snapback has occurred in a smaller time frame.

Reversion to the mean A market's tendency to move into extreme situations, then reverse back to more average prices. Sometimes used to define a trading strategy that is based on this common market tendency.

Rinse and run A reversal situation that may occur after a rinse move triggers a group of clustered stop loss orders. As faders take profits after the successful rinse, the price quickly reverses and returns to prefade levels.

Rinse move A price thrust driven by faders that takes the price up or down to test an area where many stop loss orders are likely to be clustered; a price move driven solely by the intent to trigger stop loss orders.

Risk-to-reward ratio The amount of reward realized or expected divided by the amount of risk assumed.

Running the stops *See* Rinse move.

Scalp A trade that seeks to capture a single price move within a trend, and will be exited before any correction can form; usually a trade of very short duration.

Setup The price action or chart pattern that delivers in an edge; sometimes used to state that a trade has been triggered.

Setup and flush Describes the setup of a price pattern that is quickly and successfully faded. The lack of pattern follow-through triggers a mini-panic as all the trend traders realize the faders have won the battle and rush to the exits.

Shock event A surprising bit of price movement, news, or any other market action that causes the price to sharply move or gap as it discounts the new information; often a trend-changing event.

Simple moving average (SMA) A technical indicator derived by simply averaging all the prices (usually the closing price) for the period being studied. A 30-minute, 200-period SMA would be the average price of the closing price of the last 200 30-minute bars on the chart.

Slippage The difference between the price level you wished to see filled and the actual price you receive.

SMA *See* Simple moving average.

Snapback The reversal in price (usually violent and highly volatile) that occurs after a market experiences euphoria or capitulation. Can also be used to describe a market that quickly reverses off an area of support or resistance.

Stochastics A technical indicator invented by George C. Lane. First introduced in 1984, the Stochastic Indicator is an oscillator that is based on the closing price of the market relative to its trading range for the period studied. Levels above 80 are considered overbought, below 20 oversold.

Stop The price level at which the market proves you wrong, and at which point you will exit the position for a loss.

Stop blowing Used to describe a trader who chooses not to honor a stop loss level, often resulting in catastrophic loss.

Stop jumping Used to describe a trader who chooses to exit before a stop loss level is broken, often resulting in a loss when a profit was possible.

Stop limit order An order to buy or sell contracts that will send a limit order to the exchange as soon as the stop price is exceeded; the most common order type used for entering positions.

Stop market order An order to buy or sell contracts that will send a market order to the exchange as soon as the stop price is exceeded; the most common order type used for protective stop loss orders.

Stopped out Used to describe a trade that has exceeded its stop level and has been closed for a loss.

Supply/Demand imbalance A price point at which the market has many sellers and few buyers, or many buyers and few sellers, used to describe the situation that leads to price reversal.

Support An area of price where there are more buyers than sellers.

Swing The trending price thrust between a swing high and a swing low.

Swing high The extreme high in price that is left on a chart after the market forms a reversal to the downside.

Swing low The extreme low in price that is left on a chart after the market forms a reversal to the upside.

Swing trading The trading style that seeks to capture the profit potential offered by move from support to resistance, or resistance to support.

Tape A term used to describe the flow of price and volume information contained in a time and sales window.

Tape reading The term used to describe the process of predicting a probable price moves by observing raw price and volume information.

Technical analysis *See* Chart reading.

Thirty-minute range A term used to define the range a market experiences during the first 30 minutes of trading. Most often used as a way to trigger certain reversion to the mean and gap-based setups.

Time stop An exit strategy that uses a prespecified duration of time to indicate a trade's failure and trigger an exit.

Topping tail The term used to describe a candlestick that has a large topside wick, indicating that the price rallied up and then was rejected.

Trade plan A tactical plan created to determine a trade's criteria for entry, exit, and stop loss placement; a process in which analytical trade management replaces emotional trade management.

Trailing stops The process of moving stops to reduce risk exposure or protect profits as a trade moves in the right direction.

Trap setup A trade based around a price move that will cause a widely followed setup to fail.

Trend change The transition from a market making higher highs and higher lows to lower highs and lower lows; the transition from a market making lower highs and lower lows to higher highs and higher lows.

Trend followers Traders who employ trading strategies that will align them with the current trend.

Trendline A straight line drawn through a series of swing highs or swing lows. Often used to define entries and stops for triangle-based patterns.

Triangle *See* Volatility constriction.

Trigger The level above or below which you plan to initiate a position.

Uptrend A sustained bullish environment in which the market forms a series of higher highs and higher lows.

Volatility constriction A period of time where the market's volatility steadily decreases; used to describe the action that precedes a volatility expansion breakout or triangle pattern.

Volatility expansion breakout The breakout from a period of volatility constriction which usually delivers a strongly trending move.

Volume A term of measurement used to describe the number of contracts traded within a certain period of time.

Volume spike A period of time when the market trades on higher than average volume, used as a signal of confirmation for support or resistance, euphoria or capitulation.

V-type reversal A reversal where the price moves into an area of support or resistance and reverses.

Wave *See* Swing.

Whipsaw An unpredictable chaotic move that triggers or comes close to triggering your stop loss order. Another term for rinse.

BIBLIOGRAPHY

Cramer, James. *Confessions of a Street Addict.* New York: Simon & Schuster, 2002.

Douglas, Mark. *Trading in the Zone: Master the Market with Confidence, Discipline, and a Winning Attitude.* Englewood Cliffs, N.J.: Prentice Hall Press, 2001.

Edwards, Robert and Magee, John. *Technical Analysis of Stock Trends,* 8th ed. Boca Raton, Fla.: Saint Lucie Press, 2001.

Farley, Alan. *The Master Swing Trader: Tools and Techniquest to Profit from Outstanding Short-Term Trading Opportunities.* New York: McGraw-Hill, 2001.

Graifer, Vadym and Shumacher, Christopher. *Techniques of Tape Reading.* New York: McGraw-Hill, 2003.

Lefèvre, Edwin. *Reminiscences of a Stock Operator.* New York: John Wiley & Sons, 1994.

McCall, Richard D. *The Way of the Warrior Trader: The financial Risk-Taker's Guide to Samurai Courage.* New York: McGraw-Hill, 1997.

Morris, Gregory L. *Candlestick Charting Explained: Timeless Techniques for Trading Stocks and Futures.* New York: McGraw-Hill, 1995

Oz, Tony. *How to Take Money From Wall Street: Learn to Profit in Bull and Bear Markets.* Laguana Hills, Calif.: Goldman Brown Business Media, 2001.

Oz, Tony. *The Stock Trader: How I Make a Living Trading Stocks.* Laguana Hills, Calif.: Goldman Brown Business Media, 2000.

Rudd, Barry. *Stock Patterns for Day Trading.* Greenville, S.C.: Trader's Press, 1999.

Schwager, Jack. *The Market Wizards: Interview with Top Traders.* New York: HarperBusiness, 1993.

Schwager, Jack. *The New Market Wizards: Conversations with America's Top Traders.* New York: HarperBusiness, 1994.

Schwager, Jack. *Stock Market Wizards: Interview with America's Top Stock Traders.* New York: HarperBusiness, 2003.

Schwartz, Martin. *Pit Bull: Lessons from Wall Street's Champion Trader.* New York: HarperBusiness, 1999.

Sperandeo, Victor. *Trader Vic—Methods of a Wall Street Master.* New York: John Wiley & Sons, 1993.

Twain, Mark. *Life on the Mississippi.* New York: Modern Library, 1994.

INDEX

ABOUT THE AUTHOR

Bo Yoder is a professional trader and consultant to the financial industry on matters of trading and risk management. Yoder is a frequent contributor to trading publications such as *Technical Analysis of Stocks and Commodities*, *Chartpoint* and *Active Trader* magazine, and can be seen writing for RealMoney.com's *Short Advisor* newsletter as well as the *TradingTrack*, a column featuring real time market commentary. In addition to his writing, Yoder serves as president of RealityTrader T/A, is a featured speaker at trading expos, and has worked with hundreds of individuals and market professionals as a risk management consultant and trading mentor.